Psychodynamic Theory f...

Psychodynamic Theory for Therapeutic Practice

Second Edition

Juliet Higdon

BLOOMSBURY ACADEMIC
LONDON • NEW YORK • OXFORD • NEW DELHI • SYDNEY

BLOOMSBURY ACADEMIC
Bloomsbury Publishing Plc
50 Bedford Square, London, WC1B 3DP, UK
1385 Broadway, New York, NY 10018, USA
29 Earlsfort Terrace, Dublin 2, Ireland

BLOOMSBURY, BLOOMSBURY ACADEMIC and the Diana logo
are trademarks of Bloomsbury Publishing Plc

First published by PALGRAVE MACMILLAN as From Counselling Skills to
Counsellor: A Psychodynamic Approach, 2004
Second edition, 2012
Reprinted by Bloomsbury Academic, 2023 (twice), 2024

A catalogue record for this book is available from the British Library.

A catalog record for this book is available from the Library of Congress.

ISBN: PB: 978-0-2302-4247-0
ePDF: 978-0-2303-5636-8
ePub: 978-1-3503-0594-6

Printed and bound in Great Britain

To find out more about our authors and books visit
www.bloomsbury.com and sign up for our newsletters.

For the six grandchildren, Max, Didi, Abe, Deanna, Benji and Hal who have been **'closely observed'**

Contents

List of case material examples

Preface

Though the first edition had been targeted at students on counselling courses, it attained a much wider readership. Accordingly this second edition has endeavoured to respond to a range of interests. Students, trainee counsellors, trainee psychotherapists, psychodynamic counsellors and counsellors of other modalities should find this book invaluable. Health and Social Care professionals could find the ideas extend their understanding of the relationship with their patients and clients.

The five chapters on the classic theorists are little changed as readers found their life stories fascinating and the ideas, illustrated with case studies, captivating and accessible. Readers reported that they began to understand complex theories, which had passed them by before. They could see how that understanding could enrich their practice.

A new chapter, Chapter 1, on the value of psychodynamic theory to practitioners looks at the dynamics of relationships, the idea of unconscious processes, the parent–child duo recreated in the counselling dialogue, and the notion of themes and patterns repeated in our lives.

Contemporary developments relating to psychodynamic theory are explored (see Chapter 8). These include the links with neurobiology and how attachment shapes a baby's brain; how to make sense of the anxieties contained in the organizations of hospitals and day care nurseries. Psychodynamic evidence-based theory and practice is examined.

A greatly enhanced chapter (Chapter 9) on practice gives a wealth of case study material to demonstrate how to build, use and understand the counselling relationship. Verbatim transcripts illustrate this. Theories on Brief Therapy are examined together with the ways in which they can be used with clients.

There are 39 examples of case material and like the fabled 39 steps of John Buchan's spy story they can lead to a better understanding of the whole picture.

Acknowledgements

I am indebted to my clients who have given me permission to use their material, the details of which have been disguised and changed to protect confidentiality.

I am obligated to 'Peter' who said I could reproduce his dream without alteration.

I am especially grateful to the students over the years. They inspired and convinced me that this book needed to be written.

I also want to acknowledge the encouragement of fellow professionals and friends who were keen to see a second edition.

And last, I want to thank my family for their support; in particular, my husband, David, who has challenged, invigorated and been my IT consultant without whom I could not have finished writing this book.

Introduction

This book is about Psychodynamic theory and how it can be used in counselling and therapeutic practice. The ideas are absorbing and captivating. They have so much to offer in explanation and comprehension of the world we live in, the conflicts we engage in, the relationships we treasure. A desire for understanding seems to have become part of our culture, even popular culture. Think how many Hollywood movies involve a 'Shrink'.

The book explores accessible psychodynamic ideas and suggests how they can be utilized in practice. It describes psychodynamic counselling, alongside illustrations of how practitioners from other modalities can use psychodynamic theory to enrich their work.

The psychodynamic approach

To those unfamiliar with a psychodynamic approach the terms can be confusing. Psychodynamic counselling takes its inspiration from psychoanalytic theory. This is the body of theory originally created by Freud, practised as psychoanalysis. This is, as it suggests, an analysis of the personality of an individual, who Freud, because he was a doctor, called a patient. This is described in much more detail in Chapter 2. Psychoanalysis is a long-term process in which the patient is seen possibly five times a week, for several years.

The theorists who came after Freud adapted and extended his ideas. A new way of working termed 'psychotherapy' was instituted. This was therapy for a shorter period, perhaps once or twice a week, for 1 or 2 years. The patient could sit on a chair instead of lying on the couch. Therapy was worked through in the transference (discussed in Chapter 2.)

Probably most psychodynamic counsellors would see their work overlapping with psychotherapy, but different in many respects. Some of the differences will lie in the frequency and length of time in which psychotherapists see their patients, and the long-term issues the patients bring. But this is not an absolute. Many counsellors, particularly those in private practice will see clients for months, even years when they bring long-term issues. Alternatively psychotherapists may see patients within the terms of brief therapy, usually about 15 sessions, for issues deemed appropriate (see Chapter 9). Psychodynamic ideas apply and are practised across psychodynamic counselling and psychotherapy. The ideas contained in this book can be thought about and used by counsellors of all modalities to better understand the client, and the relationship between client and counsellor.

Counselling and counselling skills – the differences between them

Counselling skills are a collection of skills and strategies used to enhance communication within a relationship. This is based on the core concepts of valuing and respecting the person, with a genuine intention by the user of the skills. Counselling skills are used particularly by workers in the caring professions. They are powerful and potentially manipulative, so ethical underpinning is essential. The client sees the user of skills as a nurse, social worker and so on not as a counsellor.

If a nurse takes off her uniform and makes a contract with a client whom she does not see in her nurse role, for example to work through a bereavement within a separate agency, this is counselling. Counselling is a contracted relationship based on ethical agreements, underpinned by theoretical concepts. The concepts are different depending on the theoretical approach of the counsellor. Within modalities there are of course similarities as well as differences. All aim to offer the client therapy, which will help the client to a more satisfying life. What is offered, and the way in which it is offered, are the salient differences between the therapies.

Similarities and differences

In deriving, from Freud's theories on psychoanalysis, psychodynamic counselling is different from humanistic counselling in many respects. Humanistic counselling is concentrated on the positive aspects of individuals, on their human potential. Its origins lie in North America and it neatly fits the American psyche, some might say the American dream. It reflects the values of the society, with its emphasis on the striving individual, with the opportunity afforded to him to achieve his potential.

Humanistic counselling was also influenced by European thought on existentialism and phenomenology. Phenomenology refers to an individual's reality, the subjective experience of each person. The thinking that humanistic counselling took from existentialism concerned the capacity each individual has for freedom and choice. Humanistic counselling is positive in outlook, which means that it relies on what is there and available, what the individual can immediately get in touch with as the truth. This is in contrast to psychodynamic theory in which the truth is layered and not immediately exposed on the surface.

Carl Rogers had a passionate belief in the goodness of man. He did not accept the Judaeo-Christian idea of original sin. Indeed he thought that the Judaeo-Christian tradition had adversely influenced the mostly secular, psychodynamic theorists, to produce a body of knowledge that is European angst ridden, negative and pessimistic!

Who would want to read such theorists? Those of us who have done so have been captivated by some astonishing ideas. We could offer Freud's notion of the unconscious, unlocking of which can pave the way to a more creative life. Or point to Klein's startling views on how the infant begins to make sense of the world, through his passionate relationship with his mother. We might cite Bion and his dazzling ideas about how we first learn to think.

We could also examine European angst, the anxiety, fear and uncertainty of human existence, a constituent of existentialism, but a constituent, which some humanistic counselling seems to have chosen to play down. Psychodynamic counsellors might say that ignoring the darker side of the self looks at only half the person. That most of the individual's battles are with his inner self, a world he cannot fully understand, where anxieties, fears and guilt can immobilize his thinking, jeopardize his behaviour and make relationships with others difficult to accomplish. It is only by exploring, bringing half-hidden experiences into awareness, achieving a measure of insight that such difficulties can begin to be managed.

Person-centred counselling counters the criticism that it is over-optimistic or naïve by asserting that aggression and destructiveness are manifestations of a person functioning under unfavourable conditions (Mearns and Thorne, 1988, p. 16). This is in contrast to psychoanalytic thought, which sees aggression as endemic to our human existence.

Psychoanalytic history

The psychoanalytic history of ideas is puzzling to those whose concepts come from a different school. Person-centred and cognitive behavioural counsellors often find the different paths of psychoanalytic history confusing, not surprisingly, because it is complex.

It starts with Freud (Chapter 2) but then leads many different ways. Carl Jung was originally a disciple of Freud, but abandoned him to create his own theoretical base, which he called Analytical Psychology, when he dissented from many of Freud's ideas. Jung was a Christian and saw his work as spiritual. He claimed a deep, transpersonal unconscious that reflects the history of the human species and the whole cosmic order. This is not something within an individual's experience, but part of a collective unconscious. While Freud saw the unconscious as very personal, something that drove an individual in particular directions, often against his conscious will, Jung saw his version of the deep unconscious as the main healing principle.

As Jung had taken Freud's concepts as a starting point for his philosophy, so did others. Melanie Klein (Chapter 3) was a disciple of Freud who powerfully added to his ideas in a particular, some would say idiosyncratic, way. She and Freud both influenced Donald Winnicott (Chapter 4) who produced his own theories on the mother–child relationship, utilized by health professionals today. Wilfred Bion (Chapter 5) was particularly influenced by Klein, and his theories on the dynamics of groups still hold sway. Freud's influence on John Bowlby (Chapter 6) resulted in an evidence-based theory on attachment and separation, which has been very useful to professionals, especially those working with loss.

The work of these commanding theorists, who, apart from Freud, worked in Britain spawned a movement of psychoanalysts that became known as The British School of Object Relations. Ronald Fairbairn, Michael Balint, Harry Guntrip contributed their several ideas. The overarching concept of the Object Relations theorists was the understanding and working with relationships, to the self and to others.

Jacques Lacan

A major psychoanalytic French theorist, who from 1951 called for 'a return to Freud', was Jacques Lacan (1901–1981). He advocated a careful rereading of Freud's work, focusing on the constant references to language. He quoted Freud having shown a link between the patient's symptoms and their language, 'symptoms joining in the conversation'. A bodily pain would indicate that something had been left unsaid.

Lacan believed language was crucial. The newborn baby cannot grasp the world of language, yet it will permeate the whole of the child's existence. The baby is bound to its image by words and names (Leader, 1995).

Lacan described three developmental stages. First was the primeval period of unconscious infantile 'desire'; next the world of the imaginary emerging from the 'mirror stage', in which the child first confronts his image (see Chapter 4 on Winnicott) and narcissistically and incorrectly assumes this to be his true self; and finally the symbolic order, arising through the use of language.

Successful therapy depends on the exploration of desire through the symbolic order of language and letting go of the world of the imaginary (Bateman and Holmes, 1995).

Lacan was a dominant figure who because of his work on language became a commanding influence on literature, philosophy, feminism and art.

Hanna Segal 1918–2011

Hanna Segal's work is momentous. Influenced by Klein, she has been distinguished as an original thinker and contributor for the last 60 years, dying on 5 July 2011. Her work on symbolism and creativity is beyond the scope of this book, but I should like to touch upon her contribution to society. She has engaged with issues of the outside world at every level. Unlike many in the therapy world, she has made it her business to challenge the political. She maintained that because psychoanalysis examines all aspects of the human mind, it has a unique contribution to make in exploring its social phenomena.

Segal believed that because analysts understand the conflict between the constructive and destructive parts of the individual, they are well placed to see its meaning at a global level. She was instrumental in setting up 'Psychoanalysts for the Prevention of Nuclear War' in 1983, horrified by the prospect that nuclear arms would be used.

David Bell says that in her 1987 paper 'Silence is the real crime' she makes the point that in the face of horrors we should scream and hope that someone hears. We must resist collusion with the various myths that society and its rulers create for our comfort.

Following the end of the cold war, Segal spoke of the danger of the 'manic triumphalism' of the Western ideologues, who now felt they could rule the world without obstacles in their way. She foresaw the imperative to find a new enemy as a justification, externally to keep the arms industry buoyant, internally to find a new object of hatred. This would be a deflection away from the misery, unemployment and poverty at home. Saddam Hussein fitted the bill (Bell, 1997, p. 32).

At the run up to the Iraq invasion, under the auspices of Medical Campaign Against Nuclear Weapons, Segal, with others, wrote an impassioned letter to *The Guardian* newspaper against the prospect of war. The arguments, which pulled no punches, were rooted in psychoanalytic theory.

'We believe that the rush to war is largely driven by irrational psychological processes which must be recognised and addressed if sanity is to prevail.' There followed nine examples of irrational thinking, one of which was, 'A tendency to replace feelings of fear, persecution and depression with those of worth, success and triumph, even if the latter are based on a delusion, such as the possibility of "winning" a war.'

Segal's (2003) paper, 'From Hiroshima to 11th September and After', published after the Iraq invasion, ends with a critique of our current position in 'the war on terror'. 'Our sanity is threatened by a delusional inner world of omnipotence and absolute evil and sainthood' (2003, p. 263).

Diversity

Classic psychoanalytic thought is criticized for being ethnocentric. This is a fair criticism as it is based on Judaeo-Christian ideas, makes assumptions based on the mores of Western society, is heterosexual and class based.

Most of the theorists of classic psychoanalytic thought have been relatively affluent, certainly more affluent than the norm. They have usually had middle- or upper-class backgrounds and have a view of society different from that of, what Freud called, the proletariat. Practices, in particular the child-rearing practices the theorists experienced, adopted or made assumptions upon, were very different from poorer groups in their own societies, let alone the rest of the world. Nannies, boarding schools, babies separated from mothers in separate cots in separate rooms and babies weaned in their first year are not the practices of the majority of the world's citizens. Yet the psychoanalytic theories espoused were intended to have universal application.

In fairness it must be remembered that Winnicott's work was primarily with 'ordinary' people and Bowlby's research was instrumental in introducing measures that enriched the lives of 'ordinary' people. But it is also true that, at the beginning, access to therapy was primarily dependent on wealth. The opening of the Tavistock Clinic was seminal in offering treatment to people unable to pay.

The Tavistock Clinic

Influenced by the new psychology coming out of Vienna, Dr Hugh Crichton Miller a neurologist developed pioneering psychotherapeutic methods for treating shellshocked soldiers from the First World War. He became convinced of the need to establish a clinic to provide similar services to civilians of limited means.

The clinic opened in 1920, at the beginning in a house in Tavistock Square, London, with the first patient, a child. It quickly established itself as a psychotherapy centre for traumatized and neurotic children and adults.

Training became more organized and a course for social workers in mental health was set up. In 1930 The Psychopathic Clinic, later called the Portman Clinic, was founded. This was the clinical arm of an institute for studies into delinquency. Freud, Jung and H. G. Wells were the early Vice Presidents. In 1935 Jung gave a series of lectures at the Tavistock Clinic, to which Bion took Samuel Becket (Chapter 5).

The Tavistock Clinic was one of the first institutions to assess its own treatment. Follow-up studies were carried out, with research always being a major part of the Tavistock's work. This may be surprising to some detractors who see psychoanalysis as nebulous. Many would not realize that psychoanalytic treatment had been subject to research from Freud onwards.

Formal supervision for all clinical staff was set up at the Tavistock in 1937. By today's standards it was not generous – supervision after 50 sessions with a patient. However, before this, supervision was informal, if clinicians experienced it at all. Another difference from other institutions was that children and parents were both treated, together and separately.

During the Second World War the clinic kept going, evacuated to a women's college in Hampstead, where the staff slept in student rooms at night and saw patients by day. There was little money with some people working for free and those clinical staff with private practices pooling their money. After the war the Tavistock Clinic became part of the National Health Service. The Tavistock Institute of Group Relations split off from the clinic so that it could charge fees and support training and research. Bion was heavily involved with the Institute with his work on groups. Menzies Lythe (Chapter 8) also did pioneering work there.

Within the Tavistock Clinic, Klein and Winnicott both gave lectures. Bowlby worked there full time from 1948 to 1972 and was still working there in 1990, the Summer of his death.

The Tavistock Clinic is known world wide for its pioneering activities and its wide range of helping professionals who have benefited from its work. Michael Balint worked with doctors, and the Balint Group composed of doctors and psychotherapists is active today. Bowlby's attachment theory was invaluable to practitioners from nursery workers to probation officers. Systemic family therapy was introduced.

In 1994 the Portman and Tavistock Clinics became The Tavistock and Portman NHS Foundation Trust.

At the time of writing, The Tavistock Adult Depression Study is being conducted. It is a randomized controlled trial investigation into the effectiveness of psychoanalytical psychotherapy on primary-care adults with long-term treatment-resistant depression. The therapy consists of weekly sessions for 18 months. The trial began in 2002 and is expected to report in 2012. It is a good example of evidence-based theory and practice, in the Tavistock tradition (see The Tavistock and Portman website).

Access to training was originally dependent on wealth. But this is changing. Psychodynamic thinkers and practitioners can now come from less-exalted backgrounds. Though psychoanalytic training is generally still costly, training as a psychodynamic counsellor is more affordable. It is a measure of the passion, which psychodynamic thought engenders, that students and trainees make huge sacrifices to enter training.

Current psychodynamic thinkers and writers are anxious to promote equality and diversity, with appropriate therapeutic response to diverse clients. Psychodynamic counsellors must be aware of bias in their interventions and endeavour to work appropriately with clients of different race, culture (see Chapter 5, 'Example: the counsellor who misunderstands'), sexual orientation (see Chapter 7) and socio-economic groups different from their own.

Psychodynamic ideas

Although psychodynamic ideas have been much expanded, adapted and developed by theorists from Freud onwards and differ in many respects, they hold common tenets:

First is an acknowledgement that our thinking and behaviour is affected by processes of which we are not fully conscious. This goes hand in hand with a recognition that past experiences, particularly childhood experiences, can help us to understand present difficulties.

Second, that there are themes and patterns in our lives of which we are often not aware.

Third, that we have a relationship with different parts of ourselves, in our internal world, as well as with other people in the external world.

Fourth, that the relationships we had with significant figures in our lives, in particular our parents, may be recreated with the therapist.

Some theorists demand that the therapist is a blank screen on to which the client can project his phantasies and therefore the therapist must remain neutral and somewhat distant. Interpretation and dream analysis are the instruments for client development.

Other theorists, particularly those in the post-Freudian Objects Relations School, think that the relationship between client and therapist can be a vehicle for change and growth. (This is a conviction held by Rogers and a central plank of person-centred counselling.) The Object Relations School believes that the need for relationships is a primary need; that the self is made up of internalized relationships at both an unconscious and a conscious level, interacting with externalized relationships. This will be explored throughout the book.

One of the principal tenets of psychodynamic thought is that the past informs the present. In Freudian terms, unresolved painful childhood experiences lie at the heart of present difficulties.

Psychodynamic counsellors use client's past experiences to work together on patterns and themes in order to help unravel difficulties in the present. Other counsellors, with different ways of working, will not ignore the past. Their treatment of it will be different. Humanistic counsellors will see the past as part of a person's whole experience. Cognitive-analytic therapists will help the client to understand past experiences, in order to make changes in the present.

One of the arguments often put forward, in the criticism of the application of psychodynamic thought, is that clients get stuck in the past and spend all their time looking at it. They never move on and after months of counselling they are still in the same place.

If this is so, then the counsellor needs to help the client to use the past to illuminate the present. The past has to be explored to understand what has happened and how this could be affecting current concerns. However, sometimes staying in the past is an escape from the reality of the present. The counsellor should examine her work, to see why she is colluding in not challenging the client.

In counselling training, students are asked to look at concepts of psychodynamic theory, either on a course, which takes a psychodynamic approach, or as part of an integrated programme. There is such a wealth of material that trainee practitioners can feel bewildered by the vast range of theories labelled psychodynamic and wonder how they can possibly apply them.

It is clearly unethical for counsellors to use ideas they do not fully understand with clients. It is particularly crucial that at this stage in the trainees' development that they are helped to use concepts within the limits of their competence.

Many students have placements in counselling agencies where the approach is not psychodynamic. At first they cannot see how psychodynamic theory can be reconciled with, for example, a person-centred approach. But as these trainee counsellors learn to be more familiar with psychodynamic concepts, they begin to realize that another perspective can add to their understanding of their clients and as a result can enhance their practice.

Structure of the book

With this in mind, I have chosen concepts and themes from major theorists, which in my experience of working with trainee practitioners can be thought about and used safely with clients. We start with Freud, before looking at post-Freudian developments in what came to be called the Object Relations School. Because they thought the need for relationships is primary, this fits more easily with most schools of counselling for which this is a central tenet. The word 'object' is confusing. It does not just mean a person. It is used to describe an interpersonal and intrapersonal relationship. It is the relationship a person has with parts of himself, with others and with the images of others, which he has taken inside himself.

The Object Relations School contains many interesting theorists, but in this introductory book I have confined myself to theorists whom students will know of, and on training courses they may be asked to study in more detail. Fairbairn (Chapter 7) Balint and Guntrip, not studied in detail here, are Object Relation theorists who would offer rewards to students who are inspired to go on to further reading.

The ideas examined in the book should be useful to trainees exploring a psychodynamic approach within the counselling relationship, or for counsellors working in an integrative way. Concepts like holding and containment, the awareness of the transference, the importance of childhood experiences should be usable, without the counsellors feeling they are trying to work beyond their competence.

I have maintained a simple structure in the chapters on the theorists, their lives, their theories, and on how the theories can be used. Case study examples illustrate the theory. I am indebted to the clients who have let me use their material, whose details have been altered and disguised. I have used amalgams of client material to illustrate some points of theory. I am also grateful to the students, who, with permission from their clients, brought material into the class group, from which we all learnt. Unless otherwise specified I have used 'she' throughout to indicate the counsellor and 'he' for the client.

Because the psychodynamic approach highlights the significance of past experiences, the life of each theorist is examined in some detail, with an exploration of how the life might have influenced the theory.

Freud and Klein are the two giants. The other three theorists, Winnicott, Bion and Bowlby have extended, adapted, modified or contradicted the concepts of the founders, contributing their own original theory.

The book is arranged as follows:

Chapter 1 examines the value of psychodynamic theory to practitioners, illustrating with practice examples how the theory could be used. It explores the motivations for being a counsellor, looks at the pitfalls, the role of humility and the necessity of thinking as well as feeling. It makes the point that there are not two camps, counsellor and client, but that to be ethical and effective, counsellors have to be clients as well.

Chapter 2 details the importance of Sigmund Freud as the founder of the psychoanalytic tradition. The theories, which can aid the understanding of the client by the practitioner, are explored. These include unconscious processes, childhood experiences, transference and defence mechanisms.

Chapter 3 charts Melanie Klein's development of Freud's theories. The relationship between the mother and the baby, and its comparison with the counsellor and client relationship are explored. Envy, guilt, love and reparation are examined.

Chapter 4 explores Donald Winnicott's development of both Freudian and Kleinian theories. The concept of holding and the counselling room as a place to play are examined. How the counsellor can make use of these concepts and have an awareness of the countertransference are investigated.

Chapter 5 looks at the role of thinking, curiosity and knowledge as power. Wilfred Bion's post-Kleinian theories on negative capability, the idea that, in order to really understand the client, the counsellor has to tolerate the feeling of 'not knowing', are examined.

Chapter 6 explores John Bowlby's development of Freudian and Kleinian concepts in his ideas on attachment and separation, with the aim of better helping the counsellor and client together to understand the client's relationships and loss.

Chapter 7 explores the legacies of Freud and Klein. It looks at the Neo-Freudians and examines Anna Freud's ego psychology and Erik Erikson's eight ages of man. Contemporary notions surrounding the Oedipus complex are reviewed with a new look at the relationship of siblings to the triangle. Feminism and psychoanalysis are probed while the second part of the chapter is given over to diverse infant observations.

Chapter 8 examines the legacies of Winnicott, Bion and Bowlby. An absorbing paper on the dangers of too-good mothering is detailed. Bion's theories on organizations are analysed in studies of a hospital and a day care centre. Fascinating contemporary developments on the links between attachment and neurobiology are examined. Evidence-based research is studied.

Chapter 9 focuses on practice. It draws together ideas on how to build, use and understand the counselling relationship. It asks the counsellor to monitor self, as well as use external supervision. A wealth of case study material and verbatim transcripts illustrate the theory.

1
The value of psychodynamic theory

The value of psychodynamic theory

In the late 1950s and early 1960s psychodynamic theory was an important part of some professional trainings. When I trained to be a teacher I learnt about Freudian concepts. Some of the students thought it would be better to spend the time learning how to discipline a classroom and when I came face to face with rebellious 14-year-olds, probably I agreed. But what those of us who were fascinated by ideas, new to us, realized was the emphasis on trying to understand the children. We could begin to see that bad behaviour had a meaning, that its roots might lie in rejection, emotional deprivation, family conflict and that this understanding could help us be more effective teachers.

A few years later I trained as a child care officer, what would now be called a child protection social worker. At university I learnt about Klein and her theories on the mother–child relationship. Again the class was divided between those who thought we should concentrate on helping parents manage their gas bills and those of us who could see that a poor maternal relationship would set the seed for future difficulties.

I cite these two examples as an illustration of the ways in which psychodynamic theory, which offers understanding and meaning, can be a useful way to enrich relationships in the caring professions. Although the focus of this book is on counselling, I maintain that the value of psychodynamic theory is not confined to a specific relationship.

Psychodynamic thought

The ancient Greeks took the word 'psyche', symbolized as a butterfly, a fragile, transitory beauty, and transferred the term to describe the human spirit, the soul, the mind. So, psychodynamic thought hinges on the essence of the person. The dynamic part means activity, so the word psychodynamic means the interrelationship and activity between the different parts of the individual's psyche. Psychodynamic counselling concerns the internal relationship with different aspects of the self and the external relationship with others.

Using psychodynamic theories in counselling

The humanistic counsellor can, if appropriate, disclose to the client from her own experience, revealing her own strengths and weaknesses. The counsellor working psychodynamically is aware of the transference (see p. 20), which means that she must be available for the client to use. He may need to explore the relationship with his mother. For this he may experience the counsellor as mother, and work through the issues with her, which he found impossible with his own mother. So the psychodynamic counsellor does not usually disclose.

The humanistic person-centred counsellor must convey to the client her positive regard. This highlights a dilemma for the psychodynamic counsellor. 'A therapist focused on conveying his positive regard for the client cannot at the same time regard the situation with the eye of a circling hawk looking for a disturbance in the underbrush' (Kovel, 1991, p. 164). However, this is not to imply that the psychodynamic counsellor wants to come across to the client as cold and unfeeling. She wants to make a real relationship with the client, and to feel his distress. But at the same time, she wants to keep a watching brief on what is happening between herself and the client. This entails being with the client, being there for him, yet simultaneously keeping a part of herself thinking and observing. McLoughlin says that the availability of the counsellor is related to her capacity for splitting, 'having a participating bit and an observing bit within herself ' (1995, p. 48). This is not easy. But if the counsellor is to be useful to the client she has to keep in counsellor role, being able to reflect on the process. What is happening within the client, what is happening between them and what is happening inside herself will ensure that she stays within the boundaries of her role.

She is not the client's best friend or his mother, whose response to the client would be primarily emotional. If the client's feelings are very powerful, the counsellor will not want to add hers. She will need to keep part of herself outside the emotion, so that she gives the message to the client that she is with him, but unlike him, not overwhelmed by his feelings. McLoughlin puts it succinctly, 'It will perhaps be clear that in order to combine effectively with the client in this way, the counsellor will need to be able to maintain the detachment of her therapeutic stance. Where the counsellor burdens her stance with too much feeling, too much wanting, she effectively renders herself less available for use by the client' (1995, p. 480).

Mearns and Thorne, in their book on person-centred counselling acknowledge it to be important 'that the counsellor monitors continually what she is prepared to offer to the client, and what lies outside the boundaries of her commitment' (1988, p. 30). The person-centred counsellor and the psychodynamic counsellor share dilemmas, but their theoretical distinctions will probably lead to different resolutions.

In spite of the differences there are similarities in concept between psychodynamic counselling and person-centred counselling, which are noted throughout the book. The person-centred counsellor could find that integrating psychodynamic perspective into her thinking should enhance her understanding of the client.

Similarly counsellors, who work in a cognitive-behavioural way, focusing primarily on the present, can find psychodynamic thought a useful contribution. An enriched understanding of the client's issues may be effective in helping the client comprehend and change his thoughts and behaviour.

Anthony Ryle developed a way of working in which an understanding of analytical psychotherapy is based on a cognitive framework. Cognitive-analytic therapy (CAT), which melds the two schools, has become important in the field of brief therapy. Clients work to defined goals, and in tandem engage with the therapist on achieving an enhanced awareness of themselves and a greater insight into their difficulties.

The psychodynamic thought that underpins practice is pinpointed below and explored in more detail within the rest of the book.

The unconscious

One of the most arresting notions in psychodynamic thought, which comes from Freudian theory, is that part of our psyche or mind is not available to us. The idea that we are driven by processes of which we are not aware is both interesting and alarming. None of us likes to feel we are out of control, or not fully in charge of ourselves. Yet it does help us to understand why we do things that seem to be out of character, or cannot stop ourselves from behaving in ways we know to be self-destructive. It helps us to understand why our clients seem stuck, not able to move on. It might stop us from offering problem-solving solutions, which the client has already thought of and discarded.

Case Example | Gavin: an angry young man with no intimate relationships

Gavin was an angry young man with no intimate relationships. His mother had been unable to offer him the preoccupation that allows a baby to feel loved. He came to therapy because he wanted to be able to form a relationship with a woman.

Working with Gavin was difficult. He wanted things to be different, but he wanted it to be fixed now. He hated the women who rejected him. He berated the counsellor for not solving his problem for him. It would have been easy to offer solutions, 'join a singles' club, date on line'.

The counsellor, working psychodynamically, spent the time exploring the present situation and looking for clues in the past. Gavin at first thought this a waste of time. He also found it painful. But over the sessions it became clear to the counsellor that Gavin had felt rejected by his mother, unloved and unlovable. They had not been able to form a relationship, though Frank thought he had tried. When Gavin understood this, he saw that he was actually frightened of trying to make an intimate relationship. The woman would reject him as his mother had. He unconsciously sabotaged any relationship, before he could be rejected.

Sometimes the unconscious can be made conscious. We try to work with unconscious or preconscious processes. This means that we have to be aware of levels of meaning and try to understand what is happening below the surface. If the client can begin to understand himself better, then he may have the option to change. At other times we have to live with the frustration of unavailable answers and do the best we can with what is accessible.

The preconscious

Freud suggested the notion of a middle layer of the mind between the conscious and the unconscious. This is where experiences lodge which are not conscious, but can be more easily accessed than unconscious memories. It is the, 'I had completely forgotten that', memory which can be brought into consciousness. This can be done through counselling and a case study example is given in Chapter 2.

The structure of the mind

As well as having some parts of the mind unknown to us, Freud proposed that the mind, or the personality, is at war with itself. Different parts of us are in conflict with other parts, which interact to disable us. Sometimes it is a straight fight, good against bad. Part of us wants to do something we know to be wrong, immoral, antisocial or even criminal. Another part of the mind says, 'Stop!', 'Don't be Stupid' or 'Look to your conscience.'

How these dilemmas are usually resolved make us the people we are. Working with clients who cannot understand why they do not 'feel themselves', why they feel 'at odds with themselves', when they are experiencing these personality struggles is helped by the counsellor's having some understanding of this whole area of conflict. A case study example is given in Chapter 2.

The past informs the present

Freud was convinced that the source of all traumatic events lay in early childhood, but it takes an event in the present to activate symptoms. Freud (1920) says that we try to safeguard ourselves against trauma, but some stimulus or trigger breaks through our defences. 'We may, I think, tentatively venture to regard the common traumatic neurosis as a consequence of an extensive breach being made in the protective shield against stimuli.'

Psychodynamic thinking uses the client's perception of past events, particularly childhood experiences, to understand present dilemmas. The counsellor, by exploring the past, helps the client to understand the links between painful infantile episodes and current trauma.

Case Example | Pauline: abandonment at four

Pauline's father abandoned her when she was four. She had been 'Daddy's girl' and spent her childhood wondering where she had gone wrong. She came to therapy because of her low self-esteem, her promiscuousness and her desire to make a lasting, caring relationship.

In the therapy, where the past was explored, Pauline realized how angry she was with her father and how, with the men she 'had loved and left', had at some level thought she was punishing him. 'They're all the same!' she had fumed. In fact she saw that she was punishing herself, by denying the possibility of a consistent relationship.

In the process, where patterns and themes were uncovered, the client began to see the part she had played in the painful drama she thought was purely of others' making. Understanding this could help her take on a new role in her life, which could prove to be more rewarding.

The counsellor as mother

The theorists who followed Freud, but adapted many of his ideas, founding the Object Relations School, made a link between the baby and the mother, and the psychoanalyst and the patient. These were theorists writing at a time when most mothers cared for the baby, with minimal input from the father. Fathers were usually seen as the authority figure within the family, while mother was the nurturing parent. Mother was the significant figure in the infant's life. She fed him, at that time mainly at the breast, so he was physically attached to her. She held him, loved him and protected him. Eventually she helped him towards independence. In the same way the analyst nurtured the patient, kept him safe, cared for him and after a period where the patient was dependent on the analyst, helped him towards an independent life.

In a rather different way, this process can be applied to counselling. It is different for a number of reasons. The main one is that the analyst will be working with the patient over a much longer time, possibly years. The relationship between the analyst and the patient who have met four or five times a week for several years is bound to be of a different quality from the counsellor–client relationship of weeks, sometimes months or occasionally years.

But the counsellor who has some understanding of psychodynamic concepts should find the idea of 'counsellor as mother' a helpful one. Clients come to counselling because they feel distressed and vulnerable. The usual adult hold they have on life may have disappeared and in its place the client feels like a frightened child. When we feel abandoned or rejected, the idea of someone being there for us is just what we need. As we feel like the powerless child, part of us will want to be held by a nurturing mother. Whether or not, in reality, we have experienced a nurturing mother will be immaterial. In fact, we are more likely to long for a mother to care for us when we are traumatized, if we have never in childhood experienced it.

So in psychodynamic theory 'the mother' is a metaphor. It stands for the relationship between the counsellor and the client. The counsellor as 'mother' can be a man. And it is not all sweetness and light. As a baby at times hates the mother, so the client will hate the counsellor. And perhaps the counsellor will, in turn, hate the client. Winnicott, in Chapter 4, says, of the psychoanalyst, that he must at some level hate his patient in order to be able to help him.

Case Example | Norma: no place for her

Norma was the eldest of three girls. Her mother, she described as a 'depressed invalid'; so Norma had to care for her sisters and her mother. Her father drank heavily and 'escaped from the house when he could'. She thinks her mother tried to show affection but was 'too wrapped up in herself'.

She had always felt weighed down by responsibility and care, so not surprisingly became a nurse. The first time she came back home from the nurses' home she found her youngest sister had been allocated her bedroom. There was no place for her.

For a client who has never had an emotionally present mother the experience of having an attentive counsellor who cares about her can be a two-edged sword. The client may feel secure and that she has value; as well she may feel resentful at what she has missed in her life and project her anger on to the counsellor as mother.

Certainly there will be strong feelings around, where frustration, anger and disappointment are in play, on both sides. Because real relationships, as against idealized relationships, do contain difficult feelings, the success of the counselling encounter may depend on how these issues are resolved. Processes identified as transference and countertransference should aid the counsellor's awareness.

Transference

Crucial to psychodynamic understanding are the two processes of transference and countertransference. The theory of transference is based on the observation of the way in which we transfer feelings from past relationships on to new relationships. For example the new boss reminds the anxious woman in the office of her father. She has hardly spoken to her boss but expects him to be critical of her in the same way that her father was. Everything he says to her she will interpret as a criticism. Similarly, an anxious client can experience the counsellor as an authoritarian figure from his past. This can lead him to experience the counsellor's reflections as an attack, even though, for the counsellor, this was not consciously intended. The counsellor has reflected on the comments she wants to make, assuring herself that they could not in any way be felt as judgemental. But she is overlooking the client's history if she is surprised by the client's defensive response.

Countertransference

Countertransference is usually understood as the counsellor's response to the client's transference. For example the client, in the transference, sees the counsellor as mother. The counsellor begins to feel like the client's mother and finds herself acting in an inappropriate, overprotective way. This needs to be reflected on by the counsellor and taken to supervision for discussion.

Another strand of countertransference refers to the response of the counsellor to something of the client's. At an unconscious level something has been transferred from the client, which hooks into the counsellor. The counsellor feels an emotion, which does not entirely belong to her. For example the client is talking about his father and how he was never there for him as a child. The counsellor listens and feels an anger, which she cannot lose as the client moves on to talk of his own happiness as a new father, and how he will always be there for his child. The feelings stay with the counsellor after the session has ended and she then takes time to examine them. She realizes that the abandoned child she was in touch with was not the client, but herself. Her father left the family when she was six and though she has tried to forgive him, she still blames him for his rejection. The counsellor has tuned into the client's feelings but transferred them to her own experience.

It is important that counsellors in their own therapy have worked through the emotions connected to the most significant experiences in their own lives, so that they do not unconsciously transfer them to their clients. This counsellor acknowledges that the counselling she had to prevent her from putting her own feelings onto the client, without fully realising it, needs a top-up. The counsellor must further explore her unresolved feelings about her own father's abandonment. This will help her to work ethically with difficult experiences which mirror her own.

Holding and containing

The idea of holding and containing the client is a strong theme in psychodynamic counselling. Winnicott, in Chapter 4, has much to say about the mother holding her baby, which can be translated into the client–counsellor relationship. In Chapter 5, Bion talks about containment. This is an idea about the way in which the mother keeps the baby safe from its unbearable thoughts. The counsellor as container of the client's worst imaginings is a useful notion.

Case Example | Laura: uncontainable anxiety

Laura was the daughter of a policeman and a passive mother. She and her sister were frightened of their father's anger, as was their mother. Laura left home after university, but could not settle at a job for long and did not seem to be able to sustain either a career or a relationship. Her anxiety was not containable and led to self-destructive behaviour.

Case Example | (Continued)

In the therapy the counsellor held the client by her consistency. She allowed the client to be angry but laid down firm boundaries. Laura began to realize that she was terrified that she might inflict her anger on others, like her father had done. This led her, as a safety measure, to inflict it on herself. When Laura understood this, the anger, and the anxiety, which went with it, began to feel more manageable.

Thinking and feeling

The relationship between emotions, emotionalism and thinking is highlighted in psychodynamic thought, particularly in Bion's work (Chapter 5). The professional distance, being with the client but keeping an observer role, is a barrier to emotionalism, the enemy of thought. Helping the client to think about his feelings has been eloquently written about by Susie Orbach, Andrew Samuels and Valerie Sinason, all current psychoanalytic thinkers.

It is important for both the counsellor and client to think as well as feel.

Case Example | Mary: the trauma of abuse

Mary, as a child was physically and sexually abused by her father. As a young woman she was raped by a colleague. In court she was not believed.

When a client is so clearly traumatized, it is hard for the counsellor to think as well as feel. She may feel overwhelmed by sorrow and anger. But it is important for the client that the counsellor holds on to the thinking part of herself. Otherwise it is not helpful for the client. She may feel that the counsellor, overcome by emotion, cannot contain her. She needs a counsellor who can help her think, so that she can eventually integrate the trauma and begin to repair her life.

Some of this thinking, for the counsellor, will take place in external supervision. As the trainee counsellor grows in experience, she will begin to monitor her own thoughts and feelings in the counselling room. She will become what Casement (1985, p. 57) calls, her own 'internal supervisor', learning from the client and the process of the counselling.

And especially the counsellor must learn, from her own therapy, the self-knowledge that comes from being a client. We learn to think and feel from the client and from being a client. There are not two separate camps, one for the counsellor, one for the client. We have to be able to take both roles.

The talking cures

As counsellors or would-be counsellors we assume that what we do is beneficial. Critics of 'the talking cures' are often vociferous in telling us we are misguided. Rather than ignoring this criticism we need to think about it, to ensure we are behaving ethically.

Jeffrey Masson, once a practising psychoanalyst, is now a relentless critic of all forms of therapy. He asserts that psychoanalysis, psychotherapy and counselling are all oppressive and ultimately harmful to the patient or client. This does not only apply to psychoanalytic theory and practice. Masson claims that person-centred therapy, while appearing to be benign, is actually abusive because it distorts the client's reality by its overemphasis on the positive. 'Reading Rogers is such a bland experience that I found myself recalling the old adage that psychotherapy is the process whereby the bland teach the unbland to be bland. This reaction points to something lacking in Rogers and his writings, and that is sensitivity to people's real suffering' (1993, p. 245). Masson is saying that the therapist cannot hear what the client is really saying because the therapist is blinkered by his own view of reality. He therefore misrepresents the client's pain.

Masson goes on to say that whatever the underlying theory, it is in the nature of therapy to distort another person's reality (1993, p. 247). This is a harsh claim. Frosh answers it for analysis by stating that psychoanalysis does not focus on reality, but with the patient's internal version of the world. Therapy works with phantasy (1999, p. 249).

Counselling of all orientations demands that the counsellor works with the client's truth. This truth might be at odds with the way others, including the counsellor, view the client and his perceptions of his world. But the good counsellor knows she must work with what the client brings. The agenda must be his, not the counsellor's and she must be aware of her own assumptions, her view of the world and the theoretical concepts underpinning her practice. That way she is less likely to exploit her power in the relationship.

But in terms of reality, most clients who come to counselling find their reality frightening. That is why they have come to counselling. They do not like the disabling feelings of anxiety or depression. They want to feel more in control of their lives. After the counsellor and client have together worked on the client's internal reality, the ultimate result of the counselling, for the client, may be a more objective reality.

> By its very nature psychotherapy must pretend to supply an objective, kindly, and humane atmosphere to those who wish to express their deepest feelings of pain and sorrow. The tragedy is that this legitimate need is exploited, even if with the best of intentions, by 'experts' who claim to offer what has never been theirs to give.
>
> (Masson, 1993, p. 47)

These are powerful statements asserting that the therapeutic relationship is based on a falsehood. This is that the pretended mutuality of the relationship is constructed with the therapist having the power and usually benefiting financially from the relationship. In this situation the 'expert' necessarily exploits the vulnerabilities of the client.

As counsellors we should examine these assertions rather than dismiss them. I do not believe that counselling is inherently harmful, but we do have the capacity to exploit our clients, so we should be keeping an ever-watchful gaze on our motivations, and a careful internal supervision of our practice. This must of course be backed up by external supervision, from a supervisor chosen for her challenging skill, rather than someone who will give us an easy ride.

Power in the counselling room

However much we may claim that we have an equal, empowering relationship with the client, we are deceiving ourselves. When a client comes to counselling he is seeking help. He may feel bitter and resentful that he finds himself in this position. He almost certainly feels vulnerable and probably powerless. We can keep this understanding at the forefront and be mindful of humility, or we can exploit our power.

The following are cartoons on power and motivation I wrote as a basis for discussion in counsellor training.

The 'I am omnipotent' counsellor

I do not want to be vulnerable or needy, so if I become a counsellor I can defend myself against these fears by making others dependent on me. They will see me as strong and different from themselves and I can start to believe it too. At its extreme I can tell people what to do and they will do it. I can change their destiny. I can play God.

The 'I can do it all myself' counsellor

A slightly different motivation, stemming from the same anxieties, results in the self-sufficient counsellor. Donald Winnicott (in Chapter 4) decided to become a doctor after he had broken his collarbone at school. He did not want to be dependent on doctors all his life. A similar reasoning affects the person who says that she is a private person who always solves her own problems. She therefore feels she is in no need of a counsellor, but is in a prime position to help others.

The 'you couldn't make it up' counsellor

Counselling encompasses an intimate relationship, in which the counsellor may be privy to the secrets of another. To be allowed to enter a stranger's world is a privilege. To be trusted with confidential information as the relationship develops is an immense honour. Abusing that privilege for our own ends is the worst betrayal of the client. In an age of confessional television, books and journals, which clearly satisfy a vicarious need in us, counselling offers a unique opportunity to satisfy this need respectably, with a professional certificate hanging on the wall giving us licence to probe. How often is voyeurism a potent force in our wish to be a counsellor?

The 'I could tell you some things' counsellor

And then, as counsellors, we may become embroiled in cases, which hit the headlines. A national disaster, a lurid court case, child sexual abuse, suicide, rape are all issues in which the public seems to have an insatiable appetite for news. Counsellors are in a preeminent position to be an insider, familiar with that news. Does sensationalism and prurience have a lure here, which we should all want to disavow?

The 'thank god it's not me' counsellor

Being a counsellor can help us to forget our own troubles. Finding that there is someone in an infinitely worse position than ourselves can make us feel happier with our lot. The hour that we sit with clients can be cleansing and reparative for us. We can feel a warm glow, which melts the anxieties.

We can feel sorry for our clients. 'Poor thing', we can think. 'Fancy getting into such a mess. Can you imagine it? Never mind, I can help her get out of it.' Arrogance and sentimentalism are other self-serving reasons to be a counsellor, what others may call a 'do-gooder'.

The 'I'll care for you through thick and thin' counsellor

The compulsive carer is a counsellor who in the past may have had little care herself. Rather than acknowledging this and asking appropriate others for care, she lavishes it on her clients. She will overwhelm them with her care and in the process threaten their independence. 'Good thing they've got me', she thinks as she envelops another client in her protection. Her clients either leave very quickly or never seem to move on.

The 'I'm riding to the rescue' counsellor

This is the counsellor who wants to save clients, from the world, from depression, from themselves. As a saviour, the counsellor knows what is best for the client and best of all is to become like the counsellor. The client will stay a long time with this counsellor because whenever he makes a bid for freedom, the counsellor will rein him in for his own good. 'It's a wicked world out there and he's not ready to cope with it just yet.'

The 'much madder than me' counsellor

'At times I think I'm a bit mad. I get very depressed and once I actually thought about ending it all. Of course that was very short lived. Normally I'm a happy, very positive person.' This counsellor thinks that working with more depressed and anxious people than herself may be a talisman, preventing her descent into madness.

The 'too clever by half' counsellor

The other extreme is the expert, the counsellor who has so many qualifications, both paper and personality, that make her full of knowledge and certainty. If she appears arrogant it is with good reason because she knows. The clients find her reassuring, if a little terrifying. Her superior knowledge and lack of any doubt ensure they feel in safe hands. Of course, the less distressed clients have not stayed around to be browbeaten and patronized. They have voted with their feet. But the remaining very vulnerable group of clients feel that this counsellor is their saviour and they will be eternally grateful to her. It makes her feel good and stifles the smallest doubt, which only occasionally assails her.

Motivation for being a counsellor

I wrote these cartoons, loosely based on observation and experience, to illustrate how essential it is to examine our motivations and to have our own personal therapy. I was aware that for some counsellors there is a horror of being a client, together with a notion that there are two camps. In the first draughty, leaking camp languish those who need counselling ('Not me!') while the other, more comfortable camp contains the counsellors. This is the camp to belong to.

The motivations in the illustrations may seem both extreme and unworthy. Yet we must acknowledge that there are elements of these motivations, which embrace power, vulnerability, loss and anxiety, in our choosing to be counsellors.

Childhood experiences

In the chapters, which follow, the biographical experiences of the theorists demonstrate reasons for their professional psychotherapeutic choices. The childhood experiences of Melanie Klein (Chapter 3), Donald Winnicott (Chapter 4), Wilfred Bion (Chapter 5) and John Bowlby (Chapter 6) suggest that they all, in different ways, felt loss and emotional deprivation, in particular from an absent mother. Klein suffered multiple losses.

I have been made aware at conferences and training events, whenever counsellors are gathered together, particularly with people they do not know, how often the subject of childhood is raised. It seems that in any given counsellor group, the majority will admit to having experienced a difficult childhood. Particularly from a psychodynamic view, early experiences are crucial in our development. We spend much of our adult life dealing with our early years. This is done in different ways. We can deny and repress, which gets us through, if we do not allow ourselves to think. We can present a difficult childhood as a justification for our lives not being successful. We can try to understand the experience and perhaps forgive the people we feel failed us. In this last position we may offer our services as counsellors in the hope that we can prevent others experiencing our distress. This is almost certainly a romantic aspiration, but realistically we may be able to help others to work through their painful, infantile experiences.

> While many people are attracted to a career as a therapist, the path towards counselling competence is often fraught with obstacles, not least those emanating from wounds that have fuelled the motivation to take such steps.
>
> (Wheeler, 2007, p. 253)

Narcissistic injury

Melanie Klein (Chapter 3) describes the narcissistic needs of a baby, who though feeling the centre of her universe, is also completely dependent on the mother. If those needs are not met the child will grow into adulthood still feeling the world revolves around her, but with an inordinate desire for love and attention. These split feelings of vulnerability and omnipotence can lead her towards wanting to be a therapist.

The wounded healer

The wounded healer was a term first used by Jung, to describe the vulnerability of the therapist. We are all to some extent wounded, some much more grievously than others. But if we can learn from past painful experiences, and integrate them, we can become effective therapists. The wounded healer can have a greater understanding and sensitivity towards the client's needs.

Sue Wheeler says that being real and vulnerable are essential components of the therapeutic relationship. 'However the therapist is a person with his own life history, traumas, wounds and difficulties sometimes no less than those of the client. Such wounds have much to contribute to the therapeutic endeavour but they can also inhibit it' (2007, p. 247).

Wheeler cites personal therapy as the way in which developmental history and past traumas can be processed. This should ensure that therapists' needs are met in their role as client, not therapist. Wheeler's own research (Wheeler and Schroder, 2005) revealed that counsellors in Britain have on average four years of personal therapy.

Reparation

A significant motivation for becoming a counsellor is reparation. Reparation, the act of repairing or being repaired is an interesting therapeutic concept. Melanie Klein suggests that from an early age a baby tries to make amends to his mother for hating her. The baby feels guilt, an uncomfortable feeling, which can be eased by making good something, which felt bad. This is the reason for the half-chewed biscuits offered as a present, but, more importantly, the hugs and kisses, proffered and demanded, that will make everything right again.

It is a truism that many people who go into the caring professions are making some sort of reparation, though the reparation will have diverse roots. In caring for others we are trying to repair something we have done or had done to us.

Research

Marilyn Barnett (2007) carried out a piece of qualitative research on therapists' unconscious motivations into their choice of profession. Nine experienced psychoanalytic and psychodynamic psychotherapists were interviewed. Two major themes of early loss and narcissistic need emerged.

She found that as children,

> they had tended to be rather introverted, often solitary, 'the odd one out'. Inner feelings of anxiety and lack of confidence had sometimes been masked by an outward show of boisterousness or efforts to amuse and entertain. A common experience seemed to be a special sensitivity to the needs of others and a readiness to comply in order to maintain feelings of security and well-being. For some, a reparative urge was in place at an early age and the roots of a desire to heal and mend lay in the dynamics of the original family.
>
> (2007)

This certainly accords with my experience as a counsellor trainer. It also highlights the benefit of being aware of unconscious motivations than merely the conscious ones offered.

Barnett says that applicants for counsellor training may defend against examining unconscious motivations. 'Applicants may initially feel indignant at the thought of needing counselling themselves but are reluctant to consider what needs of their own they might be attempting to meet by becoming a counsellor.' Barnett cites Loewenthal (2001, pp. 2–3) who 'wonders whether the emphasis on relationship is being lost and whether, attracted by the technical, they wish to avoid a personal therapy which would explore their abilities to meet the needs of others.'

Gertrude Mander (2004) says that what she is looking for in candidates for therapy training is 'a capacity for reflection, conceptualization and thinking which will enable them to read and draw on theory, to use it creatively in formulating diagnostic hypotheses, and to adjust these in the light of new material emerging during the therapeutic process. Together with empathy and intuition, thinking is the third indispensable factor in the therapeutic endeavour.'

The journey

If we become counsellors, making ourselves aware of the pitfalls, trying to curb our enthusiasm to know it all, to make it better, we could be in the privileged position to have the opportunity of making a relationship with a stranger. Here lie the rewards for the counsellor. Travelling along a path where the counsellor and client work together, gaining understanding through feeling and reflection, working through the difficult emotions like frustration and anger, and arriving at a destination that the client feels is a better place than his starting point, is rewarding.

Further reading

Barnett, M. (2007) What brings you here? An exploration of the unconscious motivation of those who choose to train and work as psychotherapists and counsellors. *Psychodynamic Practice* 13 (3): 257–274.

Mander, G. (2004) The selection of candidates for training in psychotherapy and counselling. *Psychodynamic Practice* 10.2 May 2004.

Wheeler, S. (2007) What shall we do with the wounded healer: the supervisor's dilemma. *Psychodynamic Practice* 13 (3): 245–256.

2

Freud: where it all started

Sigmund Freud was the father of psychoanalysis and so, ultimately, of counselling. Although many counsellors might want to deny it, it all started here; so it is important that we recognize his theories, even if we later discard them. We need to know what we are discarding.

Many important theorists took this route, starting as psychoanalysts and subsequently adapting Freud's theories or rebelling against them. Berne, the founder of Transactional Analysis; Perls, the founder of Gestalt therapy; Ellis, the father of Rational Emotive Behaviour therapy, all began as psychoanalysts before rejecting classical Freudian theory and going their own, very different, ways.

Melanie Klein adapted Freud's theories to found the Kleinian School, the beginning of the Object Relations School in Britain, though she always maintained that she was a Freudian. Klein saw her work as a development of Freud's, refusing to acknowledge that there were grounds for conflict. Freud, who brooked no opposition, regarded her work as heretical.

Freud's work is so fundamental to therapy and counselling that all counsellors, not just those taking a psychodynamic approach, draw on his theories, often unwittingly. This is because much Freudian thought has been adapted, almost beyond recognition. Counsellors working in bereavement agencies may not know that the models of grief and mourning they use with their clients have their origins in Freud's 1917 paper on 'Mourning and Melancholia'.

Freud's theories are not always easy for counsellors to understand, but then, of course, they were never intended for counsellors. They were written for psychoanalysts, pursuing a Freudian route, who see patients usually five times a week for several years. The relationship and the purpose are different. In analysis the purpose is often to restructure the patient's personality, a far cry from counselling.

Yet there is so much of Freudian thought that is useful to counsellors and we may be applying some of it already. It is important that we understand as much as possible of the theories that underpin our practice, otherwise we can become dangerous. So trainee counsellors, newly starting out, can gain much from an understanding of some of Freud's work, learning how to safely work with some of his principles.

Influence of Freudian ideas

A major reason for studying Freud is to learn about ourselves. Freudian theory is now so thoroughly integrated into Western culture that we cannot escape it. Freudian thought influences philosophy, sociology, art, writing, novels, plays, films – Woody Allen's film, *Love and Death* (in which Freud's life instinct, Eros, is pitted against his death instinct, Thanatos), epitomizes this. In art, movements such as Dadaism and Surrealism owe a debt to Freud. Novelists who use stream-of-consciousness techniques, like Virginia Woolf, borrow from Freud's psychoanalytic method of free association. Incidentally, when Virginia Woolf met Freud for tea, in Hampstead, in the last year of his life, she described him as 'a screwed up shrunk very old man: with a monkey's light eyes' (Gay, 1988, p. 640).

It is argued that today one can learn as much about the unconscious from reading modern literature as attending an academic course. Writers like the English Anita Brookner, the Canadian Margaret Atwood and the American Anne Tyler, writing in different ways about different societies, have in common an appreciation of internal psychodynamic conflict. Even the self-described 'low brow', Agatha Christie, played out the conflicts in her inner world in her detective novels. 'Tapping into the unconscious, she developed a range of characters who follow neither the statistical norm nor the conventions of fiction' (Gill, 1990, p. 7). In her autobiography, Christie, alluding to unconscious processes says: 'It is curious to look back over life, over all the varying incidents and scenes – such a multitude of odds and ends. Out of them all what has mattered what lies behind the selection that memory has made? What makes us choose the things that we have remembered? It is as though one went to a great trunk full of junk in the attic and plunged one's hands in to it and said, I will have this – and this – and this.' Freud himself said something similar when he talked about the amnesia of the past, what is remembered and what is 'forgotten'. Interestingly Freud, when he needed to relax, enjoyed reading detective stories like those of Agatha Christie (Gay, 1988).

Freud's nephew, Edward Bernays, was the founder of the public relations industry in the United States, an institution which permeates our everyday life. The work of Freud's daughter, Anna, was used by advertising agencies as well as for political propaganda in the United States in the 1950s and 1960s.

People who would not dream of reading Freud's work talk about 'Freudian slips'. We accept that childhood experiences shape our later life and much of social policy is based on this premise. The family is regarded as the source of emotional, as well as social development, with the dysfunctional family blamed for much of society's ills. Though not exclusive to Freud, all these are Freudian notions, often espoused by people who think Freud's ideas are 'all about sex' and repugnant. As a backcloth to Western society, exploring Freudian thought helps us to better understand ourselves and our attitudes and values in the twenty-first century. It also gives us more insight into our clients' difficulties.

Life of Sigmund Freud

Freud believed that our experiences, in particular our childhood experiences, make us what we are. Psychodynamic counselling looks at the past in order to understand the present. Therefore it makes sense to look at the experiences in Freud's life, which formed him, may have given birth to his theories, and made him, alongside Karl Marx, one of the foremost influences on twentieth-century thought.

Freud wrote so much himself, and so much has been written about him since, that it is a daunting task to decide what to include within the limitations of an introductory book. I have tried to pick out what I think will interest counsellors and help explain the man and his work. I am drawing primarily on Peter Gay's (1988) masterly biography, *Freud: A Life for Our Time*.

Early life

Sigmund Freud was born, Sigismund Schlomo Freud, in 1856 in Freiburg, a small town in Moravia, in the then Austro-Hungarian Empire, now Pribor in Czechoslovakia. In 1859 the family moved to Vienna, first staying briefly in Leipzig. The train journey from Freiburg must have been incredibly long and arduous for a three-year-old and a phobia of travelling by train (and Freud did a lot of travelling) never quite left him (Wollheim, 1971, p. 19). Freud lived in Vienna, a city, which he was ambivalent about, and at times purported to dislike, for 79 years. A long time to be ambivalent!

Lavinia Gomez evocatively describes the world Freud grew up in as an Austria embroiled in political and cultural turmoil, where social unrest was fuelled by the economic disaster of a stock market crash in 1873. 'The Hapsburgs, the longest ruling family in Europe were in the throes of self-destruction: Europe was rocked by the double suicide of Crown Prince Rudolf and his teenage mistress in 1889, and the Austro-Hungarian Empire disintegrated at the end of the First World War' (Gomez, 1997, p. 10). Cultural revolution in turn of the century Vienna produced such disparate figures as the philosopher Wittgenstein, the erotic artist Klimt and Adolf Hitler. It was in this melting pot of ideas and destruction that Freud lived.

Sigmund was the eldest of eight children, born to a father old enough to be his grandfather and a 20-year-old mother. Because this was not Jakob Freud's first marriage, Sigmund was surrounded by a confusing extended family in which his half-brother Philip was old enough to be his father. Jacobs (1992, p. 8) suggests, in terms of age, Philip would have made a more suitable partner for his mother, perhaps sowing the seeds for Freud of his attraction to the Oedipal myth. Freud had a nephew, John, who was a year older than Freud, described by Freud (Wollheim, 1971) as his 'partner in crime'. Perhaps being part of this complex family structure was an early strand of Freud's psychoanalytic view of the family, full of conflict and sexual ambiguity.

Freud was Jewish and this was the most important part of his identity. In his autobiographical study (1925, p. 7), he says, 'My parents were Jews and I have remained a Jew myself.' He never practised the Jewish religion, being equally dismissive of all religions as self-delusory.

But the fact of being part of a Jewish people, with a collective history of oppression, was seminal. He was dismayed by the story his father told of having his cap thrown into the gutter by a Christian, who ordered him to get off the pavement (Gay, 1988). Freud's dismay seems as much about his father's passivity in the face of such aggression, as the aggression itself. Freud vowed he would never be humble like his father. The scorn he felt for his father in this shaming incident is suggested by Clark (1980) as a possible catalyst for the conflict between father and son, which Freud postulated was inherent in the Oedipus complex.

Freud seemed to equate masculinity with physical force when years later he collaborated with the American diplomat William C. Bullitt in writing a psychoanalytic study of Woodrow Wilson, 28th president of the

United States (Storr, 1989, p. 73). Describing Wilson as a 'prime prig', he went on, 'Sickly, spectacled, shy, guarded by father, mother and sisters, Tommy Wilson never had a fist fight in his life.' (Prejudicial language we should not encourage trainee counsellors to use in case studies!)

As a Viennese Jew, some professions were barred to Freud, so his choice of medicine was a constrained one. He attributed his intellectual independence to the opposition he encountered at the University of Vienna where he was subject to rabid anti-Semitism. This seemed to strengthen his self-respect as a Jew. He said, 'I was expected to feel myself inferior and an alien because I was a Jew. I refused absolutely to do the first of these things.' As for being 'an alien' he says, 'at an early age I was made familiar with the fate of being in the Opposition' (1925, p. 9). Freud always saw himself very much as part of the Jewish community, had few friends who were not Jewish and regularly attended the meetings of the local Jewish society. Later he refused to accept royalties from his books when they were translated into Yiddish and Hebrew (Storr, 1989, p. 1). Psychoanalysis was at first a predominantly Jewish movement. The Christian Carl Jung is quoted as saying that it was 'too Jewish'.

Although Freud suffered discrimination outside the home, within the home he was the favourite, referred to by his mother as, 'Mein goldener Sigi' (Jones, 1954). He seems to have been both clever and hard-working from being a small child. He read Shakespeare at eight. When he complained that his sister Anna's piano playing interfered with his studies, the piano vanished, never to return (Gay, 1988, p. 14). It seems the whole family were prepared to make sacrifices for this special boy.

He attributed his success in life to the twin experiences of being Jewish and being his mother's golden boy. Freud describes little about the influence on his life of his relationship with his mother. He remembers sexual wishes towards her when he was about four, when he saw her naked in the sleeping compartment of a train during an overnight railway journey. (Perhaps another reason for his phobia about trains.) Years later he wrote about the incident in a letter to his friend Fliess, but it still embarrassed him at forty-one and he distanced himself from it by describing it in Latin (Gay, 1988, p. 11). Certainly the incident offers subjective evidence for Freud's Oedipal complex, where the young boy desires his mother and wants to be rid of his father.

As we have seen earlier, Freud felt that his father was not assertive enough. Students of Freud have noted the absence of comment on his mother as significant, indicating an unwillingness, on Freud's part, to look at their relationship. Others have variously described Freud's mother. Storr (1989, p. 1) says she was 'a vivacious and charming lady', while Roith (1987, p. 110) in contrast sees her as a 'tyrant' and 'complaining'. Ernest Jones, who had many memories of her, described her 'lively personality' as an old lady. At ninety-five, six weeks before she died, her comment on her photograph in the newspapers was, 'A bad reproduction; it makes me look a hundred.'

When Freud carried out his 30 minutes of self-analysis every night, the basis of his theoretical concepts, it was centred on his father. Maybe the death of his father in 1896, the year he introduced the term 'psychoanalysis', left feelings that needed to be worked through. Perhaps it was too difficult for Freud to think about his own mother, still alive, until 1930, or even the effect mothers in general have on their children. But it did have the effect of making psychoanalysis, at that time, very male-oriented, in both its ideas and its practitioners.

Some commentators on Freud say that he did not understand the psychology of women and found them a puzzle. However, the place of women in late nineteenth-century Europe must be taken into account. Unlike Western societies today, men did not have the experiences of working on equal terms with women and even having women as their bosses. For Freud, apart from his mother and his sisters, whom the family regarded as inferior to their clever brother, the only other women he would have come into close contact with, in his early professional life, would be his hysterical patients. Yet later there were women psychoanalysts. Freud's relationships with some of them are interestingly documented in Appignanesi and Forrester's (1992) 'Freud's Women'.

Adult life

Freud met his future wife, Martha Bernays, in 1882. He was engaged to her 2 months later and married her after an engagement of 4 years. According to Gay (1988) he was a lover so jealous, it bordered on the pathological. 'I am so exclusive where I love', he told his fiancé. 'I certainly have a disposition to tyranny.'

There is an interesting comment in his autobiographical study (1925, p. 14) to the effect that 'it was the fault of my fiancé that I was not already famous at that youthful age'. Freud then goes on to describe how he wound up his research into the anaesthetic qualities of cocaine, to go and visit his betrothed in Hamburg, 'a distant city'. He handed over his research to a friend, but on his return found that another friend had continued the research, published it and gained the credit. 'But I bore my fiancee no grudge for the interruption', says Freud. (On the evidence offered, many counsellors might disagree.)

Over the first 9 years of their marriage the Freuds were to have six children, the youngest being Anna who was to follow in her father's footsteps. Martha seems to have been a tireless wife and mother, a housewife, who devoted her life to her husband. After Freud's death she wrote that 'in the fifty-three years of our married life, not one angry word fell between us' (quoted in Storr, 1989, p. 3). We might wonder at that assertion, as most married couples would expect to have a few angry words over 53 years. But Martha never offered herself as an intellectual companion to Freud. That role was taken by her sister, Minna, who lived with the couple for most of their married life. Gay (1988, p. 753) comments on the charge, made by Jung, that Freud had an affair with his sister-in-law. The rumour, circulating at the time, was considered to be serious enough to require explicit refutation. Gay quotes Jones as saying, 'His wife was assuredly the only woman in Freud's love life, and she always came first.' Gay, having examined the available evidence, thinks the likelihood of the affair improbable.

It was because of his marriage that he set up the private practice, in Vienna, that was to have such consequence, to support both himself and a wife. Had he not married, he would perhaps have continued research, for that seemed to be his passion. However, research was badly paid; so, reluctantly, Freud embarked upon medical practice. In 1885 he was appointed a lecturer in neuropathology. For four momentous months (in 1885–1886) Freud worked in Paris, under the famous neurologist Charcot, whose teachings on hysteria stimulated his interest in the problems of neurosis and of hypnotism as a treatment. Freud at first worked with hypnotism on his patients, as a way of getting in touch with unconscious material, but abandoned it for the technique he pioneered, free association.

The main element of free association, along with interpretation of the material patients brought, was the opportunity given to patients to speak freely, without curbing their emotions, about their symptoms and anxieties. Freud's colleague Breuer had first found this 'catharsis' to be therapeutic and he had shared with Freud his discoveries. Together they had collaborated on papers, which were subsequently published as a book, *Studies on Hysteria* in 1895. For Freud, Breuer's significant patient was Anna O., who had called her treatment with Breuer, the 'talking cure'. Breuer had discussed at length his treatment of Anna O. with Freud. Freud felt disappointed that Breuer had tried to ignore the sexual implications of the case, which embarrassed him. Freud saw Anna O.'s attachment to Breuer as extremely significant, and would call it, 'the transference'.

From all these roots psychoanalysis developed, from the first use of the term in 1896. Because Breuer could not accept the way Freud's thinking was leading, particularly in respect of Freud's views on sexuality and its place in neuroses, they parted company. Freud's idealization of Breuer turned to hostility.

Freud wrote in his autobiography, 'For more than ten years after my separation from Breuer I had no followers. I was completely isolated. In Vienna I was shunned; abroad no notice was taken of me.' Then things began to change. First a circle of pupils sat at Freud's feet in Vienna, which bolstered his flagging confidence. Then from about 1906, when Freud was fifty, psychiatrists like Carl Jung in Zurich started to be interested in psychoanalysis, what Freud called this 'young science'.

The next 30 years were to see the growth and development of psychoanalysis, with it becoming a significant force, both in Europe, and later, in the United States. Freud remained the acknowledged leader, who struggled with dissent. Those who did dissent went the same way as Breuer, first idealized by Freud, then becoming a disappointment and finally a threat. Jung, Adler and Reich all went their separate ways, not without public and often vitriolic conflict on both sides. When Jung resigned as President of the International Psychoanalytic Association in 1914, Freud was euphoric. 'So we are rid of them at last, the brutal holy Jung and his pious parrots' (Gay, 1988, p. 241). Freud was prepared to say that he was wrong, but could not accept rebellion from his followers.

Anna Freud was meanwhile being groomed to succeed her father. He took her into analysis over the years from 1918 to 1925; both of them knew this to be irregular and it was not discussed in public. Anna became an analyst and worked for much of her life with children. She developed her father's theories on the ego, and ego psychology became a very important post-Freudian development in North America.

While Anna, his last child, was gaining ascendancy amongst the Freud children, Freud was dealt a devastating blow by the death of his beloved daughter Sophie, in 1920. Those who were close to him said that he never really came to accept it. It was a dark time for Freud. The palate cancer, tragically mocking the man who had given his life to the talking cure, and with which he was to struggle for the rest of his life, struck him in 1923, the same year that his little grandson, Sophie's son, died.

Freud had been appalled and depressed by the horror of the First World War. In 1929 he wrote an influential essay, 'Civilisation and its Discontents', dismayed by the rise of Nazism in Austria and Germany. The subsequent Jewish persecution was to be the reason for Freud's last journey.

In 1938, after intercession from various prominent people, the Nazis allowed Freud and his family to leave Vienna. Before letting him go they insisted that he sign a statement that they had not ill-treated him. With heavy sarcasm and recklessly exposing himself to unnecessary danger, he added the postscript, 'I can highly recommend the Gestapo to everyone' (Gay, 1988, p. 628).

The family settled at 20 Maresfield Gardens in Hampstead, now the Freud Museum, where Freud's consulting room, arranged as it had been in Vienna, can be inspected.

Freud died on 23 September 1939, shortly after War had been declared. Freud had commented dryly, 'My last war.'

The unconscious

Although Freud is often credited with introducing the concept of the unconscious, Whyte (1962) says the idea of unconscious mental processes was beginning to be thought about as early as 1700. The notion certainly gained credence during the nineteenth century. Philosophers, poets and novelists all wrote about an elusive part of ourselves that we cannot get in touch with, but is nonetheless significant to us, affecting our thoughts and behaviour. The poet Goethe and the philosopher Nietzsche, both very influential on Freud's thinking, believed the unconscious to be the source of creativity.

Novelists such as George Eliot and Henry James and poets such as William Wordsworth and Samuel Taylor Coleridge all explicitly or implicitly pay tribute to some kind of unconscious forces within us and the consequent struggle and conflict.

Wollheim (1971, p. 157) quotes Freud: 'The concept of the unconscious has long been knocking at the gates of psychology and asking to be let in. Philosophy and literature have often toyed with it, but science could find no use for it.'

The topographical approach to mental processes

What Freud did was to integrate the concept of the unconscious into his other theories in a systematic way. He produced a topographical, a layered, model of the mind in which the mind was divided into three parts, the conscious, the preconscious and the unconscious.

The conscious mind has the awareness of the moment, what we are experiencing now. We know what is happening to us in the present.

The preconscious mind contains material which can be fairly easily accessed and things that are temporarily 'forgotten' or repressed. These could possibly be remembered in counselling. Freud believed that the preconscious works through what he called secondary process. This means that there is an awareness of external reality and its limitations, which Freud called the reality principle.

Primary process rules the unconscious, which has no conception of reality, no logic, no time, no sense of waiting, for that would presuppose time in the future. The unconscious demands immediate gratification, and the pleasure principle is dominant. However, this is not as hedonist as it sounds, as Freud interpreted the pleasure principle as the avoidance of pain, maybe an example of Freud's low key, pragmatic, some would say, pessimistic approach to life.

The unconscious has two parts. The unconscious proper contains innate knowledge, which is unknowable. Primal phantasies (Freud, 1916–1917, S.E. 15) which have never been conscious, but are nonetheless there, affect us, though we are not aware of them. We cannot make this part conscious. This is a part of our human heritage.

The other part of the unconscious, the repressed unconscious, contains material which was once conscious, but we have pushed it into unconsciousness because it is too disturbing to us. Freud believed that repressing thoughts and experiences, many of them from childhood, take up much emotional energy that could be better exploited. Repressed material can make us ill. Neurotic symptoms can be the outward sign of unconscious repression. Becoming aware of this material in analysis, through Freud's technique of free association, possibly five times a week, for several years, can make the patient better. However, some repressed material may never become available to the patient, even in five-times-a-week analysis.

Although the concept of the unconscious is now so much part of our culture, it is still a puzzling idea to try to make sense of. People talk about 'knowing something unconsciously', but of course this is paradoxical. As soon as we get in touch with unconscious material it stops being unconscious. Freud is said to have chided Salvador Dali when he showed Freud a painting he said was of the unconscious. Freud replied that, since Dali had painted it, it was conscious.

So what can counsellors learn from this quite complex theory?

The first rule is not to get too involved in something we do not quite understand and then start to try to apply it. This would be both unethical and dangerous. What counsellors can learn from Freud's theory of the unconscious is a better understanding of our clients and ourselves. The idea of the unconscious does answer some of the questions counsellors struggle with. Why does this client behave in such an illogical way? Why do we all behave in illogical ways? The notion that we are driven by powerful forces that we are not fully conscious of, but which affect our behaviour, offers an explanation. We may not like the phenomenon. Acting in ways which are not entirely within our control is rather frightening to envisage. But it does mean that counsellors may begin to comprehend why it is so difficult for clients to change. It may stop us trying to impose simplistic, problem-solving solutions, which are doomed to failure. Instead we may help the client by offering a space for further exploration and understanding.

As counsellors we can try to work with preconscious material if this seems appropriate. We do see many clients who come with difficulties, the result of their traumatic repressed memories. Childhood abuse and rape are examples of such traumas. As long as we are not leading clients in ways in which we, rather than they, want to go, but offering a space to think and feel, we should be working ethically. Working ethically will include ensuring that we have adequate supervision. Not only is the task difficult, it can be traumatic for counsellors to work with such painful material. The case for personal therapy cannot be overstated in such circumstances. Providing a safe therapeutic space is essential, but it does not happen without thought and care.

Case Example | Maureen: a counsellor working psychodynamically with preconscious material

Maureen came to counselling because she was unable to go to work. She loved her job, and felt very angry with her body for letting her down. She had fainted twice at the office and was now terrified to go into work, in case it happened again. She described the humiliation

Case Example | (Continued)

and powerlessness of coming to on the office floor, surrounded by her colleagues, not knowing what had happened to her. What might she have said? What might she have done?

Her doctor had prescribed antidepressants but Maureen said that she felt no better and hated taking them. Her doctor then suggested counselling.

Maureen was thirty and lived on her own. She had a boy friend she 'knocked about with', but it was not serious. She had two elder brothers and was quite close to Peter who was only a year older than her. Maureen occasionally saw her father, but he had a second wife whom Maureen did not get on with. She did not mention her mother. Maureen went on to talk about Rita, her aunt, who had been good to her as a child. When I asked if Rita was her mother's sister there was a silence. Then Maureen said, 'My mother's dead. I wouldn't go to the funeral.'

Maureen went on to say that after leaving school she got a job, left home and had subsequently avoided contact with her mother. She remembered nothing of her childhood except going to Auntie Rita's house. It was a blank. When I said that it was a bit like her fainting attacks, she looked surprised, but then said, 'I suppose so.'

As the counselling went on Maureen began to remember more about her childhood. She remembered times when her mother had hit her. She remembered incidents where her mother had cruelly punished her, once giving her dog away. 'She always criticized me and put me down', said Maureen sadly. 'No wonder I wouldn't go to her funeral.'

It seemed to relieve Maureen to find a reason for refusing to go to the funeral. She had been the subject of opprobrium from the rest of the family for not doing 'the decent thing'. Even her brothers, whom she acknowledged also had difficult childhoods, though had never been treated so harshly as she, said that of course they must all attend their mother's funeral. But Maureen had been adamant. 'Why should I go?' she said.

During the counselling sessions Maureen was able to remember more of the traumatic incidents that had happened at her mother's hand, in her childhood. These sessions were very difficult for Maureen. She was feeling the pain that she had, unconsciously, spent much emotional energy in blanking out.

Later Maureen was able to recall some of the better moments of her childhood and her relationship with her mother. 'At times she could be nice. Sometimes she could be quite funny. She could make you laugh if she felt like it.'

By this time Maureen was feeling better about herself and felt able to go back to work. The fainting attacks were not repeated. It seemed as if making conscious some repressed traumatic memories, and looking at the relationship with her mother had unblocked a multitude of painful, repressed feelings. These repressed feelings, though she was not fully aware of them, had nonetheless affected Maureen's behaviour. Now Maureen did not feel blank any more and she did not have to blank out to escape painful feelings.

Dreams

Psychoanalysis is one way through which the unconscious can be expressed. Dreams are another. Unlike analysis, they are financially cost-free, so exploring them should be available to everyone. Freud called the interpretation of dreams the royal road to a knowledge of the unconscious. 'If I am asked how one can become a psychoanalyst I reply, "By studying one's own dreams" ' (1910, S.E. Vol. XI, p. 33).

Dreams have always been significant to the dreamer. Greek myths, Shakespearean plays, novels, poems and paintings have all portrayed the power of dreams. Sometimes they are wishful, more usually, portentous. A dream interpreter, who can see omens, is usually regarded as a person with special, maybe supernatural, gifts.

In some African societies seers, or prophets, are the link, through dreams, between god and man. 'It seems their main duties are to act as ritual elders, to give advice on religious matters (e.g. when particular ceremonies are to be held), to receive messages from divinities and spirits, through possession or dreams, and to pass on the information to their communities' (Mbiti, 1969, p. 68).

So the duty of the interpreter is to communicate his special knowledge to his listeners. However, if the interpretation is not to the listeners' advantage, the interpreter can be in danger. In the *Biblical Book of Genesis* (Chapters 37–47), we see how Joseph is dispatched, by his envious brothers, for interpreting dreams in which they are subservient to him. In the dream the brothers took most exception to, they all, as sheaves of corn, bow down to Joseph. He is sold to strangers, but in the way of portentous dreams, the brothers do all end, years later, bowing down to Joseph, beholden to him for food. Joseph has become influential because of his interpretation of dreams. Pharoah's dreams of fat cows and thin cows have been interpreted by Joseph to forecast famine. Joseph utilizes the dream to manage the existing resources, so the people do not starve. (The success of the musical, 'Joseph and The Amazing Technicolour Dreamcoat' is, in part, a tribute to our fascination with the dream.)

If, in the past, dreams were useful to tell the future, in Freudian theory, because the unconscious has no truck with time, this is not the function of the dream. Freud's first book to be published was *The Interpretation of Dreams* (actually published in 1989, though dated by the publisher as 1900). In it Freud discusses the function of the dream. He suggests that since the rejection of mythological hypotheses, dreams have needed some explanation. What is the relationship between waking life, the stimuli for the dream, the contents, which Freud says are often repugnant to waking thought, and the transitory nature of the dream? Above all what is the significance of dreams, and does an individual dream have a meaning? (1900).

Freud answered his own questions. He posited that the content of a dream is the representation of a fulfilled wish, altered by the censorship we impose, so that we do not find the wish shocking. Because this repressed material would disturb us, if it were not transformed by the dream, the function of the dream is to guard our sleep. This notion is confirmed by later scientists, who in their research into REM (rapid eye movement denoting dreaming) sleep reinforce the necessity of dreaming to good mental and physical health. Torturers know that to deprive victims of sleep invites psychotic behaviour, and of course sleep deprivation means dream deprivation.

In counselling, clients often bring their dreams. Perhaps influenced by Hollywood, where the therapist usually holds the answers, they ask us to interpret them. This is a trap to avoid. Within a 'standard' counselling training we do not have the knowledge or skills to do this. This should not stop our encouraging the client to give the dream meaning. We can also work with the client on the meaning, just as we would do with any material the client brings. But how an analyst, with years of training studying dreams, works with dreams is way beyond our scope.

Below is an example of a client who brings a dream, and works on it in the counselling session, until it has meaning for him.

Case Example | Peter: learns from a dream

This is the dream of Peter, a 31-year-old man who originally came to counselling because he was depressed. During the counselling he brought the dilemma that he constantly wrestled with, the conflict between freedom and security. Which should he choose? Freedom was epitomized by the ability to take off and live in another country for several months, which had been his recent pattern. Security, which at some level he longed for, though was frightened by, was represented by his girlfriend and the possibility of marrying her, settling down and having a family.

Peter dreamt that he was walking through a wood and saw a lioness in a tree. The lioness was large and beautiful and she was watching him. She had a tail in her claws, which seemed to be the remains of her dinner.

Then the dream changed and Peter was at a fair. He was having a good time playing on the swings and merry-go-rounds; when he looked up he saw the lioness watching him from the top of a tree.

Peter said he thought the dream was very clear. He had dreamt his dilemma. Should he choose security or freedom? I asked him what he thought about the lioness, in the two halves of the dream. He said that he thought in the first part of the dream she was frightening, and the meal she had finished might have been him. But in the second part of the dream he could feel she was protective.

Yet Peter felt that the dream did not set out his dilemma fairly. In the second part, freedom, epitomized by the swings, taking off into the air, and the merry-go-rounds, having fun on something that takes you round, perhaps round the world, is offered. Surprisingly the lioness/girlfriend seems to give him her blessing.

In the first part of the dream the lioness/girlfriend will devour him and perhaps emasculate him, the image of the tail (his?) in her claws. There is freedom in the second part of the dream, but no security in the first.

I wondered what meaning Peter could get out of the dream that would make sense to him. Peter said that he had been thinking a

Case Example | (Continued)

lot about it. The dream was so vivid that he carried it around in his head. He thought he had turned his girlfriend into a frightening predator in the first part of the dream, whereas the reality was much more like the second part of the dream, where she is protective.

What he had been thinking was that perhaps the choice was not so stark. Perhaps he had made it into opposites, freedom on the one hand, security, which maybe he saw as a prison, on the other. Perhaps there was a compromise. He had assumed that his girlfriend wanted security, while he wanted freedom. But they had met when both were travelling overseas. Maybe she wanted freedom too. They needed to properly talk together.

Peter had got out of his dream some meaning for himself. I might have read it differently. But, because I believe it is important when clients bring us their dreams that we do not try to interpret them. I listened, trying to help Peter explore the dream, both then and in subsequent sessions.

The dream belongs to the client, and it is not for us to play expert. We can use what the client says about his dream as a basis for further discussion, and this can be very helpful. The worst we can do is to be influenced by the books that purport to give a standard meaning to particular dreams. What the client is bringing in his dream is a glimpse into his internal world. It is individual and precious and should be treated as such.

The structure of the mind

Over the years Freud wrestled with a structure of the mind as he felt the layered map of the mind, divided into the conscious, preconscious and unconscious, incomplete. It was not until 1923 that he put forward his three-part structure of the mind, in which the components were the 'It, I and Over I'. Unfortunately when it was translated into English from the German, the Latin terms id, ego and superego were substituted. The translations were carried out by James and Alix Strachey and Joan Riviere. James Strachey was anxious to make Freud's work acceptable, not just to the psychoanalytic community but to a wider academic readership and in doing so turned Freud's everyday terms into something much more obscure. Bettelheim (1983) goes further and says that the translations, endorsed by Anna Freud and accepted by Freud himself, conceal and distort Freud's humanity.

The three elements, of the structure of the mind, the id, the ego and the superego are closely associated with the conscious, preconscious and unconscious but are further defined and described.

The id is the repository of our darkest instincts and desires. It has no concept of reality or morality. Murky sexual wishes lurk there, demanding instant gratification. Freud described it as a seething cauldron of drives, many of these repressed drives left over from infantile sexual desires. Because the id resides in the unconscious, it cannot be explicitly experienced. However, because it seeks pleasure, or alternately the avoidance of pain, it influences our behaviour, though we do not know why. Freud following the idiosyncratic psychiatrist George Groddeck, the self-proclaimed 'wild analyst', said he would call this entity of unknown and uncontrollable forces, the 'it'.

The superego, mostly unconscious, contains all the strictures from our youth. Parental voices are there in abundance, in particular a harsh, punitive voice, almost a caricature of the father. This is the voice that chides the client, making him feel guilty because he has not lived up to what he believes were parental expectations. He can become the embodiment of the critical father and will not forgive himself for being flawed. The superego is bound up with a morality, which Freud said could be 'super-moral' and then be as cruel as the id can be. Some of the work of the therapist in working with a harsh superego is helping the client towards an ego ideal and reality.

The ego ideal is the representation of the mother, seen by Freud as the gentle parent. The ego ideal helps the individual to aspire to ways of living and being that make him feel content with himself. 'What he projects before him as his ideal is the substitute for the lost narcissism of his childhood in which he was his own ideal' (Freud, 1914). The reality principle of the ego tells him as an adult he has to encompass the concerns of others, not just his own self-absorption as a child.

Freud describes the ego as 'a poor creature' because it is bedevilled by danger from all sides. It aims to keep the individual safe, but is the seat of anxiety, trying to serve three masters, the id, the superego and reality, while being the mediator for the perils they may bring. The perils lie in the external world, which may threaten the person's security and identity. Danger springs from the libido of the id, which may demand risky self-gratification; and hazard from the severity of the super ego, which may unhinge a personal sense of self and torture the individual's conscience. Keeping everyone happy is the impossible task of the ego. Freud (1923) said of the poor benighted ego, 'In its position midway between the id and reality, it only too often yields to the temptation to become sycophantic, opportunist and lying, like a politician who sees the truth but wants to keep his place in popular favour.' The ego is the lynchpin. We depend upon it for our survival. The aim of therapy is to strengthen the ego. As Freud said, 'Where id was, there ego shall be.'

The theories Freud put forward about the structure of the mind are complex, but it is helpful to understand Freud's ideas of different parts of the mind in conflict with each other. A diagrammatic example I have given to students does not cover all the complexities, but throws some light on the differences between the three structural components.

You come into the seminar room during a break. You are the only person in the room. There is a ten-pound note on the floor.

> The id would say, 'Take it.'
> The ego would say, 'Someone might see, and you would be branded a
>   thief.'
> The superego would say, 'It's wrong.'

Here there is a conflict between the different elements of the personality. What counsellors can learn from Freud's ideas is the awareness of the individual in conflict with himself. If the ego is not strong enough to triumph over the id, the result will be a person who feels chaotic, out of control or mad because he does not understand what is happening to him. In his saner moments, when the ego can take back some control, he will say something like, 'I'm not myself at the moment and it frightens me.'

The counsellor's task is to help the client strengthen his ego, by getting back in touch with reality and starting to protect himself again. It may also be about acknowledging the claims of the superego, in order that the client feels he is acting morally, so that he can feel good about himself again.

Case Example | Charles: a client at war with himself

Charles was a country solicitor married for 20 years with three children. He was a serious man, took his responsibilities to his family extremely seriously, worrying about his children's education and whether his wife was happy. He worried about his clients and he worried about money. Sometimes he felt weighed down by his cares. His wife was also a solicitor, successful and efficient, effortlessly, it seemed to Charles, balancing home and work.

Then Charles did something completely out of character. He met a woman 20 years younger than himself on the Internet. She was called Carol and lived about 50 miles away. The Internet relationship developed and Charles started to meet Carol in her tiny, student-like flat. Charles found the whole experience desperately exciting. He found himself telling lies about having to stay late at the office, while normally he abhorred lying. He even forgot an appointment with a client, when he tore 50 miles down the motorway to see Carol, who unexpectedly had a free afternoon. Then Carol said to him, 'All this tearing about isn't good for you. Why don't you just move in?' Carol said this on the phone to Charles, while he was at the office. Charles had told her not to ring him on the office phone, but she ignored it. He sat in his office waiting for his next client and thought, 'What on earth am I doing? I've gone mad.'

Charles had told Carol that it was difficult to talk and he would ring her back, but he knew he would never speak to her again. He rang a florist and sent Carol a large bunch of spring flowers. The message read, 'Thank you for everything. Sorry I can't do it.'

Charles thought he knew Carol, that she would shrug her shoulders and not pursue him. A message on his office answer phone next day merely said, 'Your loss!'

What Charles brought to counselling was his horror at what he had done and his panic that he no longer knew himself. He could not understand himself. Look what he had almost thrown away. How could he think of abandoning his children? And yet there were times when he wished he could have left all his responsibilities behind, and thrown in his lot with Carol. Being with her was like being young again except that he felt he had never really been young. He had always felt responsible.

In Freudian terms what Charles was experiencing was the conflict between his very strong superego where duty, responsibility and moral imperatives held sway, and the id where sensuality and desire sought fulfilment. Charles had managed to repress this part of himself, but just briefly it had emerged to destabilize him. And

Case Example | (Continued)

because the id had taken over, he had felt out of control, out of his mind, mad.

Perhaps we could say that the ego, the reality part, turned out to be the strongest element, for this was the part that said, 'Are you going to throw away your security, your family, your position in society for a 20-year-old who will probably soon tire of you? You've got away with it so far. Quit, while you're ahead!'

Charles is still struggling with the guilt, but the whole experience has triggered for him a kind of review of his life. He had not been aware of his frustrations, his longings, his desire for the responsibility-free youth that he never had. Charles realizes that he needs to reassess his relationships, particularly with his wife.

Now that he understands himself a little better, maybe his wife can become a more real person to him, rather than the superwoman he currently sees. Perhaps she has needs and vulnerabilities, which he has been unable to acknowledge. Charles has begun an exploration of himself, which he hopes will prove to be both enlightening and beneficial.

Defence mechanisms

Because the ego is the seat of anxiety, trying to keep the libidinous desires of the id in check at one moment, worried about the intrusion of the conscience of the superego at another, various mechanisms are deployed to protect the ego from its ultimate fear of annihilation. These defence mechanisms operate at an unconscious level working to protect the ego and keep it in touch with reality.

Repression

The most important defence is repression, where inappropriate, painful and uncomfortable desires and experiences are kept at bay by being repressed or 'forgotten'. An example of this may be a traumatic experience like childhood abuse, or abandonment, where the reality is too painful to contemplate. The child is in any case powerless, so the experience is managed by being repressed into the unconscious. But although it may be 'forgotten' at a conscious level, it does not go away and may manifest itself in other ways. As Freud saw with his hysterical patients, one way in which repressed material makes itself felt is in physical symptoms. His 'hysterical' patients, the label taken from the Greek word for uterus, as only women were deemed to be hysterical, presented a range of hysterical symptoms, such as paralysis of a limb. Freud claimed that he 'cured' the physical symptoms, when the repressed, sexual material, was made conscious.

Denial

Freud later posited other mechanisms, which the ego used to defend itself. We see these in the counselling room, as we all use them, though we are not aware of it. We use denial to protect us from unpleasant reality, for example when we receive bad news about illness or death and cannot believe that it is true.

Regression

Regression is a retreat to an earlier stage of development, when we feel we cannot cope with the situation we find ourselves in. We want to be looked after and rely on someone else to care for us, as life seems unmanageable. This is the situation for clients who come to therapy after a trauma. This defence mechanism ensures that their dependence on the counsellor will keep them safe until they are able to face reality.

Projection

Projection is an important defence mechanism, which those who came after Freud found crucial to their particular application of Freudian theory. In projection we project onto others the bad bits of ourselves and then abhor them in the other. This leaves us feeling good about ourselves, rather than ashamed of what we have become, if we had been able to own it.

Introjection

Alongside projection goes introjection. Here we take in good or bad bits of the other and make it our own. This can help us make sense of what may otherwise seem painful or irrational situations. For example, a child who is physically abused defends herself against the unthinkable feeling that her father cannot love her, because of the pain he inflicts on her, by believing that she deserves it. If she is sexually abused she has to believe that this is the way the parent shows his love. She has taken into herself, or introjected, the father's justification for his actions.

Reaction formation

Reaction formation is a defence in which the unconscious thought or feeling is so painful to us that we cannot bear it, and have to consciously change it to its opposite. An example may be a man who is unconsciously drawn to other men, but denies this at a conscious level, by vociferously espousing homophobic sentiments.

Displacement

A defence we may see often in bereavement counselling is displacement. Here the real object of our anger and fury is the dead person who has abandoned and rejected us. However, these feelings are too painful to be consciously felt, so we direct the fury at a less-risky target, the doctor or the hospital that failed to protect our loved one and let him die.

Sublimation

Sublimation is a defence we all use and is essential to civilized culture. Here our instinctual sexual impulses, from the id, are redirected from their target of sexual activity and diverted to socially acceptable goals. Sport, literature, theatre, painting and the arts, generally, are some of the beneficiaries of these retargeted sexual desires.

We all use these defence mechanisms, so of course we see them in the counselling room. For counsellors it is important that we are aware of the deep-seated anxiety that we only see the tip of, along with the often irrational behaviour, thoughts and feelings that are its manifestation. It means that we try to understand the underlying feeling, rather than taking all that is presented to us at face value.

Defence mechanisms have a function, but using them all the time instead of facing and managing reality becomes ineffective. Much emotional energy goes into keeping the painful thoughts, feelings and experiences battened down in the unconscious. It could be better used in learning to live with these powerful emotions in a conscious way.

Sometimes there is no choice. There is not enough emotional energy available for the task of holding down everything that is disquieting in the unconscious, so sometimes, when we are particularly fragile, it all spills over into the conscious. Then we break down and are ill.

As counsellors, much of our work is to help our clients manage reality; so some awareness and understanding of the defence mechanisms, we all habitually use, is crucial to this aim.

Psychosexual stages of development

Freud saw development of the individual as a series of psychosexual stages, in which sexual gratification was the chief goal, a controversial claim, and one which made Freud enemies. Though the Victorians were castigated as being prudish about sex, by Freud amongst others, sex was explicitly written about. Freud in his *Three Essays on the Theory of Sexuality* (1905) credited sexual pioneers such as Havelock Ellis and Kraft-Ebbing and acknowledged his debt to them. Freud's opposition came, not primarily from writing about sex, but suggesting that infantile sexuality was central to the young child's development. For most people the linking of children with sexual gratification was abhorrent. The fact that it was autoerotic, that is the child induced gratification through his own actions, did not make it for many people any less distasteful.

However, Freud was convinced that he was right and expounded his theories, difficult though they were. He posited that throughout our lives we pass through several psychosexual stages. 'There seems no doubt that germs of sexual impulses are already present in the new-born child, but that the sexual life of children usually emerges in a form accessible to observation round about the third or fourth year of life' (1924).

- **The oral stage:** birth to about 2 years
  First was the oral stage where gratification was centred on the mouth with sucking and biting the means to obtain both food and bodily pleasure.

- **The anal stage:** 2 to about 3 years
  Next was the anal stage where the giving and withholding of faeces became the source of pleasure. This coincides with potty training in Western society.

- **The phallic stage**: 3 to about 5 years

  The most important stage for psychotherapists and counsellors is the phallic stage, because this is the stage that encompasses the Oedipus complex, Freud's significant psychosexual landmark. In the phallic stage, the child discovers the pleasure in genital stimulation. Again this is mainly autoerotic, although in the handling of the child by a carer, usually the mother, normal washing, rubbing and drying can produce stimulating effects. The phallic stage, in spite of its name, applies to both boys and girls. Freud believed that the clitoris in the girl was a lesser version, a substitute, albeit a poor one, for the penis.

The Oedipus complex

Freud was convinced that this stage in the child's development was crucial. If we look back to Freud's life we remember that in a letter to his friend Fliess he recalled that at about the age of four he had sexual wishes towards his mother and these thoughts were at the basis of his daily self-analysis. He has been criticized for basing his theory on such scanty evidence, but of course he had the sexual material from his hysterical patients as reinforcement.

Freud had experienced a classical education, so he was steeped in Greek myth and legend. He used the legend of Oedipus as a metaphor to illustrate the rivalry, conflict and incestuous feelings that families wrestled with. In the legend, the protagonist, Oedipus, was the son of King Laius and Queen Jocasta of Thebes. Before the baby was born his mother had consulted an oracle, which had prophesied that Oedipus was doomed to tragedy. He would kill his father and marry his mother. Consequently, at his birth, Oedipus was abandoned by his parents, who left him to die. In the way of Greek myths he did not die, but as an adult, unaware of his true identity, killed the man who was his father and married his wife, Oedipus's mother. Oedipus, when he discovered the enormity of what he had done, in remorse blinded himself.

The story is about the horror of incest and patricide and how, even though inadvertent, it has to be punished. Freud posited that during the phallic stage the small boy has an overwhelming desire to penetrate his mother after having got rid of his father. This is the time when little boys will say that they want to marry Mummy and little girls are in love with Daddy. The parent of the same sex is resented. The little boy is terrified that his father will castrate him. The little girl suffers from penis envy.

In reality it is not surprising that the boy wants to protect his penis, when he sees what he imagines has happened to his sister. The girl, particularly in Freud's day, quickly realized that the acquisition of a penis would confer more power, than she had as a mere female.

The Oedipal situation is resolved by the child eventually identifying with the parent of the same sex. Freud suggested that if the tumultuous feelings in the family were not determined in this way, then the child would suffer the consequences in psychic pain. One of the ways in which the Oedipal triangle becomes a threat to subsequent mental health is when it is played out in reality. The father actually seduces his daughter, and the mother actually seduces her son.

Freud was originally convinced that all the women patients he saw with hysterical symptoms had been seduced by their fathers. These patients were women who displayed physical symptoms, for which there seemed no cause, other than a physical manifestation of a mental illness. Because it was mainly women who suffered from hysteria, and because so many women told Freud of sexual abuse by a father, Freud concluded that here was the cause.

Then he began to be anxious about his own father. In a letter to Fliess he says that he has become convinced that his own father was one of these men, for he sees the evidence in the hysterical symptoms of his brothers and sisters. He might have included himself, for he admitted to being prone to hysterical symptoms at certain times in his life. However, after intense self-analysis, together with reflection and reinterpretation of his patients narratives, Freud concluded that the seduction of women by their fathers is generally not real, but a phantasy illustrating the extreme love that a daughter has for her father and a way of explaining sexual conflict and ambivalence in families.

Counsellors working with survivors of abuse may conclude that Freud's original conclusion was the right one. They know only too well that childhood abuse is the source of untold misery, self-destructive behaviour, lack of self-worth and inability to trust others. At its extreme the victim can feel she no longer exists. It is an annihilation of the self. Working with the results of abuse can make therapists feel very angry with Freud's revised position and his followers' acceptance of the seduction phantasy.

Whatever counsellors make of the Oedipal complex, it does provide a starting point for an examination of the warring factors which divide families, as well as the juxtaposition of love and hate which is the source of much anguish.

Case Example | George: conflict with the father at the Oedipal stage

George came to counselling because he was depressed. He had embarked on an academic course and felt he would fail it. He had no evidence for his worries, his marks were reasonable but his illogical anxiety threatened to overwhelm him. He knew where the anxiety came from. As soon as he sat down in front of his computer, he could hear his father say, 'You'll never make anything of yourself.'

He was the second child of a family of four children. His elder brother had died at a few weeks old. When George was born, 14 months later, he was given the name of his dead brother.

As a child George tried hard to please his father, but he was aware from a very early age, about four or five, before he went to school, that it was impossible. Everything George did was wrong. George's mother tried to protect him from his father's anger, but that was not enough for George. He wanted his father's approval. His two sisters had it. George's mother was irritated and hurt that what she said or did seemed meaningless to George. George felt increasingly stuck and frustrated. He was powerless. He could not have the very thing he wanted, however hard he tried.

George did well at school, but his father refused to recognize it; so somehow the doing well did not count. Eventually George gave up. He left home when he was 16. He is now thirty-eight and has nothing to do with his father, though he keeps in touch with his mother.

In the counselling he repeatedly said how angry he was with himself because, at his age, he should not be stuck over what happened to him as a child. He hated his father for what he had done, for he felt it had disadvantaged him for life. He would never escape his father's disapproval, going round and round in his head. He felt stuck. This phrase was used so often; I suggested to George that it must have a meaning. By this time I too was feeling stuck, convinced that the counselling could never move on. This was a countertransference feeling and it went alongside a feeling of irritation with George. Why could he not move on? But there was also a feeling of irritation in me. Why was I not a better counsellor? We were both well and truly stuck.

As I talked about the case in supervision, my feelings of frustration and how I was caught up in the countertransference, I began to think aloud about the relationship between George and his father and me. We were stuck in an Oedipal triangle. I was playing out the mother who is not heard, although she tries to protect George from his father's disapproval.

This was a helpful insight, as it took us further along the road to understanding what may have happened. It seemed as if George and his father were stuck at the Oedipal stage in never-ending conflict. For some reason they could not move on.

I began to think I had some idea what the reason might be. George and I had talked at length about his dead brother. He could never remember his being talked about in the family. George was quite old, about seven or eight, before he even knew he had a dead brother, who shared his name. George, he was told, was in Heaven. George had not seemed to think it strange that he was given the name of the dead brother. In fact, true to family tradition, he did not really want to talk about it.

COUNSELLOR: So there were two Georges. You and your dead brother.
GEORGE: (*Long silence*) Yes I suppose so. I'd never really thought about it though.
COUNSELLOR: One George died as a baby, and so could do no wrong. Perhaps for your father, the other George couldn't ever get it right.
GEORGE: (*Angrily*) Well I certainly couldn't.
COUNSELLOR: I suppose you can't compete with a dead angel.
GEORGE: Well I was very much alive and needed a father.
COUNSELLOR: And tragically he wasn't there for you.

When I speculated that perhaps it was impossible to compete with a dead angel and get it right, it did not seem to resonate with George. Maybe George was too angry. Perhaps it was too painful to contemplate. It seems that of the two Georges, one was the good dead George, and the other, the live George, into whom all his father's anger, frustration and powerlessness about his brother's death had been projected. It seemed as if in this situation, where George's

Case Example | (Continued)

father could not move on, whatever George did to try to placate his father, George could not win.

Freud said that the conflict between father and son, engendered by the Oedipal complex, was eventually resolved and the child moved into the latency stage. It seems as if George's father could not resolve that conflict and George was the loser. It says much about George's father's hold on reality that he could bear to see George's suffering, which he himself had inflicted, while hanging on to his image of a perfect child.

George said his father was capable of making relationships, as he had done so with George's sisters. George also talked about his father making good relationships with his nephews. So if George is able to make an unbiased judgement, it would appear that his father could make relationships with George's sisters, which means he was able to make relationships with his children. If he can also make relationships with his nephews, he can make relationships with boys. It is just George he cannot, or will not, make a relationship with. It seems as if George's father could not forgive George for living, when his perfect brother had died. George suffered the consequences.

- **The latency stage**: 5 to about 12 years
  After the Oedipal conflict, within the phallic stage, comes the stage of latency where sexual desires are temporarily dormant. It could be described as the lull before the storm of urgent adolescent sexuality and conflict.

- **The genital stage**: 12 years to adulthood
  Finally the genital stage is reached where sexual fulfilment, within what Freud, at the time, saw as a specifically heterosexual relationship, is the culmination of adulthood. Homosexuality, he regarded, as psychosexually immature. For counsellors it can be useful to reflect on Freud's stages when we are struggling with a client where there are issues of development.

Erikson, a neo-Freudian, enlarged these life stages, adding developmental tasks and highlighting the conflicts that have to be resolved by the individual in each stage before he can move successfully to the next.

His work can be illuminating to counsellors, where clients are struggling with feelings of missing out, or unable to move on.

Instincts Life force and death drive

Freud believed that we are driven by our instincts and that our instincts are in opposition to each other. Chief amongst these are the Life and Death instinct, which Freud, again led by his classical education, called Eros and Thanatos.

Eros is the life force, the instinct within us that heralds good. As Bettelheim said, 'It was our love for others, and our concern for the future of those we love, that Freud had in mind when he spoke of eternal Eros' (1983, p. 109).

' "Psyche" is the soul – a term full of the richest meaning, endowed with emotion, comprehensively human and unscientific' (Bettelheim, 1983, p. 11). Psyche and Eros are joined in love. For a rich and vibrant life force, Eros's charm, cunning and beauty must be twinned with the soul.

Eros is in constant conflict with the destructive power of the death instinct, and uses the libido as a force for good against the malevolent energy of the death instinct. Life and love, through sexual energy, can be creative and prevail. Reflecting on the collisions between Eros and Thanatos, for Freud, came to be a battle between good and evil, with a commitment to trying to understand the role played by the death instinct in the origins of aggression.

Freud's insistence on the death instinct produced much controversy. Freud believed that the counterforce to Eros, the life instinct, lay in the death instinct, which Bettelheim (1983) says should be translated as the 'death drive'. This was a longing to return to a prebirth state of nonexistence. In all his thinking on this, Freud kept returning to the problem of aggression. He believed that aggression 'constitutes the greatest impediment to civilisation'. He thought the origins of aggression lay in the death drive, with a perpetual conflict between the drive for life and the drive for death, as a fight between good and evil. The 'hippy' slogan of the 1960s, 'Make love not war', encapsulates this.

When Freud wrote about the death drive and aggression in 1920 the world had just been through a period of mass destruction. Seen through twenty-first-century eyes, the chaos and decimation of the First World War does look like a collective death wish. Freud was haunted by wasted lives throughout his lifetime. He was not to know the awful aggression that lay ahead, in the general destruction of the Second World War and the particular destruction of his people in the 'final solution' of the Nazis. Four of his sisters died in concentration camps. Though when he wrote his essay 'Civilisation and its Discontents' in 1929, the power of the Nazis was already grimly in evidence.

In the animal world aggression is regarded as a necessary tool to protect the territory and the young, and so preserve the species. In this sense it has more connection to a life drive than a death drive. Freud was a great admirer of Darwin who put forward the notion of survival of the fittest, which would presumably include the most aggressive. Many of Freud's followers thought his view on the death drive illogical because the whole animal kingdom, which includes the human animal, is bent on survival.

Yet interestingly, in lay terms, people often refer to someone who is behaving dangerously as having a death wish. Young motorbike riders doing 150 mph must be testing something. We talk of 'dicing with death', and at this speed survival is a gamble, a toss of the dice. Maybe they are testing their own mortality and it is a truism that most young people do, at some level, think they are immortal.

Yet counsellors who work with young people who have tried to kill themselves either deliberately, in taking an overdose, or more ambiguously in doing extremely perilous activities that could end in death know that there is, if only for some people, an attraction towards self-destruction.

It means that we should take seriously any thoughts or intentions towards self-harm that our clients express. Self-harm is sometimes described as para-suicide and is thought by some practitioners to be a kind of lesser alternative to suicide. But there is danger in self-harm because of the illogical belief that the client can control it. Death from anorexia is the proof that the rationale of control is illusory. Instead it lies in the, often disordered, thought patterns of illogical reasoning.

Case Example | Judi: self-harm in response to a fragmented internal world

Judi was a 19-year-old student who came to her university counselling service because her tutors were worried about her. The worry concerned her being upset in seminars and they thought she might be depressed. Judi made it clear that she was only coming to please her tutors because she did not want them to worry about her. But it turned out that everyone was worried about her and the counsellor was soon added to the list. Judi had a history of depression, self-harm and eating difficulties. She was painfully thin and liked herself that way. In fact, as is common with people with disordered eating, she thought she was too fat. She had a psychiatrist, a community psychiatric nurse, her doctor and a counsellor anxious about her, but all the professionals trying to work together, felt powerless. The main reason they all felt powerless was that Judi did not want to change her behaviour, at least not at a conscious level. Judi felt that cutting herself, taking laxatives and making herself sick kept her in control of her body. The counsellor imagined, from the little Judi told her, that her internal world was chaotic and fragmented and felt out of control. Judi seemed to believe that if she firmly controlled her external world she could manage her life. Of course the danger lies in this being an illusion, and the professionals worried about her cutting herself too deeply, or starving herself to death, while mistakenly convinced that she was in control and knew exactly how far to go. Judi threatened suicide and for a short time went as an inpatient into a psychiatric unit. But she was soon back and everything went on as before.

If Freud was right about the existence of the death drive and it being constantly in conflict with the life drive, then it seemed as if Judi sided with death and the professionals stood for life. It is very common in cases of this nature where the client ostensibly does not consciously worry about her behaviour, but acts it out in perverse ways that she raises anxiety and powerlessness in everyone she is in contact with. A stream of worried tutors continued to bring their frustrations to the counselling service insisting that 'something be done about Judi' epitomizing the powerlessness of everyone concerned.

But I do wonder about the function of the worry and have heard other professionals speculating on this. Perhaps it is other people's worry that keeps the client going, perhaps keeps them alive. If, as often happens, the client's difficulties have their origins in the family, then the family will not be a source of help. Instead what the client gathers around her is a new 'family' of doctors, nurses and counsellors who will care about her and try to keep her safe. However, it is not an easy task and counsellors finding themselves in this role have to be prepared for a lot of hard work and little overt reward.

Mourning

Freud wrote his significant paper on Mourning and Melancholia in 1917. It was 3 years before his beloved daughter, Sophie, died, whose death, those who were close to him said, he could never fully accept.

In the 1917 paper he compares mourning with a similar, though separate state, which he calls 'melancholia'. Melancholia, we might term today extreme depression, obsession or hysteria. Freud says that mourning, like a mental illness is fully absorbing and both the internal and external worlds are occupied in this working through, to the exclusion of all else.

Freud examines the role self-reproach plays in melancholia and of course in mourning. We know how guilt is an important factor in loss and that guilt is a function of the superego or the conscience. Freud believed at this point that there was 'normal mourning', and 'pathological mourning'; the pathological mourning was evidenced by the mourner believing that he was to blame for the loss of the loved object. Yet most theorists and practitioners working with bereavement today would say that blaming oneself for a loved one's death is very common, 'I should have tried harder', 'I should have seen it coming', 'if only . . .' Freud said a pathological response is to think, 'I willed it'. But most loving relationships contain hate at some point, 'I wish you were dead', 'I'd be better off without you', yet the flip side, 'I love you', 'I can't do without you', are seldom far away.

In 1923 Freud, in 'The Ego and the Id', put forward the idea that withdrawal of the libido, which is the channel through which one person attaches himself to another, can only happen when the lost object is reinstated in the ego. This means that if someone dies, the mourner can only move on, perhaps making a relationship with a new partner, when the mourner has taken inside himself the lost loved person and identified with it.

Transference and countertransference

Freud's work was based on the acceptance of unconscious processes. For psychodynamic work, one of the chief uses of the unconscious lies in recognition of the phenomena of transference and countertransference.

Freud's consultancy with Breuer on his work with Anna O. had led him to see the importance of the transference. Bertha Pappenheim (Anna O.) had revealed an erotic transference to Breuer within the sessions of the 'talking cure'. The culmination of this was an indication to Breuer that she was pregnant by him and was delivering his child, a phantasy at which Breuer had taken fright. Freud had been disappointed by Breuer whom he felt had not taken the opportunity afforded him to explore it further, but had terminated the therapy because Anna O.'s behaviour alarmed and embarrassed him.

In contrast Freud realized that the erotic transference was part of the process and had to be worked with in some way. He had come to this conclusion when a patient of his had thrown her arms around his neck when coming out of hypnosis. After Freud had discontinued the hypnosis, he found that the talking cure produced the same result; female patients were in love with him. 'I was modest enough not to con- tribute the event to my own irresistible personal attraction', he says dryly (1925, p. 27).

He wrote a paper 'Observations on Transference Love' (1915b) that was addressed to analysts, not patients, and was in a somewhat 'mind your back' mode. He was aware that some analysts acted out the transference and slept with their patients and his paper was an attempt to show how analysts could manage the erotic transference, it being 'an unavoidable consequence of a medical situation'.

Freud talked about the 'positive transference', which apes real love, and the 'negative transference' where the analyst has hostile feelings from the patient projected onto him. Both these states are intensely emotional and only resolved by the analyst 'convincing him' that he is re-experiencing emotional attachments, the source of which lies in his childhood (1925, p. 43).

Countertransference

Freud believed that the countertransference, when the analyst feels something, which really belongs to the patient, should be avoided. He was particularly speaking of the analyst allowing himself to respond to his patient's transference love and regarding the patient's feelings towards him as a 'conquest'.

However, theorists who came after Freud thought that the countertransference provided clues to understanding the therapeutic encounter. This is described in more detail in later chapters.

The basic rule

Working with free association, Freud's rule for his patients in analysis was that they had to say whatever came into their heads. Patients tried to resist this and censor material. Freud wanted patients to get in touch with their infantile sexuality and repressed unconscious mental processes. Freud was determined that the patients must 'know all the things which had hitherto only been made accessible to them in hypnosis' (1925, p. 28).

As counsellors, what we can learn from this is to give the client free rein to say what he wants to say, without too much comment. Too much intervention sets a counsellor agenda, rather than a client agenda. If at the beginning of a session we wait for the client to start, as Freud would have done, the client will bring the thing that is uppermost in his mind. This may make little sense to the counsellor, or have nothing to do with what the client brought last session. But it belongs to the client, and is significant to him, even if he and we are not sure why. It is important that material is not counsellor led, and even something, as neutral, in many counsellors' eyes, as starting the session with, 'How are you this week?' means that the counsellor has set the agenda.

Freud believed that the patient would speak his anxieties. He may not mean to do so because he could find it too threatening and may try to cover up his anxieties. But Freud thought that, even disguised in another story, an attentive therapist could hear the anxiety.

Counsellors can learn from this. Suppose a client arrives at the counselling room and immediately launches into an account of how fed up he is with the vet. He had taken his dog for the third time, paid a fortune for more injections and still the dog seems no better.

Now the client may justifiably be angry with a vet, whom he perceives as incompetent, or his fondness for his dog may make him unfairly blame the vet for not working miracles. What the counsellor, influenced by Freudian theory, may pick up is a client, unwilling to confront his counsellor, who feels that he has been coming to counselling for a long time, has paid a fortune for the sessions, and still he feels no better.

Talking about this with the client, his disappointment at not making the progress he had hoped for, his anxiety that he has wasted his money, and the fear that the counsellor is not competent, could prove to be very useful. It could make the relationship more meaningful because the counsellor has shown, he is so in tune with the client that he can deduce feelings the client may not have been able to put into words. The client may not even have allowed himself to think these thoughts, and may deny them. Whatever the response, the exchange will be more fruitful than merely taking the client's story at face value and saying, 'You seem angry with your vet.'

The Rule of Abstinence

The Basic Rule went alongside 'the Rule of Abstinence'. 'The treatment must be carried through in a state of abstinence' (Freud, 1915b) 'by which he meant that the patient must be given unconditional acceptance and nothing else' (Malan, 1995, p. 162). Malan's assertion of unconditional acceptance ties in with Rogers person-centred approach, though Rogers might disagree with Malan's proscription on the expression of love. For Malan goes on to say that advice, interventions in the client's life and of course no expression of love, above all, not physical love, are permissible.

'Nothing else' also means for psychodynamic counsellors, no reassurance, and no offering of approval. This is partly because of the transference relationship. The client may try to appease the counsellor, who in the transference may be the authoritarian parent, by 'being a good boy' and doing as he thinks he has been told. For the counsellor to say, 'Well done', is very powerful, and how will he face her, if he has not done so well next week? The psychodynamic counsellor wants to provide a therapeutic space, in which the client is able to express negative thoughts and feelings. Once the counsellor and the client can acknowledge the anxieties and the terrors, they have more possibility of being worked through.

Case Example | Dea: a counsellor works psychodynamically with an 18-year-old student

(The client and counsellor sit down. The counsellor waits for the client to start.)

DEA: It's been a better week this week. (This is said in a social kind of way. The client smiles brightly as she says it.)

COUNSELLOR: It sounds as if you feel you should bring some good news.

DEA: Well the things in my head...

Case Example | (Continued)

COUNSELLOR: (*Waits for client to say more.*)
DEA: The things in my head ... I seem calmer.
COUNSELLOR: So the demons seem more controlled.
DEA: Well, the demons are better ...
COUNSELLOR: But?
DEA: Not controlled.
COUNSELLOR: It's frightening that you can't control them.
DEA: It scares me to hell.

This is a very short encounter but it goes a long way into the client's fears. Had the counsellor after the first client comment;

'It's been a better week this week.'
Offered praise;
'You have done well.'
Or reassurance;
'Things never stay bad for long.'
Or reflected on the statement with,
'You've managed to make it a good week.'

It would have been difficult for the client to confess the negative, terrifying aspect of himself once the client–counsellor encounter had started on this positive road. It means that the counsellor and client have got a basis to work from. The counsellor knows that the client is still wrestling with demons, and the client does not have to pretend that everything is all right. In some ways, life is better for the client, but there is still work to do. It is easy for the inexperienced counsellor to take what the client says about things being better, and hustle him into 'health'. If the client is given the space to 'tell it as it is' there is a better chance of a real resolution of the issue, based on time, discomfort and a real relationship.

Comment

However unpalatable the idea may be to hero-worshippers, the truth has to be stated that Freud did not always possess the serenity and inner sureness so characteristic of him in the years when he was well known.

(Jones, 1954, p. 334)

Sigmund Freud, the father of psychoanalysis and ultimately counselling, one of the most significant influences of the twentieth century, was, as well, a man of frailties and vulnerabilities. He needed affirmation and reassurance. He put his mentors and friends on pedestals, only to knock them down when he felt they had failed him. The more one reads his work, the more one sees his struggles and doubts with himself. Here is a man who is thoroughly human, not the righteous, godlike figure his detractors portray.

That he could be arrogant and distant there is no denying, but he could also be warm and engaging. His letters show his intense interest in the welfare of others, while his family photographs portray his pleasure in close relationships.

Freud is lambasted by his critics, for being a practitioner, who was not interested in his patients, and consequently, not very skilled. Sandor Ferenczi in his diary quotes Freud as saying that psychoanalytic patients were a rabble, but at least they provided analysts with a living and material to learn from (1988). Although this is not particularly edifying, one wonders if it were said tongue in cheek. Professionals, amongst themselves, can sometimes be disparaging of their clients. Perhaps it is something about resenting having to be a servant to the client.

Peter Swales, an independent Freud scholar, in documenting the case of Anna von Lieben, an early patient of Freud's, comments on the learning Freud gained from Anna's 'material' and the importance she had for him as his 'teacher'. However, Swales says that her family had completely lost confidence in Freud as a clinician. He seemed powerless to help Anna as she showed no sign of permanent improvement (1998, p. 33). This was after Freud had seen Anna twice a day, for 3 years, a long, and presumably lucrative, encounter.

It is significant that Freud was so enthusiastic about learning from his patients, as their 'material' was part of the building blocks of his theory. It seems that he was more interested in the workings of the human mind than effecting cures. And that was his chief legacy. It is acknowledged, even by his detractors, that literature, the arts and philosophy owe a great debt to Freud. The philosopher, Herbert Marcuse, a radical political commentator, in his book, 'Eros and Civilisation' says of Freudian concepts that their importance lies in their philosophical and sociological implications.

For him the theoretical construction aims 'not at curing individual sickness, but at diagnosing the general disorder' (1972, p. 25).

The critic, Jeffrey Masson, briefly worked as projects director of the Sigmund Freud archives. He therefore had access to Freud's letters and other documents. So he was in a prime position to comment on Freud's writing. Masson finds the case study of 'Dora' elegant and eloquent, and says what impressed him about Freud was the way in which he did not try to hide the complexities in all the cases he saw (1993).

However, Masson slammed Freud for his change of view about the seduction theory. Freud had first believed that his women patients had been sexually abused and that this was the cause of their trauma. He then changed his view to a phantasy seduction in which the women had desired their fathers unconsciously, persuading themselves that they had been seduced. Masson, thought that Freud had changed his views for spurious reasons and felt Freud had ill-served his patients. Masson claimed that Freud's women patients, and those who came after, suffered grievously at not being believed when they told a therapist of their trauma of rape and abuse.

It is certainly true that it is only comparatively recently that sexual abuse has been recognized as being more common and more traumatic than previously accepted. However, it is also true that the therapy world has responded to these findings with an acknowledgement of past mistakes and a readiness to make reparation. Survivors of abuse are now offered counselling routinely, as trainee counsellors working in the field know. Psychodynamic thought has recognized the significance of sexual abuse in trauma, with psychotherapists such as Valerie Sinason (1992) eloquently writing of the feelings of annihilation of the self.

Classic psychoanalytic theory and practice has generally been perceived as homophobic, with homosexuality being seen as deviant and a perversion. Even today one can read letters, in professional journals, from gay and lesbian trainees who feel they have been stigmatized because of their sexual orientation.

However, it is unjust to lay everything at Freud's door. Freud had, by the mores of the day, an unusually liberal approach to homosexuality. In his autobiographical study he says, 'The most important of these perversions, homosexuality, scarcely deserves the name. It can be traced back to the constitutional bisexuality of all human beings and to the after effects of the phallic primacy. Psycho-analysis enables us to point to some trace or other of a homosexual object choice in everyone' (1925, p. 38).

Twenty years earlier he had published a case study of Dora, which he admitted was a record of an analytic failure. Within the case study he writes about sexual instincts and perversions, taking his colleagues to task for their moral condemnation. 'We surely ought not to forget that the perversion which is the most repellent to us, the sensual love of a man for a man, was not only tolerated by a people so far our superiors in cultivation as the Greeks, but was actually entrusted by them with important social functions. The sexual life of each of us extends to a slight degree-now in this direction, now in that – beyond the narrow lines imposed as the standard of normality' (1905, in 1995, pp. 197–198).

Gay and lesbian therapists and clients will doubtless feel that Freud's comments fall lamentably short of an acceptance of homosexual identity. However, it does seem that Freud attempted to begin a dialogue, which his colleagues and followers were loth to continue.

Some critics suggest that the whole of Freudian theory, on which psychodynamic thought is based, is spurious. They ask for evidence of the unconscious and claim that asking followers to take it on trust is akin to accepting the kind of religious fundamentalism that Freud rails against. One of his critics, Cioffi (1998), says that Freud 'the relentless seeker after truth was no better at detecting his own essays in self decep-tion than the rest of us.' This criticism is not confined to those outside the psychoanalytic world. Many of Freud's supporters acknowledge that although preaching a readiness to face uncomfortable truths, he did not always live up to this himself. 'In practice, however, Freud himself was no paragon of self criticism. He was unusually intolerant of outside criticism too' (Holt, 1989, p. 341).

However, this does not make his ideas vain. The notion of the uncon-scious had been around for well over a hundred years before Freud capitalized on it. He was not the first person to look to the unconscious to answer the question of why we often seem driven by forces outside our-selves, or why we behave in irrational ways. If this notion seems useful to us in our work, helping us to understand ourselves, and our clients, better, then it has served its purpose.

Bruno Bettleheim (1903–1990), a psychoanalyst and child psycholo-gist, was born in Vienna to a middle class, assimilated Jewish family and had an upbringing very similar to that of Freud. However, one big dif-ference lay in the fact that in 1938, when Freud had was in England, having fled Austria, Bettleheim was in Dachau concentration camp. This experience, not surprisingly, had far-ranging effects.

Bettleheim was heavily influenced by Freud's writings, which of course he read in the original German. In middle age he moved to the United States and began to read Freud in English. He was shocked to discover that it was like reading the work of another man. The essential humanism that permeated the original was missing.

Bettleheim says, 'All his writings are gentle, persuasive, often brilliantly worded intimations that we, his readers, would benefit from a similar spiritual journey of self-discovery' (1982, p. 4). Freud shows us, says Bettleheim, how exploring the lowest depths of the soul, the hell we might suffer, is not easy, but the rewards lie in becoming more fully human. This makes us more compassionate and gives us a deeper understanding of our fellow men.

Unfortunately if we read Freud in English we could not guess this. Bettleheim says that the many references to the soul have been excised in translation. The result is that Freud's direct and personal appeals to our common humanity appear to readers as abstract, depersonalized, highly theoretical, erudite and mechanized. He thinks the translators want us to develop a scientific attitude towards man and his actions, and a scientific understanding of the unconscious and how it conditions behaviour.

This is an interesting idea. Certainly there was motivation to make psychoanalysis more respectable to its detractors and making it scientific probably fitted the bill. But maybe Bettleheim did not want to acknowledge how much Freud with his ideas on psychoanalysis, which he called this 'young science', his admiration for Darwin and his interest in research wanted psychoanalysis to be seen as scientific.

Freud's work was monumental, yet his stated aspirations, to turn neurotic misery into ordinary human unhappiness, seem pragmatically low-key. Perhaps his life experience, fighting anti-Semitism, reviled by his colleagues, living in chaotically turbulent times, the horror of war an ever-present backdrop, made for disillusionment. Add to this his serious, driven personality and the result is a man who can seem pessimistic and world-weary. But it is his search for meaning which never lets up and which we have benefited from, his dogged quest for the truth. As for his disillusion, it helps us acknowledge the dark side of ourselves.

Like many of his patients, Freud suffered at times from a neurosis, which Jones (1954) described as anxiety-hysteria. However, Freud did his most original work when the neurosis was at its height, as neurotic symptoms were one of the ways in which unconscious material was trying to emerge. Ernest Jones said it was the only way, but costly. Freud also admitted to being depressed, but he did not work well then.

One has only to look at the 24 volumes of the Standard Editions of the Complete Psychological Works of Sigmund Freud, taking up more shelf space than almost any other writer, to realize how much work Freud did accomplish and what he achieved in his writing.

First was the theory of the unconscious. Nineteenth-century thinkers were aware of this as a concept, but Freud was the first to capitalize on it, exploring its role in normal and abnormal life.

This led to the notion of transference and countertransference, experiences in the unconscious. Patient and therapist meet in the unconscious. Freud thought that transference, where the patient transfers relationships from the past on to the therapist, was useful to the therapy. Countertransference, where the therapist hooked into something from the patient, was an obstacle to therapeutic work. Subsequent psychoanalytic thinkers disagreed, finding the countertransference a useful tool in the therapy.

Then Freud gave us two versions of an analysis of the personality. The first version he called the topographical, or layered, approach where the mind was divided into three layers, the conscious, preconscious and unconscious. He was later dissatisfied with this alone and devised an additional structure of the personality, in which the id, ego and superego were in constant interaction and conflict. Defence mechanisms, like projection, ensured that repressed material does not reach consciousness.

Freud posited five psychosexual stages, significant aspects of the development of mental life, in which the critical Oedipal conflict was rooted in the third, or phallic stage. Childhood experiences were the source of difficulty in later life. Infantile experiences need to be brought from the unconscious and worked through so that life can be managed. 'Where id was, there ego shall be' (Freud, 1933).

What can a trainee, or a counsellor versed in other ways of working, learn from Freud that can safely be incorporated into thinking and practice at this stage in their professional development?

If a counsellor has some awareness of the notion of the unconscious, it should help her better understand what seems irrational behaviour in the client and why he finds it difficult to change. It may stop the counsellor offering simplistic problem-solving solutions, while the exploration of the irrational behaviour could be much more profitable.

This leads to the acknowledgement of defence mechanisms. How we try to protect ourselves from unpleasant and painful thoughts and experiences by denying them, repressing them. Counsellors should be aware of client defences, but also know that it is not their job to try and break them down.

Then there are the phenomena of transference and countertransference. Clients bring unconscious experiences from the past and transfer them unconsciously on to the counsellor. The counsellor can respond at an unconscious level in the countertransference. If counsellors are aware of this, it could help them better understand the counselling dynamic.

In reflecting on the theory of the structure of the personality, counsellors could be more aware of dynamic conflict. It helps to understand the idea of opposing aspects of the mind and offers insight into the client at war with himself.

Because in Freudian theory the past informs the present, there is a weight of importance laid on childhood experience. If the counsellor is aware that current problems may have their roots in the past, then it will affect the way the counsellor views what the client is offering. The client's talking of his childhood may be the key to his present difficulties, not something getting in the way of the here and now, as may have been previously supposed. For example, the Oedipal triangle, where the child felt locked out of the parental bedroom, might be the source of the anxiety and feelings of rejection that he has carried into the present.

And last, the practice of Freudian psychoanalysis lay in free association, the patient saying whatever came into his head, without censoring it. Counsellors have a different purpose from the psychoanalyst, but what we can learn from this is to follow what the client says and let him have the freedom to go where he wants to go. The antithesis of this is a counsellor-led agenda.

Further reading

Gay, P. (1988) *Freud. A Life for Our Time*. London: J. M. Dent and Sons Ltd.
Gay, P. (ed.) (1995) *The Freud Reader*. London: Vintage. (A collection of Freud's key texts.)
Jacobs, M. (2003) *Sigmund Freud*. London: Sage Publications.

3
Klein: mothers and babies

Melanie Klein always claimed she was a Freudian, though Freud did not. He thought her ideas were in conflict with his, while she saw them as a development of his work. However, for us, as readers of her work, it does seem that there is a divergence. Where Freud saw life as biologically driven, Klein saw it as psychologically driven. She was less interested in biological drives than the relationships a person has with himself, including the different parts of himself, as well as with other people.

In fact, Klein believed the internal relationships of the individual were more influential than the external relationships. She suggested that we have, within ourselves, images of others who are significant to us. This will certainly include parents, probably siblings, authority figures in our lives, as well as others who have meaning for us. The images may be driven by phantasy (unconscious fantasy) and bear little relationship to the reality. But these 'internalized objects' as Klein called them have a tremendous impact on our behaviour, and reinforce the way we see the world.

Klein's main contribution lies in the work she did with infants and children, a reason for some adversaries to regard her clinical practice as not proper evidence. As from her observations of childhood experience, she extrapolated theories of human development, which she and her followers regard as having universal application.

For Klein, nurture was the blueprint for adult life. It was not always so. People have always argued about the factors that make us what we are, and what we want to be. Buddhism, six centuries BC, taught that existence is unhappiness, and man is unhappy because of his selfish desires. Only right living will help him towards Nirvana, a merging with the universe, in his cycle of lives. Plato, 350 BC, agreed that temperance and self-control made for human happiness.

Traditional Christian teaching says that original sin has to be expurgated, in some way, for people to be made whole. For many Christians it is through baptism that they can be purified. In the sixteenth century, Calvinism taught the doctrine of predestination that the protestant God ordained some to eternal salvation and others to eternal damnation. People were either chosen or not. It was out of their control.

The nature–nurture debate has raged for centuries and continues to do so, particularly now in the age of the human genome project, when some scientists suggest that genetics alone is responsible for the way we are. In the nineteenth century, John Stuart Mill had posited the opposite view, that everyone is born a 'tabula rasa', a blank slate. He meant that babies are born with nothing, and what they become is a result of their experiences. This was a position similar to Klein's, except that she believed that babies have an innate experience of 'mother' and 'breast', together with a terrible anxiety about their own annihilation, of existing no more. So did Klein's ideas come from her own experiences? We can look to the life of Melanie Klein to provide some clues.

Life of Melanie Klein

I am drawing on Phyllis Grosskurth's (1986) monumental biography, 'Melanie Klein', which includes Klein's autobiographical material.

Melanie Klein seems a tragic figure. She suffered multiple losses; especially cruel were the deaths of her brother and her son. Her daughter, significantly, also a psychoanalyst, publicly humiliated her at professional meetings. Many of her male medical colleagues refused to accept her theories because she had the twin handicaps of being neither a doctor nor a man. Freud, whom she regarded as her guru disowned her, as he thought her ideas heretical. His daughter Anna embarked on a campaign of what might be seen as sibling rivalry, again of the most public kind. And yet in spite of, or perhaps because of, such opprobrium, Klein stiffened her body of knowledge to ward off all attackers and became a significant, even heroic, figure.

Early life

Life never appeared easy for Melanie Klein. She was born in Vienna in 1882, the last and, as she was later told, 'unexpected' fourth child, to a Jewish family living in straitened circumstances. Her father Moriz Reizes had trained as a doctor, but probably because of anti-Semitism, practised as a dentist. Her mother Libussa kept a shop to make ends meet. Most of the letters between Libussa and her children in later life revolve around money. Melanie sent a long letter to her mother when she was twenty, whose main purpose was to beg money for a pair of fingerless kid gloves (Grosskurth, 1986, p. 28).

Like Freud, Melanie seems to have had an unassertive father and a very powerful mother. The family appeared riven with envy and rivalry. Moriz made no secret of the fact that the eldest daughter, Emilie, was his favourite and Libussa made no secret of her adoration of her son, Emmanuel. Emilie and Emmanuel closed ranks against Melanie, and her only champion, her sister, Sidonie, died when Melanie was four. Add to this the later knowledge that she was an 'accident', who was farmed out to a wet nurse, it is perhaps not surprising that Melanie felt she had to fight her corner to survive. She seems to have spent much of her childhood very actively seeking attention. Perhaps her feeling that she had to prove her existence is tied up with her later theories about the baby's fear of annihilation.

Adult life

Moriz Reizes died when Melanie was eighteen; so her plans to go to medical school were shelved. Instead Melanie became engaged to Arthur Klein, who seemed the most suitable bet of the young men around her, with the prospect of money, the most important attribute. In fact, when Melanie, in 1903, eventually married Arthur, after numerous postponements by him, they hardly knew each other and the marriage seemed doomed from the start. Melanie appears to have been caught up in the appurtenances of marriage, excited about her trousseau and the impression she made on her in-laws, without appearing to have let herself think what marriage meant.

About 10 years later Klein wrote a story, seemingly autobiographical, in which she describes 'the shock experienced by a young woman, Anna, on her wedding night. "And does it therefore have to be like this, that motherhood begins with disgust?"' (Grosskurth, 1986, p. 40). In fact, Klein did not seem to feel much better about motherhood. In her autobiography she says, 'I threw myself as much as I could into motherhood and interest in my child. I knew all the time that I was not happy, but saw no way out' (Grosskurth, 1986, p. 42). Interestingly 'the child' was Melitta who was to become an analyst herself, publicly, challenge her mother, and refuse to go to her funeral. Perhaps the cycle was being repeated, and Melitta, like her mother, wanted for attention.

It may be that the main difficulty with Melanie's marriage to Arthur was that her real emotional attachment was to her brother Emmanuel. From their letters (see Grosskurth, 1986), she seems locked in an emotionally incestuous relationship, where he was quite cruel to her. When he died, just before her marriage, she was distraught. As Grosskurth says, 'He was her surrogate father, close companion, phantom lover – and no one in her life was ever able to replace him' (1986, p. 39).

The early years of her marriage were very difficult for Klein. She was listless and depressed. Her mother, who seems to have been both controlling and manipulative, sent Klein off on cures for her health, while she looked after Klein's husband and children. Klein seemed quite relieved to be dispatched. However, it did mean she lost control of her children, and was the locked out child in the Oedipal relationship, with her husband and mother as authoritative parents. She did worry that her place in the affections of both her mother and her husband was in danger of being usurped by her daughter. In her later theories Klein claims that the baby is envious of the mother. The reverse, the mother's envy of the baby does not seem an issue, yet Klein did seem to struggle with her envy of Melitta.

The marriage never seemed to be fulfilling for Klein. She found an outlet in her passion for psychoanalysis, first going into analysis with Sandor Ferenczi, the closest of Freud's associates, when the family moved to Budapest in 1910. Ferenczi seems to have provided the father figure she felt had been denied to her. Under Ferenczi's tutelage she blossomed, and decided, on his encouragement, to concentrate on child psychoanalysis. Ferenczi also gave the same advice to Anna Freud. Perhaps he thought it a fitting occupation for a woman.

Klein had originally sought psychoanalysis after the death of her mother, Libussa. She had been devastated by this death, for Libussa was such a dominant figure in Klein's life. It must have been a convoluted relationship, with Libussa's control and Klein's dependence at one level, and Klein's rage at her helplessness, fury at her manipulation, and a passionate attachment, at another. Love and hate, the two sides of this enmeshed relationship, were the emotions that later Klein was to assign, as paramount, to the tiny baby.

Earlier in 1914, the year of her mother's death, Klein had become a mother again, after 7 years. Melitta was ten, Hans was seven, when Erich was born. It sounds as if this was a difficult time for Klein, as it seems that

Erich, like Klein, was 'unexpected'. Due to 'circumstances' (unspecified by Klein) Erich, too, had a wet nurse.

When Erich was seven, Klein moved with him to Berlin and eventually went into analysis with Karl Abraham. He was another father figure, and described as the most stalwart of Freud's early colleagues. Klein had met Freud at the Berlin Congress in 1922, delighted to have the opportunity to tell her hero about her theories of the infantile psyche. She was bitterly disappointed. 'He seemed uninterested in what she was telling him, and gave the impression that his mind was occupied elsewhere' (Grosskurth, 1986, p. 127). Of course his own daughter, Anna, was making herself a name as a child analyst, so Freud may have had a vested interest in finding his daughter's rival uninteresting.

Klein had felt guilty about leaving her two elder children under the care of her in-laws when she moved to Berlin, and her husband Arthur worked in Sweden. The couple decided to seek a reconciliation, for the sake of the children, and so the whole family moved into a comfort-able house in Berlin. However, the tensions and rifts in the home were impossible. Hans was bullied by Arthur, and there were ugly quarrels between the couple. Melitta, surprisingly, took her mother's side but that was because her father disapproved of her suitor. Melitta, now a medical student, had fallen in love with Walter Schmideberg, 14 years her senior, with an addiction to alcohol and, her father claimed, drugs. Schmideberg, also involved in psychoanalysis, was, more importantly, a friend of Freud's. Grosskurth (1986) speculates that Klein, harking back to when Melitta was small, was again envious of her daughter, and well she may have been. Melitta was beautiful, as Klein had been, a medical student, which Klein had wanted to be, and romantically entangled with a rich, well-connected, and charming man. At twenty Melitta was training to be the analyst her mother was still striving to be, and Melitta had access to Freud. No wonder Klein felt envious. Her daughter had everything handed to her on a plate. Klein had had to struggle, felt betrayed by lost opportunities, and still felt she had not been accepted in the psychoanalytic movement. It must have been galling.

Professional life

In 1924 Melanie and Arthur finally parted and Melanie threw herself into her professional life. She delivered two papers on child analysis, one in Salzburg and one in Vienna. In her autobiography she does not refer to the Vienna paper, so we do not know if there was any communication between Klein and Freud. Anna Freud said the audience response to the paper was very critical (Grosskurth, 1986, p. 126). It does seem that Klein dealt with criticism by trying to ignore it, though like many abrasive people, was secretly very hurt by it. She described being wounded, and humiliated, by Sigmund Freud's earlier treatment of her.

In 1925 Klein lectured for 3 weeks in London. As a result of the interest she engendered, Klein was asked by Ernest Jones, founder of the London Psychoanalytical Society in 1913, and thereafter a prominent figure on the British Psychoanalytical scene, to come to live in Britain. One stipulation was that she analyse, not only Jones's children, but also his wife, reporting to Jones on their progress. For counsellors, this would seem to be a huge boundary issue. Even more questionable, from today's viewpoint, is Klein's analysis of her own children, presented in papers as other people's children. But it was not uncommon for psychoanalysts at that time to treat each other, and each other's families. Klein's son, Erich, was psychoanalysed by Donald Winnicott. Klein in turn later analysed Winnicott's second wife, Clare.

Klein moved to London in 1926 and was joined by Erich, and 2 years later by Melitta. Abraham, Klein's beloved mentor, had died in Berlin and she was very upset to lose this father figure in her life. She had begun an affair with a younger, married, journalist, which also brought her pain. Their love letters (Grosskurth, 1986), where he calls her Mel, and she chooses to call him Hans (curiously not his name, but the name of her elder son), show how she put more store by the relationship than he did, and eventually he jilted her. By the age of forty-three she had lost, by death, a sister, a father, a brother, a mother and a substitute father. She had also lost a marriage, a love affair, and was beginning to lose a daughter. Life must have seemed very bleak at the end of her stay in Berlin. Perhaps the arrival in London felt like a fresh start.

Klein in London seems to have concentrated on making herself a place on the analytic stage. She may have been rather disconcerted by her daughter's arrival, particularly as it was not long before it was evident that Melitta was a professional rival.

Klein had a further loss in 1933 with the death of her first psychoanalyst, and father figure, Sandor Ferenczi. Eleven months later came a devastating blow. Klein's elder son, Hans, was killed while walking in the Tatra mountains. Arthur Klein went to the funeral, but Melanie was too distraught to travel. Erich Klein said she never recovered from this trauma. The trauma was compounded by Melitta's claim that Hans' death was suicide, a claim for which there was no evidence, but which generated much controversy.

Over the next few years Klein was establishing herself as a powerful figure. In 1937 she published with Joan Riviere, a friend and fellow analyst, a small volume of their public lectures, 'Love, Hate and Reparation'. Klein was set to have things her own way, when everything changed with the arrival of Sigmund and Anna Freud. They had escaped persecution in Nazi Germany and arrived in London in 1938. Other Jewish analysts had taken the same route. Klein, realizing the horrific way Nazi Germany was going, had already become a naturalized British Citizen. Erich Klein changed his name to Eric Clyne.

Suddenly, in London, there were too many analysts chasing too few patients, but for Klein, the personal rivalry, that existed between herself and Anna Freud, was the all-consuming factor. Sigmund Freud died a year after his arrival in London. Klein had no social contact with the Freuds, though her daughter, doubtless annoyingly for Klein, was a frequent visitor. Klein spent the following years in open conflict with the Anna Freudians, an episode termed with considerable understatement, 'The Controversial Discussions', for the psychoanalytic scene was torn apart. Klein seems to have won, for John Bowlby said about the 1950s, that 'it was as clear as a pikestaff that it was advantageous to be a Kleinian' (Grosskurth, 1986, p. 428). However, though respectful of Klein, Bowlby and the Kleinians did not see eye to eye. Others were less respectful and openly reviled her, which Klein seems to have met with stoicism. However, even her supporters at times were frustrated by her intransigence. Winnicott, close to tears, after being snubbed by her, is reported as saying, 'If only Mrs Klein just once would acknowledge an idea she has borrowed from someone else!' (Grosskurth, 1986, p. 374).

What must have been most upsetting for Klein was not Anna Freud's expected refusal to accept Klein's theories. After all she was following in her father's footsteps. What was humiliating was Klein's own daughter publicly decrying her. Melitta stormed out of a scientific meeting after accusing Klein of trying to deprive her of her psychoanalytic practice, and of analysing a year old child. Klein denied treating any child under two and a half. Melitta's parting shot to Klein was, 'where is the father in your work?' (Grosskurth, 1986, p. 214) an accusation with which, no doubt, others agreed, for Klein had banished the father, in her preoccupation with mothers and babies. Klein died in 1960. Melitta did not attend the funeral. Instead she gave a lecture a few miles away wearing a pair of brilliant red boots.

The mother and baby relationship

Freud was never interested in tiny babies, or, if he was, he never wrote about that stage in much detail. The Oedipal stage, which came much later, occupied his attention. Perhaps as a man in the late nineteenth century he did not know too much about babies. They were women's territory, brought down to the drawing room when they were rather more civilized, not puking and bawling in the nursery.

Yet this was the stage that fascinated Klein, the stage she regarded as being the template for future development. For Klein believed that the early relationship between mother and baby laid the foundation for what was to follow. A satisfying, good relationship meant that the baby was set up, with the resources to flourish and grow into an individual, able to make relationships with others. A fraught, unsatisfying, relationship sowed the seeds for a lifetime of neurotic interactions.

There are a number of ideas Klein put forward, which, over 70 years ago, were regarded as fanciful, but are accepted today. For example she thought that the relationship between mother and baby started in utero. Today women's magazines suggest that pregnant women should play soothing music to the foetus.

She posited that babies are full of hate and rage. A far-fetched notion at the time, decried by those who clung to Victorian sentimentalism and preferred to idealize the gentle, innocent babe. However, many mothers and other carers who have frantically tried in vain to soothe a red-faced, furious, baby tyrant will probably agree with Klein that babies are no strangers to rage.

The paranoid schizoid position

So why should the baby be so angry? The baby may feel like a tyrant to the mother but the reality is that he is powerless. As Winnicott (1952) later said, 'There is no such thing as a baby', meaning that a baby has to have a mother, or mother substitute, to survive. Melanie Klein suggested that, in focusing on survival, the tiny baby cries bitterly to ensure his needs are met. The baby sees the carer, usually mother, as 'good' when needs are met promptly and 'bad' when he is left wet and hungry. He is too focused on self to give her the benefit of the doubt, a stage which Klein, following Freud, called narcissistic. (This is named after the youth Narcissus in the Greek myth, who fell in love with his own reflection.)

Klein said the baby sees the mother as an object to satisfy his needs, not even a whole object, but a 'part object', the part he is focused on. He sees Mother as 'good breast' or 'bad breast'. The 'bad breast' experience could be immediately followed by 'good breast', but the baby cannot experience both together. The baby's emotions are split. The good breast experience is the baby's version of love, the bad breast is experienced as hate. Klein thought the baby had aggressive feelings towards its mother, which were acted out in biting the nipple or furiously arching away from the mother's breast.

Envy

To many mothers, carers and watchers of babies most of this would make sense. What may be more difficult to understand is Klein's theory of envy because this assumes that unconscious fantasies drive the baby's responses. Klein (1957) describes how the infant envies the feeding breast, which he imagines has an endless supply of milk that he wants to keep for himself. Klein says she is reminded of the saying, 'to bite the hand that feeds one'. The baby attacks the breast thus spoiling the thing he loves.

But what about bottle-fed babies? Klein talks about the breast as feeder and that would be her experience at a time when most babies were breast-fed. She herself had a wet nurse, which, according to her own theories, must have affected her significantly, at an unconscious, if not conscious, level. In fact, one wonders what part that experience played in her later hypotheses. As far as the bottle is concerned, Klein sees it as a symbolic representation of the breast (paper published posthumously 1963). However, Klein (1952) also thinks that babies are born with unconscious knowledge of the breast. This means that bottle-fed babies feel deprived and envious. Klein claimed her experience of bottle-fed patients led her to believe that they had a greater yearning for an unobtainable object, in later life.

For counsellors, I think what can be taken from this is the idea of envy as a primal, potent force, something to be handled with great caution. For, alongside this, is the concept of spoiling the thing we want, and cannot have. It is destructive to self and others. Envy is an emotion we all feel but also feel ashamed by it. Because we yearn for what we cannot have but are loath to admit it, we deny the envious feelings by spoiling. 'I didn't want the job anyway.' 'He was a bastard and there's plenty more fish in the sea.'

Only young children are allowed to be envious. 'I want his tricycle', stamps the angry 2-year-old, and parents look on adoringly. So, when we admit to envious feelings, we feel infantilized. Klein said that by acknowledging the envy we can allow ourselves other emotions, sadness being one of them. This seems more grown up and manageable, but most of us avoid sadness. It is too painful. Better to hang on to envy and anger.

Case Example | Maggie: from envy to sadness

Maggie had thought she was happily married. She had just had a second child. When her husband, John, said he was moving out, to go and live with a work colleague, she was stunned. It was unbelievable that he could do this to her and his children. The ultimate betrayal was to abandon his new baby. Maggie was overcome by fury and envy of the new woman. She took to passing her flat, in the hope of seeing them together, though she was not sure what she would do if she spotted them. Then one day, when travelling on the underground, she saw the girlfriend standing by the edge of the platform. Maggie had an overwhelming desire to push her on to the track. 'I wanted to kill her,' she said.

Instead she wheeled the baby past trying not to cry. It was her fear that, if she allowed herself to be sad, she would collapse. She had to keep the anger going, to keep the family going. Months later, when she had acknowledged that John would not return and that she had managed to survive, she allowed herself to be sad. She began to grieve for what she had lost. The emotional energy, she had put into keeping herself angry, could be redirected. Eventually she was able to take up the career she had left behind on marriage, rebuild her circle of friends and slowly begin to have a satisfying life again.

A trainee counsellor had this case. She was overwhelmed by the client's anger, and felt helpless. She also felt stuck because Maggie refused to do anything other than rail at her betrayal.

The counsellor took the case to supervision, and was surprised when her supervisor asked her what she thought was the function of the anger. She had not thought of the anger having a function, merely seen it as a normal reaction to rejection. But when she did think about it, with help from her supervisor, she saw how the anger was a shield, protecting Maggie from the hurt and pain of what had happened.

The counsellor was inexperienced, but, like so many trainee counsellors, she spent much of her time thinking and worrying about the case. She kept the client in mind and, consciously or unconsciously, the client knew this.

Some years later the counsellor bumped into Maggie, who told her how well her life was progressing. Maggie also said how crucial the counselling had been to her development. The counsellor was genuinely disclaiming, thinking that this had been a case where she had felt mostly out of her depth, and had done very little. 'Oh no,' said Maggie. 'You were my life line.'

The counsellor had been for the client a potent figure. The client felt destroyed by her rejection, powerless and childlike. She felt like a child, who runs home to mother, seeking validation and security. Maggie would not have voiced this. She was probably not even aware she wanted a mother figure, but unconsciously she sought it in the person of the counsellor.

But like the good mother, the counsellor had not colluded with Maggie, but had gently challenged her anger and bitterness. The counsellor had helped her to be sad. In being sad, Maggie had let go of some of the envy. This had helped Maggie to move on, beginning to accept that she must take her life in a different direction.

Anxiety

Another emotion which can wreak havoc on people's lives is anxiety. Klein believed that the baby is racked with anxiety. First the trauma of birth is anxiety-laden. Added to this is the baby's fear that he could destroy himself and others. Klein, from her child observations, believed that the infant had a phantasy, that he could be annihilated. His anxiety about not existing was fuelled by his murderous rage, which could annihilate his mother, and therefore himself.

Given this perilous start, Klein felt it was little wonder that clients brought anxiety as a primary issue to their therapy sessions. Counsellors, too, know that much of their work lies in helping clients in their lifelong struggle to manage anxiety, so that it is not disabling. Trainee counsellors need to be aware that anxiety is very powerful and to treat it with respect. It can be the catalyst for extremely self-destructive behaviour.

The baby's self-destructive thoughts, together with his paranoid thoughts of annihilation by the mother, make for an anxious first 3 months of life. As the baby's feelings are also split between love and hate at this time, Klein called this 'the paranoid schizoid position'. She did not call it a stage but a position. This was because she believed that we all take this position throughout our lives, particularly if we feel infantilized with the world against us.

Splitting

Psychodynamic counsellors have found these positions useful to help understand their clients and the issues they bring to counselling. I believe counsellors, of whatever persuasion, can benefit from some of these ideas. The notion of splitting as found in the paranoid schizoid phase is a useful concept. Klein said that whenever we feel childlike and powerless, infantilized by the experiences of our lives, we can take refuge in splitting. This means that clients can polarize events and people. Things can be either idealized or demonized. This can include the counsellor, who at times can be an ideal mother, while at other times the most critical, neglectful and punishing of mothers.

Sometimes the counselling is about reconciling the two extremes and finding some common or middle ground. Sometimes the counselling will be helping the client to live less narcissistically because he does not feel so threatened.

Case Example | Kathleen: splitting as a defence against trauma

A client, Kathleen, whom the counsellor saw over a long period had been subject to gross trauma. As a result she felt that no one could be trusted. Because of the horrific experiences she had suffered, she took refuge in splitting, and seeing others as objects, whose sole purpose was to fulfil her needs. This included the counsellor, who spent long hours in supervision, alternately worrying about how to get close to this client, and being furious about the way she felt manipulated and deskilled by the client. Because of Kathleen's experience she was suspicious of anyone who came close to her and was convinced that everyone was out to get her.

Working with a highly defended client like Kathleen needs stamina. The counsellor has to be careful not to collude with the client, but also, because of the nature of the client's trauma, not to be unconsciously abusive. Very forceful challenging, where the client feels she is not understood, can come into this category. Challenging the client is important, but it has to be sensitively done.

It is important that part of the counsellor keeps a watching brief on what is happening in the session, and the other part is with the client. Being there for the client, in terms of the counsellor's concentration, monitoring how the client is using the counsellor, being aware of the process, are all necessary elements. Holding all this together, as well as accepting the client's hostility and anger, is not easy. It does call for experience. A trainee counsellor who finds herself in this position will need excellent supervision and may have to think about referring.

For Kathleen, counselling presented an enormous challenge. Eventually she was able to trust the counsellor and begin to work with her. As a result of this relationship, Kathleen was able to live less narcissistically. As time went on she was able to make other relationships. This was in part through her being able to rally her not inconsiderable, but denied, resources.

The other part lay in having a consistent counsellor, seen unconsciously as mother, to challenge her, keep her in touch with reality, be able to accept her anger and between sessions hold her in mind. Both client and counsellor learnt an enormous amount about relationships from this encounter.

Projective identification

Like Freud, Klein believed that projection and introjection are useful defences against emotions too powerful to cope with. In projection, the baby splits off, in phantasy, the unmanageable feelings and believes he has thrust them into another, most usually the mother. The feelings can be both good and bad, bad feelings he wants to be rid of, good feelings he wants to protect from his bad self.

Introjection is a way of taking into himself goodness from the mother, to make himself feel better. Alternately he can take into himself the bad parts of the mother, to make the world, he has to relate to, seem a safer place.

Projective identification is a more complicated and intense form of projection. 'Much of the hatred against parts of the self is now directed towards the mother. This leads to a particular form of identification' (Klein, 1946). The baby projects the parts of himself, which he cannot bear, into his mother. She identifies with the baby's hated self and feels his pain. By recognizing and then responding to his destructive anxieties, the mother can make the baby feel that he does still exist and will not be annihilated.

Klein was not persuaded by the therapeutic use of her theory of projective identification. She lectured students on their claim that the patient, through projective identification, had made them confused. 'No, you are confused', she is quoted as saying.

However, her Kleinian followers found it a very helpful therapeutic concept. Hanna Segal called it 'the earliest form of empathy' (1988, p. 36) and a way of putting oneself into another person's shoes. Patrick Casement graphically describes his response to this happening (1985, p. 79) and demonstrates, throughout the book, *On Learning from the Patient*, the efficacy of projective identification with his patients.

In psychodynamic counselling, the use of this Kleinian concept, in therapeutic practice, shows that this is a most useful phenomenon. A useful clue to the operation of this process is the way in which the client tells his story. Sometimes he describes the most dreadful events with a complete lack of emotion. His voice is devoid of life and his tone is monotonous. Alternately, he may not speak at all, relying on the counsellor to intercept his unexpressed pain. Whatever the way, unconsciously chosen, the client projects his unbearable feelings into the counsellor, and the counsellor feels them for him. It means that the counsellor can identify with the experience, which the client cannot manage. This presupposes that she allows herself to be available to the client, rather than ignoring his cry for help. It assumes the counsellor can bear to feel the split-off feelings.

If the counsellor can hold on to the feelings of despair, rather than try to give such uncomfortable feelings straight back, she can be very helpful to the client. Not only can she learn a good deal about her client, which she would otherwise not know, but also can get a glimpse of what it is like to be him. Over time she can help the client to take back the, once unmanageable, feelings in a way that is manageable for him.

Case Example | Luke: the counsellor feels the split-off feelings of the client

Luke came to counselling because his brother had died. Luke was twenty-one and his brother was twenty-three. He had died in a motorbike accident.

Luke had come to counselling because his friends had suggested it. He said he did not see what good it would do. His brother was dead and that was that. Nothing would bring him back. So what was the point?

Luke told the story of his brother's death in a monotonous tone, devoid of any emotion. Luke had been backpacking in South America when his brother had been killed. He had collected his emails from an Internet café and received the horrific news. By the time he was able to get home, the funeral was over, and all his relatives had begun to accept that his brother was dead. Luke still could not believe it. He did not want to believe it.

Luke came for a second session and we talked more about his brother. It was still very distanced. To try to make it more real to Luke, I asked the name of his brother. 'Paul', he said reluctantly. I thereafter used Paul's name, but Luke still talked about 'my brother'. Luke said that he had taken his brother's music tapes and he played them a lot. I wondered if that made him feel closer to Paul. 'Well, it's just music,' said Luke.

I took the case to supervision. I told the traumatic story outlining Luke's emotional denial of the death. I started to describe what Luke had said about playing Paul's music tapes. I realised I felt distressed and was holding back tears. I wanted to cry.

I think this is what counsellors can learn in practice from Klein's theory of projective identification. The client cannot bear to feel the feelings, so the counsellor feels them for him. Eventually if the counselling goes on, and the counsellor and client can form a relationship, the client can begin to take back the feelings.

For Luke the shock of his brother's death was too much for him to take in. Not only had he and Paul been very close to each other, but the manner of Paul's death had added to the trauma. Luke had left behind, at home, a vibrant, fit and very alive elder brother. He returned to a dead brother, already cremated. Luke hated

Case Example | (Continued)

himself for being alive. His family had already begun to accept the awful tragedy. Luke could not do that, so unconsciously he shut down his emotions. He refused to feel.

After weeks of counselling Luke felt safe enough to begin to allow himself to feel. Luke began to grieve for Paul. It was a very painful process, but Luke knew he had to go through it. 'I couldn't go on feeling like a zombie,' he said.

Managing the paranoid schizoid position

Melanie Klein saw the world as a place where raw, primal emotions are not far beneath the surface of civilized living. Envy, greed, rage, hate and murderous thoughts are emotions we can all feel, though we are loath to admit them. Because we spend much emotional energy in pushing away these frightening urges, we have less energy left for the business of living. The Kleinian answer is to acknowledge that they are there, and then we can manage them.

The depressive position

After about 4 months the baby becomes more accommodating. As he grows and slowly becomes less dependent on his mother (this is the time when some babies begin to eat solid food), he starts to see her as a whole person. My Mother good and bad! My Mother right and wrong! He can love her, and he can hate her, and be aware of both emotions. He can feel his mother's hate at times, while experiencing how much she really loves him. Klein termed this holding of two conflicting emotions, 'ambivalence' (a word usually used these days in a pejorative way, 'You're ambivalent. You can't make up your mind'). But with this development of the personality comes mourning and guilt, two very painful feelings. The baby can feel guilty if he has distressed his mother and can mourn her loss when she is away from him. He can mourn his fall from grace, when he perceives she is angry with him, and try to win favour by pleasing her. Klein called this whole experience 'the depressive position'. Winnicott (1963), later, called it, 'the stage of concern'.

Klein thought that through life we gravitate between the paranoid schizoid position, and the depressive position, according to our personalities and experiences. She thought that the baby, who never gets his needs met, can rarely move on to the depressive position, and at the extreme can become psychotic. Neurosis is the likely outcome for the individual who cannot handle the perpetual conflict of the depressive position.

Klein (1959) thought that the internal depressive anxieties in babies are outwardly displayed in their sad and melancholy expressions around the end of the first year. She associated it with weaning, and the loss of the mother's breast, at that time. But of course, this is an ethnocentric view, as in the Third World countries babies are routinely breast fed until they are about 3 years old, as breast milk is more nutritious, cleaner and cheaper than any alternatives.

The concept of the depressive position is helpful to many clients. The idea that guilt and mourning are a central part of the human condition can be reassuring to people who, influenced by the twenty-first-century Western culture, feel that if they are not happy there is something very wrong with them. Counsellors can help clients, wracked by guilt, or overcome by painful feelings associated with loss, to work through them and try to integrate them. This can lead clients to feel less depressed and be able to take more satisfaction from their lives.

Ambivalence

Ambivalence is a useful concept as a way of working with conflicting emotions. The notion of holding two contradictory concepts, at the same time, is novel to many. That both of the opposing thoughts and feelings are legitimate can be very illuminating for clients who have been locked in emotions like blame and bitterness. We do not have to choose one position forever. For example 'My mother was not there for me when I was small and I felt abandoned' is one position. 'She was ill and did her best' is another. Both are true. Both can be held together. Both can be worked with and both can be integrated. This is useful for those of us who as children have felt abandoned, rejected or ignored by parents whom we felt were not there for us. This will include many clients and many counsellors. We can hold on to these feelings while acknowledging that perhaps for all sorts of reasons our parents did their best. It may not have felt good enough, but when we can forgive, we can move on. The bitterness of 'It's my parents' fault that I'm like this' is a hiding to nowhere. It can be freeing to cast that aside, though it is never easy. It does enable us to begin to take responsibility for our own lives, less cumbered by the past.

Case Example | Anita: from blame to ambivalence

Anita felt she suffered from low self-esteem. She blamed it on her mother who had always been critical of her as a child. Nothing Anita ever did seemed to be good enough. When she came home at 9 years old, saying that she had come second in the maths test, her mother had snapped, 'Why not first?'

Anita felt her mother's criticism had dogged her adolescence and made her shy and submissive. She had taken refuge in her studies and though feeling underconfident had done well, first at school, then at university.

Anita's mother had died when Anita was twenty, but Anita had taken on the mantle and become her own harshest critic. It was as if she had internalized all the negative bits of her mother, while forgetting that, at times, her mother could be warm and accepting.

When, with the counsellor, Anita looked at her mother's life, Anita saw her mother, left a widow at thirty, struggling to give her daughter a decent life. Anita's mother had been made bitter by what she felt were missed opportunities, never feeling that she had been able to achieve her educational potential. Anita, significantly, now thirty herself, began to understand why her mother had been so anxious for her daughter to succeed, though it had never been explained in those terms. In fact, Anita wondered if her mother had ever understood that she was trying to achieve her own goals, vicariously, through her daughter. Anita, eventually, acknowledged that though her childhood had been difficult, her mother, too, had had a tough time.

For perhaps the first time Anita was able to put herself into her mother's shoes and feel sad. She realized her mother had probably done her best. Anita began to grieve for her mother, something she had not allowed herself to do fully before, because of her anger. Anita had felt tremendous anger towards her mother and would not let it go. She had hung on to the anger, perhaps as a defence against sadness and pain.

However, with the counsellor, Anita was able to get in touch with the pain, and try to work with it. Anita decided that she should learn from her mother's bitterness. She did not have to go along that road. In relinquishing blame she began to take back responsibility for her own life. Anita saw that she, and she alone, could allow herself to take pride in her achievements. Integrating painful childhood experiences takes time, but Anita is working on it. She thinks that she is now better able to understand herself and begin to move on.

Ambivalence is ever present in the counselling room. The whole process of counselling carries ambivalence. As clients we want to use the counsellor to improve our lives, yet part of us resents having to be a client. Admitting to needing help, particularly to oneself, is difficult, and who wants to go through the pain? We can love the counsellor when things are going well in the counselling. We can hate her when it is going badly. This is made clear in the counselling exchange. As counsellors, we have to learn to understand the process, rather than react defensively to what can feel a personal attack.

Case Example | Lorna: acknowledging ambivalence

Lorna, an only child, is now a 33-year-old woman, with two young children. She has been coming to counselling for nearly a year, after the break up of her marriage. Her husband had been violent towards her, but when she had turned to her mother for support, it had not been forthcoming. Lorna's mother's approach had been, 'You've made your bed, he's a good provider and nothing's perfect in this world. You'll have to learn to cope with it.' Consequently when Lorna had finally managed the monumental step of leaving her husband, she felt very much alone. She came to counselling, where much of the work centred round her feelings of betrayal by her mother. The counsellor in the transference was often the idealized mother, but at times the abandoning mother. This is the start of a session after a break.

Case Example | (Continued)

LORNA: Did you have a good holiday?

COUNSELLOR: Yes, thank you. I did.

LORNA: (*There is a long silence.*) Something awful always happens when you go away. (*Lorna sounds tearful.*)

COUNSELLOR: And I've left you to manage on your own.

LORNA: (*Pulls herself together.*) Well, I know you need your holidays.

COUNSELLOR: But that doesn't stop you feeling mad with me for leaving you.

LORNA: (*Lorna sits in silence while she thinks about it.*) It's so childish - but yes I was bloody furious with you. But it is childish.

COUNSELLOR: But isn't that what it feels like at times? Back to being a child.

LORNA: You mean feeling that you can't cope on your own.

COUNSELLOR: Yes. And also that your mother isn't there when you want her.

LORNA: (*Angrily*) Well I know my mother hasn't been there for me. (*Lorna looks as if she might cry. There is another long silence.*) But you have. Well usually.

COUNSELLOR: But not on this occasion.

LORNA: (*Angrily*) There's no comparison!

COUNSELLOR: The feelings are the same. Abandonment. Betrayal. They remind you of how you felt about your mother.

LORNA: (*Spiritedly*) But that's unfair. You've been supportive.

COUNSELLOR: But it doesn't stop you feeling I failed you.

LORNA: Well, nobody's perfect.

COUNSELLOR: That's what your mother said.

LORNA: (*Tearfully*) Yes. And that's what I sometimes think. When it all goes wrong. That I should have stayed with him. (*The counsellor and client sit in silence while Lorna wipes her tears.*)

COUNSELLOR: You've talked about the feelings of being abused and betrayed by your husband, of being betrayed and abandoned by your mother, and feeling abandoned by me.

LORNA: Well, yes. I felt a bit the same, but it's different.

COUNSELLOR: How different?

LORNA: (*Fiercely*) You didn't thump me against the wall and put me in hospital.

COUNSELLOR: Nor did your mother.

LORNA: No. But she did other things.

COUNSELLOR: So the feelings are the same but the situation is different. You can accept that I can do my best, but still get it wrong for you. And it's sort of O.K.

LORNA: Yes. I suppose … Yes. On a good day it's O.K.

COUNSELLOR: So is it O.K. to beat you up and put you in hospital?

LORNA: It is not O.K. No Way! Definitely not.

COUNSELLOR: So you've reminded yourself why you left.

LORNA: I sometimes need you to remind me.

COUNSELLOR: And I go away on holiday. And leave you with awful things.

LORNA: Well at times I did feel that. But I coped on my own.

COUNSELLOR: And that's something to hang on to, isn't it? That you do manage on your own.

LORNA: Yes, I always doubt myself. But yes I do.

The session then moved on to examine the 'awful thing' that had happened when the counsellor was away, and how Lorna had managed it, or, in her, and her mother's words, coped with it.

The first part of the session highlighted the ambivalent feelings of the client. It started with a seemingly neutral question of one adult to another, about her holiday. But then, this exchange is not merely two adults talking together. They have different roles, with the adult in the counsellor role knowing that her holiday has probably produced strong feelings in the other, the client. The counsellor knows that it would certainly not be helpful to go into details about the holiday (the hotel was awful, my partner got food poisoning). On the other hand, the counsellor could counter the question with another question. 'I wonder why you are asking me about my holiday?' But this could sound both patronizing and attacking. It also projects the exchange immediately into what may be risky areas for the client. She may find it difficult to admit to the feelings she has about the counsellor's holiday.

As it was, the counsellor gave Lorna the space and opportunity to play it her way. After the start, in which Lorna asks about the counsellor's well-being in terms of the holiday, Lorna makes what appears to be an observation. Lorna says that when the counsellor goes away something awful always happens to Lorna. But the counsellor reads it as a loaded statement, blaming the counsellor for neglecting the client. She lets Lorna know that she acknowledges her abandonment of Lorna. Though Lorna struggles to be the understanding adult, recognizing that counsellors need holidays, she eventually capitulates, conceding her childlike feelings and making plain her fury at the counsellor's desertion.

Case Example | (Continued)

This provides a platform for the counsellor and client to look at these mixed feelings. The counsellor helps Lorna to see that it is valid to acknowledge what the counsellor has done, that has felt supportive for Lorna, but it is also valid to acknowledge that at times Lorna can feel betrayed by the counsellor. The counsellor can do her best, but the counsellor is not perfect. This reverberates with what Lorna's mother said about the world not being perfect, with the implication that you have to put up with it. In her darkest moments Lorna sometimes believes her mother was right. Lorna and the counsellor discuss this, setting the subjective feelings of betrayal against the objective reality of being betrayed and abused. It is reasonable to accept that the counsellor sometimes gets it wrong for the client. What it is not reasonable to accept is a husband's violence.

This fraction of a counselling exchange shows how the counsellor, using her awareness of the concept of ambivalence, can help the client explore her conflicting feelings about the counselling. She can get in touch with the childlike parts of herself, but she can also use the adult parts to develop greater independence.

Reparation

The capacity to feel guilt over hating the mother makes the baby want to make it better. He wants to make amends. He wants to show his mother he loves her and his attachment to her. As he grows and his conflicts with the mother are played out, in temper tantrums or mute refusals, he will want to be forgiven afterwards, demonstrating his love for his mother, and seeking reassurance that he is still loved.

Reparation is a useful Kleinian notion. Klein ties it with identification (1937) saying that being able to put ourselves in the place of others is a precursor to love. When we love, and feel guilty that we have injured our loved one, we want to make good the injury. Making reparation is a fundamental element of human relationships.

This is a helpful concept to clients who feel they are too destructive to make reparation. Their belief in their ability to be loved and lovable is tenuous. Counselling, usually long term, with a consistent counsellor, who can stand in for the good parent the client never had, can sometimes help him to get in touch with his own goodness. The counsellor will have to bear the attacks, when the confidence in his capacity for reparation ebbs. It is not for the faint hearted and it demands skilled supervision and preferably an experienced counsellor.

Klein suggested that in caring for others we are making reparation. Certainly her own early life, where she desperately sought love and attention, envied her siblings and hated her parents, made a good breeding ground for guilt and reparation. As workers in the caring professions, perhaps we should reflect on what we are trying to repair.

Mourning

Klein wrote her influential paper on 'Mourning and its Relation to the Manic-Depressive States' in 1940. She was then fifty-eight. She had experienced the death of her father, her mother, her two sisters, her brother, her son and her two mentors cum father figures. She had also lost the love of her daughter, and been spurned by her lover. She was alienated from her homeland by war, while the most terrible persecution was being meted out to her Jewish friends and relations. Klein was no stranger to mourning.

Klein compared the process of mourning with the infantile depressive position. Klein suggests that the object being mourned is the mother's breast. As discussed earlier this is an ethnocentric, Western view, as in world terms, the majority of babies are not weaned from the breast by the time they are a year old. I suppose we could say that developmentally, babies at this stage are beginning to walk and can walk away from the mother. Although this is part of the beginnings of independence and clearly sought by the toddler, it involves a loss of constant closeness, of being held by the mother. This is particularly so in less-developed countries where small babies are not separated from the mother in cots or prams. The baby is tied to the mother's back and pulled round to the breast for feeding. As the baby also sleeps with the mother the contact is enduring. This is partly lost when the baby starts to walk.

In 'normal mourning' Klein suggested that the mourner goes through a temporary psychotic manic-depressive state, where he is 'ill'. The greatest danger lies in the mourner projecting all his feelings of distress, as hatred, against the dead person. This hatred can be expressed as triumph over the dead person. Klein in her paper talks about a dream as if it were a patient's, but it is actually her own dream about her son's, Hans, death. She dreamt that she was flying with her son and he disappeared and drowned. She, too, felt that she had drowned, but she made an effort and drew back to life. She had survived. This survival, in turn, leads to guilt. Klein traces this back to childhood where the infantile cries of 'I wish you were dead' are projected into reality.

Klein identified a passing manic state of elation, which was present between sorrow and distress. She said it was due to the feeling of possessing the perfect, loved object, inside oneself. However, when the hatred against the loved person, for punishing the mourner by leaving him, wells up again, the perfect idealized internal object is disturbed. Klein says that it is only by regaining trust in external objects and values of different kinds, that the mourner is able to strengthen his confidence in the lost loved person. (It is quite surprising for Klein to direct mourners to the external world, which she habitually ignored. However, Klein, herself, sought consolation after the death of her son, Hans, in looking at nicely situated houses in the country [Sayers, 2000, p. 22]. She thought she might like one for herself.)

Eventually, like the baby who realizes that mother can be both good and bad, the mourner can bear to realize that the loved object was not perfect, but is still lovable and trustworthy and will not be an object of fearful revenge. When this stage is reached Klein believed that 'important steps in the work of mourning and towards overcoming it have been made' (1940, in 1988, p. 355). This sounds as if all mourning is pathological and must be 'overcome'. However, Klein, herself, knew that grief cannot be 'overcome' in the sense of vanquished. It can be made less raw and eventually it can be integrated.

In fact, Klein went on to say that when grief is experienced to the full and despair is at its height, the love for the lost person is reactivated and the mourner feels that life will go on, with the lost loved object preserved within. Klein compares this to the infantile depressive position. This means that mourning can make us feel childlike and lost. However, as the mourner preserves his loved object inside him, he also reinstates his first loved objects, usually his parents, that he was in danger of losing, 'he overcomes his grief, regains security and achieves true harmony and peace' (ibid., p. 369).

Again this use of the word 'overcome' makes it sound as if it is gone for ever, which does not accord with Klein's other thoughts on grief. I would think that she means the manic state of mourning is overcome, with the mourner left with good memories of the loved person, which he can hold inside him. This develops alongside a grief or sadness, which Klein thought could be enriching.

Counsellors can learn from these ideas of the value of grief, of not pushing clients into a false recovery. It is also salutary to remind ourselves that bereaved people do feel 'mad', may exhibit bizarre behaviour, and that it is a normal part of the process. Once we can hold the image of the loved person inside us as a good memory, we can begin to feel less fragmented and more whole. Klein had more than her fair share of loss, yet she used her grief in the creative, enriching way she advocated for others. Perhaps both we and our clients should take hope from this.

Transference

We all transfer experiences from the past onto the present, in ordinary life not just in the counselling room. If we come from families where parental authority was an issue, we will probably continue to struggle with our relationships with authority figures, as well as with organizations, which spell authority to us. People we meet for the first time 'remind' us of someone from the past. Often the first indication of this is our reaction to them. Why do we feel so envious of this person, why do we feel so fearful of that person? It does not make sense and here lies the answer. It is not usually sensible. We may hardly know someone, yet already we have strong feelings towards him.

It is the unconscious talking. Experiences, we are hardly aware of, trigger what seem irrational responses to a new person, but they really belong to a different person from the past.

Like Freud, Klein thought that clients transferred to the therapist figure experiences from the past. Counsellors are, unconsciously, seen by the client as parent, sibling, authority figure, friend. This can be very useful to the counsellor as it can be a pointer to a denied or dependent relationship, which the clients may not be aware that they are struggling with. The way that the counsellor is treated, by the client, can be a clue to the habitual ways of relating for this client. The external client–counsellor interaction can be symbolic of interaction in the client's internal world. The more distressed, damaged or out of touch with reality the client is, the more likely he is to operate in the transference.

Case Example | Jack: the counsellor as mother

Jack came to counselling because he wanted to 'sort out' the relationship with his mother. He knew he was too enmeshed in his family, but felt he could not escape them. Particularly he felt bound up with his mother in what he thought was an unhealthy way. He was thirty-five and although he had his own flat he spent much of the time at his mother's house. He had no job so could persuade himself that going to see his mother was a good use of his time. However, every time he left his mother, he felt worse than when he arrived. He left feeling depressed and worthless. Each time he vowed that he would not return, at least not for a long time. Then he started to feel guilty. He was the only one of her children who was not married with a family, so it really was his responsibility to make sure his mother was all right.

He looked towards his siblings for support, but they were dismissive. His elder brother told him that it was his own fault. His mother had him on a string. She was manipulative and domineering. 'Leave her alone. She doesn't need you. Get yourself a life' was his brother's advice. His sister was equally direct. But she added that she thought that visiting his mother was not good for Jack. 'It does nothing for your self-esteem', she said. But Jack continued to visit. He thought his mother might be lonely since his father's death. Each time he went with the hope that, this time, his mother would appreciate him show she loved him and not criticize him. He tried hard not to upset her or make her angry. He was compliant and appeasing.

In the counselling he treated his female counsellor with great deference. He always agreed with her, and altogether showed he wanted to please. The counsellor found it very frustrating and discussed it at length in supervision. She realized that Jack was transferring on to her his experience of being mothered, and his response to it. To begin with the counsellor was idealized, and treated almost with reverence. But as the counsellor, after discussion with her supervisor, started to challenge Jack, he began to be angry towards her. He accused her of not caring about him, and on one occasion stormed out of the room. The next session he came back looking fearful, and seemed astonished when his counsellor merely commented that he was angry last week. This was a revelation for Jack. That his counsellor (mother) could contain his anger and not seek retribution was an experience he had never had before. Like a child he started to test the counsellor (How much do you love me?) and began to be rude and aggressive in the sessions.

The counsellor told him firmly that she would not tolerate this because she cared about him. She reminded him that he had come to feel better about himself and behaving badly made him hate himself. After this demonising of the counsellor, subsequent to the initial idealization, Jack started to have a more-balanced relationship with her. He was able to tell her when he was disappointed when the sessions did not seem to get anywhere. He agreed with her that he was cross with her when she went on holiday and left him. But he also began to take more responsibility for his behaviour, including the way the sessions went, and became less dependent on his counsellor.

As his relationship with the counsellor developed, he began to treat his mother differently. He went there less often, and was able to stand up for himself better. He said that he felt more adult with his mother, not like a little boy, at least not all of the time. The development in his relationship with the counsellor, whom he had treated like his mother, had enabled him to have a better relationship with his mother. He had transferred what he had learnt with the counsellor, to the relationship with his mother, and was delighted with the result.

He feels so freed from his enslavement to his mother that he is beginning to think that a sexual relationship with a partner might not be beyond him. He is beginning, at thirty-five, to feel an adult.

Countertransference

Countertransference feelings can be the other end of the client's transference. The counsellor unconsciously accepts the strong feelings transferred from the client and may act them out. For example, she starts to feel like the client's mother, and may begin to behave maternally. The second way that countertransference feelings can be evoked in the counsellor is when something from the client hooks into something from the client. Klein, like Freud, thought that countertransference feelings, stirred up in the therapy and felt by the analyst, were an obstacle to the patient's development within the therapy. The feelings demanded more therapy for the analyst, so that they could be mastered.

Paula Heimann, Klein's one-time disciple, who asserted a place outside Klein's shadow, disagreed. She said that the feelings unconsciously communicated by the patient are a key to the patient's state of mind. They can provide deep insights into the patient's unconscious mental processes. This is a means to understanding the patient's experience, which he may, otherwise, be unable to communicate.

For psychodynamic counsellors, it is useful to see the countertransference as a response to the transference. It is usually assigned to the counsellor, though clients can also have a countertransference reaction to the counsellor's transference. Very vulnerable clients who have been traumatized are likely, at least at first, to operate, almost solely, in the transference. They feel very fragile and fragmented, torn apart by the trauma. This lack of control over their lives makes them feel like a powerless baby, so unconsciously they seek a parent figure, to depend on. Counsellors can find themselves unconsciously responding in the countertransference, as a nurturing and sometimes overprotective parent.

Counsellors often have countertransference feelings, when someone they are working with brings issues that mirror something from the counsellor's past. It might be a difficult relationship with the mother the client is talking about, a mother who was never there for him. The counsellor also had a difficult relationship with her mother and before she realizes what is happening she is offering to the client the experience of an ever-present mother. This can extend to the counsellor being worried about abandoning the client to go away on a holiday, or offering the client telephone calls between sessions. She will need to take this to supervision. She will also need to make sure that she really has worked enough on this issue in her own therapy.

That is why the client's personal counselling is so crucial for the psychodynamic counsellor. Not all schools of counselling would agree with this. However, the counsellor who is trying to work in a psychodynamic way needs to understand the significance of transference and countertransference issues. If the counsellor has not worked on the difficult relationship with her mother and the client presents her with a similar situation, two things can happen. First she finds herself thinking about her own history and switches off from the client. The client realizes this and feels abandoned by another 'mother'. Or, second, the counsellor swings into a sympathetic-mother mode to comfort the client and protect him from his past. This can mean that the counsellor becomes unhelpful. She can end up colluding with the client and her identification ensures that she is at some level trying to come to terms with her own past history, rather than working with the client on his. She can collude with the blame, so that the client can feel there is no way forward. He is doomed. His life is forever ruined because of his difficult childhood. But if the counsellor has worked through her own abandonment, learned to accept it, integrate it and move on, she is in a stronger position to help the client work through his own past.

Case Example | Karen: acknowledging countertransference

A trainee counsellor, Karen, had been very reluctant to go to personal counselling herself. She worked in the caring professions and knew she did a good job with her professional clients. She felt that, as she had got by without counselling so far, there was no reason why she should need counselling herself, just because she was now seeing counselling clients.

Then she saw a client, Irene, who was a woman about her own age, who had grown up in her area. 'In fact', Karen said, when she brought the case to the case discussion group, 'I was surprised that I did not already know her.' The issue the client had brought was her difficult relationship with her father. Irene had found him cold and distant and she felt that he had always put her down. Now, in late middle age, he was dead of a heart attack. Irene had thought she would have had time to effect some sort of reconciliation, 'I just put the problem on the back burner, but I did want to do something about it eventually. The time never seemed right and now it's too late.'

Karen tried to work with her on the difficult grief and guilt, but found herself thinking a lot about her own father. He, too, had died, killed in a car accident when she was fourteen. He, too, had seemed distant from her when she was a child. She had tried very hard to be 'Daddy's girl', but had felt rejected. In her early teens Karen had

Case Example | (Continued)

given up and become rebellious and difficult. In the middle of all this he had died. As an adult she had talked about it to friends and family and decided that she had no reason to feel guilty. 'After all my behaviour was typical teenager. If he'd lived we might eventually have been the best of friends.' But he had not lived and Karen as she heard Irene's story became locked in her own.

At first she did not realize what was happening. She took the case to supervision and the supervisor challenged her on the work. What made her offer the client extra sessions? Why was she being so sympathetic and reassuring to the client? How was the client ever to work through her grief in this cosy climate of protection and collusion? 'Nothing grows in honey', said the supervisor. 'And why have you given the client your telephone number? You know it's against agency policy? What's happening here?'

Karen and the supervisor talked. The supervisor suggested that there was some sort of identification going on. Did Karen have a similar story to the client? Karen admitted that they had both lost their fathers and as she began to explain the circumstances, realized that she could not hold back the tears. Without prompting from her supervisor, Karen said that she must get some counselling for herself straight away. 'I can see I need it personally, but I also need it so that I can give a professional service to clients. I haven't been behaving professionally recently and that appals me.'

The trainee counsellor had been locked in countertransference because the client's grief had hooked into her own unresolved issues. She became at times the child desperate for protection from an unresponsive parent. In the counselling this made her into the overprotective mother wanting to make it better for the client, with whom she identified. But because the rejected child part of the counsellor was never addressed, she was not consistent. As the overprotective parent she had given Irene her telephone number, but was actually furious with her when she used it. Unconsciously Karen was the child who needed love and protection and was envious of the client who was getting all this attention for herself. At some level she felt murderous towards Irene for demanding more.

Perhaps Irene had unconsciously picked this up and wanted to make reparation. Before Karen could ask the client at the end of the counselling if she might use her material in a case study, Irene offered it. For Karen this case had been a huge learning experience. She is now impassioned in her belief that counsellors must have counselling themselves before they can be sure that they are working ethically.

It is not just trainee counsellors who get caught in countertransference reactions and take some time to learn from their own responses. Some time ago I had a client who had been traumatized in an abusive situation which then escalated into more trauma and abuse. Her mother was dead. The loss of her mother and her feelings of abandonment ensured that she sought a mother in me. I became for her a mother figure. In the counselling sessions I began to feel like her mother and then without being conscious of it, started to act like her mother. I got entangled in the whole feelings of powerlessness and unfairness that she held. I felt very stuck.

So I became more available. I started to worry about how she would manage when I was on holiday. As I talked this over in supervision, I realized I had taken on the client's feelings and was hurt and angry. I had lost the boundaries. My wise supervisor urged me to take back the counsellor role and start to be useful again.

If the counsellor can learn from the countertransference feelings, the counselling can be more effective. If, like me, she gets swept along without realizing what has happened, she becomes ineffectual. All that happens is that both client and counsellor share the same problem, with the same way of looking at it. They are not separate but joined in paralysis. If the client could have worked through it on his own, he would not be in the counselling room. He has sought counselling because he wants another perspective, he wants to understand, he wants to move on, he wants to feel less anxious and he wants to integrate the bad feelings. The counsellor's role is to help him do this by being with him, yet objective. The things he projects on to her in countertransference are the signposts to the way the work should be heading. The things the counsellor feels are the clues to his emotions and his method of interacting with others.

Kleinian application

Kleinian theory has been very influential in Britain, though not nearly so much in the United States. Maybe it is regarded as too pessimistic for a nation whose culture is more approving of the positive. Also, Anna Freud has been very influential in North America, and we are back to the split with Klein. Kleinian theory is significant in South America.

In the 1960s, in Britain, training in child protection, in some universities, was informed by Kleinian thinking. My training as a childcare officer concentrated on looking at the relationship with the mother, rather than, as in the past, the cleanliness of the home. These ideas were taken into policy and influenced the move from taking children out of the home, to improving relationships and conditions within it.

Today at the Tavistock Centre in London, a leading training institution in Britain for mental health, the Kleinian approach is very influential, although other theoretical approaches are taught, studied and practised. One of the keystones of the Kleinian approach is the Infant Observation. This was set up by Esther Bick, an analysand, and later colleague of Klein's, who was very influenced by Klein's work.

Students and trainees have to find a baby to observe, usually for an hour each week. The aim of the observation is to get a glimpse of the baby's internal world and try to see how the external world is filtered through and juxtaposed with his internal world. The observer watches how the baby relates to his carer, usually the mother, and starts to make sense of the world. The observer tries not to influence the process by asking questions or commenting on the baby's progress. It is a difficult role, particularly when confronted by an anxious mother, who naturally wants an observer's opinion on her baby's development. Sometimes one goes to the house to watch a sleeping baby and by watching every tiny movement, tries to imagine what is going on in the baby's internal world.

Comment

Kleinian theory was built on Freudian theory, but where Freud sees the individual driven by biological drives, Klein sees an inner world of relationships, peopled by internal objects. The external world is lived through the subject relations of the internal world. This is the beginning of the Object Relations school, where Klein's followers developed her ideas, extended, modified and changed them.

One of the areas for disagreement from other theorists and practitioners has been Klein's perceived insistence on ignoring the reality of the external world. Winnicott's wife, Clare (Chapter 4) when she went into analysis with Klein, was troubled by Klein's total disregard for the environmental factor. 'It's no good your talking about your mother', she was told by Klein, one day. 'We can't do anything about it now' (Grosskurth, 1986, p. 451). Klein would only be interested in Clare Winnicott's phantasy relationship with her internalized mother figures.

Clare Winnicott also accused Klein of imposing her own ideas on the patient. 'She implanted her own theory on what you gave her. You took it or left it.' Klein never greeted her or said goodbye. She found her a brilliant theoretician, but not a clinician (Grosskurth, 1986, p. 451).

Clare Winnicott also believed that in the analytical situation it was very hard for Klein to accept love and reparation. She always emphasized the destructive side so that positive acts were interpreted as a disguise for hate (Grosskurth, 1986, p. 452).

Yet Klein wrote eloquently about love and reparation. She was the inspiration for the theorists who came after her. Perhaps we have to accept, that like Freud, for these two giants, above all, theory is their legacy. They have been the pillars from which other theorists have chipped bits off and made them their own.

Clare Winnicott was not the only adult patient to find Klein difficult, but perhaps Klein ought better to be judged by her work with children. This was her passion and from all accounts it encompassed a mutual liking and understanding. The work was child based with Klein responding to the child's playing with dolls, soft and hard toys, and creative tools like drawing materials and clay. This is a very different arena from the patient on the couch.

Critics of psychoanalytic theorists complain that the focus is solely on the internal world. They particularly cite Klein as someone bound up with the inner world and suggest that counsellors influenced by her ideas will not take into account external factors which impinge on the client's life.

Klein did not say that the external world was unimportant but that it is interpreted through the internal world. Counsellors who find Klein's ideas generally useful do not need to agonize too much on this point They could cite Donald Winnicott (Chapter 4), as a follower of Klein, who believed that the internal and external world had to be regarded as an entity, with one influencing the other.

The idea of an internal world offers a new dimension to clients who have never come across the notion before. In our Western world where accusations of the 'dumbed down' acceptance of trivial beliefs and superficial behaviour are routinely levelled, clients can find the idea of a deep, personal part of themselves, where relationships with self, as well as others, can be explored, exciting and enriching.

It may be unfair that Klein was accused of being preoccupied with the internal world to the detriment of the external.

Hanna Segal says that Klein was very interested in the Arts. She read widely, went to concerts and played the piano. She also 'liked a good party, liked a good drink, a good laugh. She was also very jolly.' Unusually, for a woman, she won a wine tasting competition in the Dordogne! (Interview with Hanna Segal, 2001).

A criticism that counsellors outside the psychodynamic school sometimes make is that the psychodynamic counsellor is distant and cold, working in a rigid way. They point to Klein's blank screen on which the client can project his phantasies, seeing the therapist as uninvolved and impersonal.

Today psychodynamic counsellors, like person-centred counsellors, would highlight the relationship between client and counsellor as the overriding element in the counselling process. This precludes being distant, impersonal and cold. Although psychodynamic counsellors may have a stronger allegiance to 'the frame' (that is the consistency of time, setting and purpose) than other counsellors, it does not mean that the process is rigid, merely structured. If appropriate, psychodynamic counsellors can be flexible and stretch the frame, though this will not be done without a good deal of thought, usually in consultation with their supervisor.

Linked to the idea of the psychodynamic counsellor being distant is the criticism that psychodynamic counsellors want to be the powerful expert. This is a criticism that all counsellors must heed. Psychodynamic counsellors like person-centred counsellors, must make a real relationship with the client and this is impossible if the counsellor feels superior. Fairbairn (Chapter 7), the Edinburgh-based theorist, isolated from the supportive or acrimonious debate of his London colleagues, believed a real relationship was crucial to the therapy. He accepted the notion of the transference, and the transference relationship. The patient may see him, as the analyst, in transference terms, as the authoritarian father. However, he was adamant that for change to occur in the patient, a genuine relationship was more important than the transference relationship. This brings Object Relations therapy closer to Person Centred counselling.

Winnicott (Chapter 4) set a good example by teaching that he and the patient, whether adult or child, had equal status. In his account of his psychoanalytic treatment of Gabrielle, a little girl who was only just over two when he started treating her, he says that there was much that he did not understand, and that only she knew the answers (1980).

Bion (Chapter 5) wrote about negative capability, and that to 'not know' is a more honest and creative position to be in than to be the expert who 'knows'. Counsellors can learn that being there for the client is considerably more important than keeping a check-list of every detail, and thinking one knows it all. Otherwise it can be a question of missing the wood for the trees.

What can trainee counsellors learn from Melanie Klein's concepts of the mother–baby relationship, which can be related to the counselling room?

The baby's internal world provided for Klein an insight into the world of the adult. Klein's thoughts on the darker side of life, the side of ourselves we would prefer not to acknowledge, either as clients or counsellors, are very helpful in understanding ourselves and others. When clients come to counselling it is often because the world seems a very frightening place in which everyone is out to get them. This may of course be true, but usually it is more about the client's perception of the world and his place within it. It is useful to understand that when we feel rejected, abandoned and infantilized, we resort to splitting and seeing people as part objects. Other people are demonized, idealized or used in a narcissistic way. It can feel as if the world is against us.

Klein's theories on the paranoid schizoid position are helpful for an understanding of primitive emotions in both clients and counsellors. Clients who have wrestled with envy, rage and murderous thoughts spend a deal of emotional energy on denying these feelings. Once they can be admitted and worked with, clients can move on. If we can accept that we are capable of, for example, murderous thoughts, then we can see others around us as culpable, rather than evil. Distancing others into nonhuman categories (animals! devils!), just makes us feel more scared about what lies in wait for us, and our own powerlessness. Newspapers, particularly the sensational ones, make money from our terrors and encourage us to see the world from a 'them and us' position. 'We are good. They are evil.'

Once a client can see that the man in the office, whom he sees as a demon wanting to destroy him, is no more than a bully looking for a willing victim then, possibly with support, the bully can be faced. Victims of rape and abuse can start to be survivors, when they can see the perpetrator as a culpable human, whom they can see in court, rather than a monster they have to cower from. In facing the bad parts of ourselves we can more readily face the bad parts in others.

Klein's theories on the depressive position suggest that ambivalence is a helpful concept as a way of working with blame. It is possible to hold two opposing thoughts and feelings at the same time. For example, 'My mother was not there for me when I was small. I was farmed out to relatives and I felt rejected. But she was a single parent, had to work long hours and did her best.' Both are legitimate. The client does not have to choose one position. Both can be integrated. Development and growth lie in integrating the opposites, good and bad, love and hate, rather than remaining split.

Klein herself engendered both love and hate. The psychoanalyst Hanna Segal, the great Kleinian, described her as 'generous, warm, passionate, even explosive – such defects as she had were defects of her qualities and did not detract from her lovability' (Grosskurth, 1986, p. 462).

Yet many of her colleagues found her arrogant and abrasive. She seems to have had a flair for making relationships with other people's children, though struggled to have good relationships with her own. Being a grandmother seemed easier and her grandchildren found her very affectionate. Most significantly she suffered an inordinate amount of losses, and had to learn how to live with them, while continuing to function in an extraordinarily creative way.

Perhaps the most important point that we, as counsellors, can learn from Klein and her theories is the resourcefulness of the human spirit. That in being human we not only experience the happiness, which in the Western world we have come to expect as our right, but also have to learn to manage suffering and despair.

Further reading

Grosskurth, P. (1986) *Melanie Klein: Her World and Her Work*. London: Hodder and Stoughton.

Segal, H. (1988) *Introduction to the World of Melanie Klein*. London: Karnac Books.

Segal, J. (1992) *Melanie Klein*. London: Sage Publications.

Klein, M. (1988) *Love, Guilt and Reparation, and Other Works 1921–1945*. London: Virago Press.

Klein, M. (1988) *Envy and Gratitude, and Other Works 1946–1963*. London: Virago Press.

Melanie Klein Trust. *Memories of Melanie Klein: Part 1. An Interview with Hanna Segal* by Daniel Pick and Jane Milton, both psychoanalysts belonging to the British Psychoanalytical Society http:/www.melanie-klein-trust.org.uk/segalinterview2001.htm.

4
Winnicott: holding within boundaries

Counsellors in training invariably find Winnicott attractive. Whether it is his one-liners which appeal, 'the good enough mother', 'there is no such thing as a baby', 'the transitional object', or whether the criticisms, from some of his colleagues and commentators, on the dearth of a comprehensive theory, become positive approval from trainees struggling to make sense of other theorists.

Winnicott's optimism may be another attraction, particularly for those counsellors whose favourite word is 'positive'. Other counsellors may find Winnicott's optimism a nice balance to Freud's world-weariness and Klein's dark view of humanity. However, Winnicott's theories were primarily based on the work of both Freud and Klein, with his adapting their concepts where they did not agree with his own experience.

Because of his experience, Winnicott seems a more ordinary, more accessible figure than Freud or Klein. As well as seeing a small number of private patients during a long working life, as Freud and Klein had done, Winnicott, in his role as a paediatrician, is estimated to have seen 60,000 patients within the public sector. This gave him a much broader picture of 'ordinary' people's experience than most psychoanalysts normally have. So what led Winnicott to this very different path?

Life of Donald Winnicott

I am primarily drawing on Kahr's (1996) biography, *D. W. Winnicott. A Biographical Portrait*, and Phillip's (1988) biography, *Winnicott*.

Early life

Donald Woods Winnicott was born in Plymouth in 1896. Like Freud, Winnicott was a favoured son with admiring sisters. He was apparently doted on by a bevy of women, who, as well as his female relatives, included the domestic staff of nanny, governess, cook and maids. Winnicott's colleague, Charles Rycroft, said that though the family had money they were not 'top drawer' landed gentry, so did not employ male servants (Kahr, 1996, p. 6). Therefore Winnicott was surrounded by women, whom he called his 'multiple mothers'. He described himself as 'in a sense . . . an only child with multiple mothers and a father extremely preoccupied in my younger years with town as well as business matters' (Phillips, 1988, p. 23). In his unpublished autobiography he commented that his father 'left me too much to all my mothers. Things never quite righted themselves' (Kahr, 1996, p. 10). Although Winnicott suggests that his situation was not beneficial, he continued to recreate it in his writings. The importance of the mother with a peripheral father is reflected in his work, where, unlike Freud, the emphasis is on the twosome, mother and child, rather than the threesome of the Oedipal relationship.

Winnicott's father, Frederick, was a merchant who, amongst other things, sold corsets. It is not surprising that commentators have found it significant that Winnicott, given a lifetime of empathizing with the female, was brought up in a household whose livelihood partly depended on women's intimate garments. Frederick Winnicott was not only a successful businessman, but was heavily involved in civic affairs and became a successful public man. He was twice the mayor of Plymouth and was knighted in 1924 when he was sixty-nine.

Like Freud, Winnicott was born to an older father. At Winnicott's birth in 1896 Frederick was forty-one. Like Freud, Winnicott is described as feeling rivalrous towards his father and in later life felt that he must compete with his father's successful achievements. Also, like Freud, Winnicott wrote little about his mother, which is surprising, for, unlike Freud, Winnicott's theoretical work centred on the mother. It has led commentators to speculate that Winnicott's mother, Elizabeth, was not able to be there for him, emotionally absent, because she was depressed. At sixty-seven Winnicott wrote a poem, about his mother which he sent to his brother-in-law, James Britton, with a note saying, 'Do you mind seeing this hurt that came out of me?' (Phillips, 1988, p. 29). The poem was called 'The Tree', the tree being Christ's cross, a wooden symbol of anguish. Perhaps significantly Elizabeth Winnicott's maiden name was 'Woods' (hence Winnicott's full name, Donald Woods Winnicott). Phillips describes the images in the poem as 'chilling', the child's desolation at the inability of his mother to hold him. The poem reads as a lament to the absent mother, who can neither hold her child physically nor hold him in mind. Kahr offers confirmation from an associate of Winnicott's that Elizabeth Winnicott did indeed suffer from bouts of depression. Kahr suggests that Winnicott's choice of profession was influenced by his childhood. 'But the experience of ministering to the needs of a sad mother might have stimulated rescue phantasies in young Donald, prompting him to devote his life to the care of other sad individuals' (Kahr, 1996, p. 10). However, Winnicott always maintained that he had a happy childhood, which suggests that his mother and/or multiple mothers must have provided a good enough nurturing experience to allow him to grow up optimistic and creative.

When Winnicott was fourteen he was sent away to boarding school. The apparent trigger for his banishment was his keeping poor company with boys who were not considered 'decent friends' by his father and taught him to say words like 'drat'. Kahr wonders if Winnicott felt very young and vulnerable after this dismissal from the family home as he wrote of it happening when he was thirteen, when he was in fact fourteen (Kahr, 1996, p. 13). Winnicott also puts a conciliatory gloss on his father's decision, seeing it in retrospect as being all for the best. Phillips describes Winnicott's memories of his father as 'suspiciously cheerful' (Phillips, 1988, p. 26) and one wonders if the same could be said of his childhood memories in general.

Whatever Winnicott's feelings at leaving home, he seems to have thrived at boarding school, making friends, developing a reputation as a runner and enjoying learning. Like Bowlby he was fascinated by the work of Darwin and this may have been one of the influences that led to his decision to be a doctor. He is also quoted as saying when he broke his shoulder bone at school, that in order to avoid dependency on doctors, he would have to be a doctor himself. Winnicott asked his headmaster if he thought medicine a suitable career for him and received the rather discouraging response, 'Boy not brilliant but will get on' (Kahr, 1996, p. 27). In spite of this faint praise he was determined to go ahead, adamant that he had never wanted to be anything else but a doctor. Like Bowlby, Winnicott first had to persuade a reluctant father to allow him to study medicine. Presumably the only son would have been expected to carry on the family firm, and his father may have felt betrayed by Winnicott's decision, but permission was eventually given.

Adult life

Winnicott then embarked on his medical career. This coincided with the First World War and although as a medical student Winnicott was exempt from conscription, he presumably caught the patriotic fervour that was around and enlisted in the Royal Navy. He became a Surgeon Probationer, not yet a qualified doctor but the only medical officer on a destroyer (Kahr, 1996). At twenty-one this must have been an alarming position to be in as his destroyer saw active service and Winnicott had to deal with the casualties. One of the things it did teach him, which was to be useful to him as both a doctor and a psychoanalyst, was how to communicate with people outside his own class.

On his return to civilian life Winnicott studied at St Bartholomew's Hospital. There he was very much influenced by a celebrated physician, Dr Thomas Jeeves Horder, who taught Winnicott to listen to his patients and let them tell their own stories (Kahr, 1996). This was to constitute Winnicott's way of working with psychoanalytic as well as paediatric patients. At about this time he came across the work of Sigmund Freud and was captivated by reading 'The Interpretation of Dreams'. He felt Freud's ideas were very helpful to him in understanding the difficulties he was having in remembering his dreams after the trauma of the First World War. This was to be the beginning of his lifetime passion with psychoanalysis.

In 1923 he became a consultant paediatrician to two London hospitals and married Alice Taylor. She was beautiful and artistic and worked as a potter. But she was also fragile and fragmented, suffering from psychotic episodes. Masud Khan in describing the Winnicotts' relationship said that she 'went mad and taking care of her took all his youth' (Kahr, 1996, p. 44). It is interesting to speculate on why Winnicott chose her as a wife, rather than a patient. Perhaps he thought that he could rescue her, but although they stayed married for 25 years it was clearly not an easy relationship. It was ended in 1949 when Winnicott divorced his wife and 2 years later married the social worker Clare Britton, with whom he had been working as a colleague, but also with whom, it was alleged, he had carried on an affair, long before his divorce had been finalized (Kahr, 1996). Much of the biographical detail of Winnicott's life was supplied by his second wife, which of course included a description of his first marriage. Clare Winnicott was, presumably, not a disinterested observer and others have suggested that the marriage may have been a more rewarding enterprise than it was painted. For example, Alice at times heavily supported Winnicott in his work by taking in difficult children whom Winnicott thought needed fostering. Jacobs quotes Margaret Little, in analysis with Winnicott at the time, who saw Winnicott's depression and second heart attack as the result of his distress from the break-up of his first marriage (1995, p. 13).

At the time of his first marriage Winnicott went into analysis with James Strachey, the analyst who had translated Freud's work into English. Winnicott had originally gone to Ernest Jones for a consultation because, as he later described himself, he was 'ill'. In what Kahr notes as 'a shameful breach of confidentiality' (1996, p. 45), Strachey had hinted to his wife that Winnicott had sexual difficulties and, because he never fathered children, there was some general speculation that he was impotent. Whatever the truth, the psychoanalysis lasted 10 years and during that time Winnicott decided to be an analyst himself, perhaps for the same reasons he had originally decided to become a medical doctor, a horror of being dependent on the knowledge of others.

During his psychoanalytic training, Winnicott had a second analysis. Having had the first with a Freudian, the second was with a Kleininan, Joan Riviere (a woman severally described as extremely tall, glamorous and difficult). These two strands of psychoanalytic thought were to be the basis of Winnicott's work on which he formulated his own theories. Consequently when psychoananlytic training later became structured into Freudian or Kleinian divisions, Winnicott allied himself with a 'middle group' of independents.

He was very influenced by Klein's theories on early childhood, but because of his observations as a paediatrician, he disagreed with much of her thinking. He was particularly in conflict with her views on the primacy of the internal world feeling that the external world was equally important. In this he agreed with Bowlby whose work with deprived children highlighted the importance of a consistent nurturing environment. During the war Winnicott, like Bowlby, had worked with evacuated children. Winnicott realized that the children suffering the most difficulties were those who had not had the advantage of a good nurturing environment and came from 'unsettled homes'. Where Winnicott and Bowlby might have disagreed was in Winnicott's belief that both the internal and external world was crucial to development. Bowlby was criticized for disregarding the internal world.

However much Winnicott publicly spoke of his debt to Kleinian theories, many Kleinians resented his independence. Kahr (1996, p. 77) says that some tutors at the Tavistock Clinic in the late 1960s forbade their students to attend Winnicott's public lectures. Kahr also quotes Klein as referring to Winnicott as 'that awful man', even though she had earlier chosen him to analyse her son Erich. Klein had in a reciprocal arrangement analysed Winnicott's second wife Clare. Kahr also notes Charles Rycroft's observation that the relationship between Klein and Winnicott was an 'exercise in mutual non-comprehension'.

One of the reasons for the noncomprehension may have been their different professional experiences. Klein worked solely in the psychoanalytic world, whereas Winnicott, as well as being the only analyst who was a paediatrician, also worked with childcare professionals such as social workers and residential childcare officers. He was keen to spread his message to all who worked with children and that of course included parents. He broadcast on the radio and his addresses were down to earth, informative rather than advice giving and easily understandable by the lay person. The fact that in his writing he often neglected to attribute the theories to their original authors did not always endear him, but he was very open about it. In addressing the British Psychoanalytical Society on 'Primitive Emotional Development' in 1945 he said, 'I shall not first give an historical survey and show the development of my ideas from the theory of others, because my mind does not work that way. What happens is that I gather this and that, here and there, settle down to clinical experience, form my own theories and, last of all, interest myself in looking to see where I stole what. Perhaps this is as good a method as any' (1945).

Although he never got a knighthood like his father, a source of disappointment to him, Winnicott was professionally successful and received many awards and distinctions in the psychoanalytic field. At the same time he won the James Spence award for paediatrics, so on both fronts he received acclaim. He was very sensitive to criticism and, where his work was not acclaimed, took it very much to heart. In 1968 he went to America and lectured to the New York Psychoanalytic Society, a venerable institution, which he failed to impress. He was devastated by the criticism and returned to his hotel room where he had a massive heart attack. This was his third, the first after his father's death and the second after the break-up with his first wife. Unfortunately it seems he did take distress 'to heart'.

Winnicott recovered, but he was not well. He spent the last 3 years of his life getting his papers in order for publication and overseeing the erection of a statue of Freud, close to the Tavistock Clinic in London. He died peacefully in his London house, in the company of his wife Clare, on 25 January 1971. He was seventy-four.

The mother–baby relationship

Primary maternal preoccupation

Influenced by Klein, Winnicott saw the therapeutic relationship in terms of the nursing dyad, mother and baby together in a nurturing relationship. Because fathers are peripheral for Winnicott, Freud's Oedipal triangle is not so relevant to Winniicott. He had exceptional opportunities to observe mothers relating to their children and postulated theories that were different from Klein's. He suggested that when the baby is first born the mother goes through a state akin to madness, where the mother focuses on the baby to the exclusion of everything and everyone else. Winnicott called this state 'primary maternal preoccupation' (1956), its purpose being for the baby to feel secure through the mother's identification with him. Like Bowlby, Winnicott was influenced by Darwin, so another strand to this state could be biological. The baby's survival is ensured by the mother, who, tigress-like, constantly guards her offspring, protecting him from any danger. Husbands and older children may be able to recognize this state, which, though temporary, can feel both bewildering and excluding to the rest of the family.

Winnicott says that this extreme state lasts for a few weeks after birth. Observers will be aware of the mother gradually relaxing both her physical hold on the baby and her emotional exclusivity. At 3 months the baby could be 'taking solids' and others may be involved in the spooning-in of cereals. Although the mother may still be breast feeding and the holding and closeness remains, she may now have the emotional space to be there for others in the family.

As the mother intuitively meets the needs of the infant during the phase of primary maternal preoccupation, so the therapist can offer a form of maternal preoccupation in being there for the client and offering, in the session, a concentrated focus on him and the issues he brings, which few else can do. This is particularly relevant for the client who has been through a trauma where he has felt powerless and regressed. The meeting of counsellor and client can be a mini-recreation of his early mother–baby relationship. Like the mother with the dependent new baby and her older children, the counsellor will give this client more thought and attention while he comes through his regressed state. She may not mean to do this, but his extreme dependency at this time will ensure that she thinks about him more than usually between sessions because she is anxious about him.

The mirror

When a mother looks at her baby, her look says all. For the fortunate baby it says, 'You are the most important person in the world.' Winnicott was influenced by the work of Jacques Lacan, who postulated that the baby looking into the mother's face sees himself. The mother's role lies in giving back to the baby its own self, reflected in the mother's face. In the mother's face he sees, as if in a mirror, himself reflected in the love and concern written there. So for the infant, there is confirmation that he exists, and that he is lovable.

Observational development studies have shown that a newborn baby is attracted to the human face and that eye-to-eye contact and mutual gaze seems important to both mothers and babies. However, most studies come from Western industrialized societies, where a baby may be lying in a crib, pram or on a piece of furniture, facing the mother for long periods. In the Third World rural societies most mothers and babies will not be face to face except at feeding times, when eye contact will be more limited, at least on the baby's part. The rest of the time the baby will be attached to the mother's back while she works.

As Winnicott himself suggested there must be other means of reflecting back the infant self, other than eye contact. My own observations when living in African countries would suggest a contented, soporific baby, his head lying against his mother's bare shoulders and neck, his whole body in contact with hers, moving in consort with her, both seemingly in tune with the other. In these circumstances it is rare to hear a baby cry, a restless shuffle from the infant and he is brought round to the breast immediately. That baby must have a sense that he is important, that he exists.

In counselling it is sometime suggested on skills courses that the counsellor mirror the client. But this is a strategy and the client may feel it so. This can lead to the client feeling patronized or that the counsellor's concern is not genuine. A counsellor who is attending to the client and his story may unconsciously mirror the client's gestures and mannerisms.

But more importantly the client will read in the counsellor's face her attention and concern. Like the baby he will know that he exists for the counsellor.

Holding

This holding of the client both in the physical attention given to him in the session and the holding in mind between sessions gives the client a feeling of security. Like the baby who is physically held by the mother as a tiny infant, the counsellor is providing a facilitating environment in which the client, like the baby, can begin to grow. As the baby grows into a toddler, he becomes less dependent on his mother if he feels he can explore safely. The security comes about through the toddler intuitively knowing that the mother, though not physically holding him, holds him in her mind. That concern, attention and identification with the baby's needs keep him safe. In the same way the counsellor working with the traumatized client can offer a secure place in which the client can be heard.

Case Example | Emma: a client who is held

Emma came into the counselling room warily, fearfully looking around, and before I could direct her to the 'client chair', sat in a chair by the window as far away from me as she could. She spent the entire session looking at the floor, avoiding any eye contact and saying very little. She dutifully answered the questions I asked her but ventured little else. Much of the session we sat in silence. By the end of the session, I had learnt that 'something terrible' had happened to her, but she could not bear to talk about it.

These sessions of mainly silence went on for several weeks, but things had changed. Emma without any prompting chose the client chair for the second session and was able on occasion to meet my eye. I acknowledged that it was difficult to trust people when something terrible had happened to you and that I was not going to force her to talk before she was ready. I deliberately used the word 'force' as in a previous session she had indicated that what had happened to her was against her will. I was very much aware that I could be intrusive and if the terrible thing were rape or abuse it could feel as if the counsellor, too, were being abusive.

As the weeks went on I learnt that 'the terrible thing' was indeed rape, but it was 6 months before she could trust me enough and bear to tell me the details. By this time we had a relationship that felt constant, we met at the same time every week, she began to feel safe, she knew she was thought about, and she knew I cared about her. Like the baby who is held by the mother, at first physically and then, when a toddler, is able to move away from the mother, knowing that the mother holds the baby in mind. Emma began to feel less passive and began to move slowly towards feeling less dependent on the counsellor. As time went on she was able to begin to work with me in the counselling sessions. Eventually she felt confident enough to challenge me, and at times, safe enough to be angry with me. By now she knew I would not willingly abandon her, so like the child who knows the mother will not reject him, however bad he has been, she felt more secure in the relationship. She felt held.

Winnicott's concept of holding had been very useful to me. Otherwise I might have regarded those early sessions in the counselling relationship as not very useful to the client. This could have resulted in my jumping ahead, trying to persuade a reluctant client to go where she was not ready to and a pace at which she could easily have taken fright. This is a case for going with our intuitive feelings and ignoring the voice that says, 'You should be doing more.'

Omnipotence

Freud believed that the relationship between the baby and the mother is based on the gratification of instinctual drives. Winnicott disagreed, believing that the infant from the start is involved in primitive object-relating. At the beginning the 'object' is himself, where he has a relationship with parts of himself, sucking his hands in the same way he sucks his mother's nipple. If the nipple is there for him he will find it and feel that he has made it be there. A mother who is in tune with her baby will let him find the nipple rather than intrusively pushing it in his mouth. As the baby's needs are met by the mother, so he has the phantasy that he has ordained it. He has created his world. He feels omnipotent.

This stage does not last, as disillusion sets in when the baby's mother does not anticipate his every desire. But the omnipotent stage is the beginning of less primitive relating, in which eventually the child and his mother have a relationship as separate people. The experience of omnipotence also helps the baby to tolerate his disappointment with his mother.

Disillusion

As the mother's primary preoccupation lessens and she engages herself in other activities, the baby feels disillusioned. This mother was there for him all the time and now she is no longer. He feels disappointed in her. But if she is there for him enough, his disappointment at her lack of constant presence allows him to tolerate her short absences, and begin to rely on his own resources. He is growing and developing, beginning the long separation process from her. The capacity to be alone is something that the child begins to develop when he is actually with the mother who is not intrusive. He can begin to be separate and be himself, while physically being with his mother. The good enough mother will let him begin that separation. This is the mother who does not have to possess the child who wants to grow away from her, if only for a few minutes.

Counsellors can learn from this disappointment and disillusionment about relationships with our clients. As the mother necessarily disillusions and disappoints her child, by not being perfect, by having another child, and by being generally found wanting, so counsellors disappoint their clients. They are not always available when the client needs them. They have holidays and are ill. Counsellors can get it very wrong and misunderstand the client. They may not have enough experience, or they may try too hard. But as the child grows and develops through the mother's mistakes and omissions, so the client learns to become independent from the flawed counsellor. We necessarily have to fail our clients.

Winnicott (1963) said, 'So in the end we succeed by failing – failing the patient's way.' He went on to say that patients make the analyst fail in ways dictated by their history. The patient remembers that his mother failed him when he was a child, just like he felt the analyst did. Fortunately we cannot be the perfect mother. We can be the good enough mother and our clients can grow away from us because we are not perfect.

Absence of the mother

So as the baby grows, his capacity to be alone grows. He does not have to be with his mother all the time. He can survive. Winnicott believed that the baby can manage the absence of his mother, if it is not too long.

However, an absence that is 'too long', for example when the mother is ill, can make the baby doubt his capacity to be loved. He will try very hard to be compliant, pleasing and persuasive, so that he can be loved again. This may explain Winnicott's always wanting to be liked, his compulsion to amuse and his distress when his ideas failed to meet with approval. If, as has been suggested, his mother was an absent mother for too long, then his childhood desire to please her may have become a way of life.

A trainee counsellor, Jennifer, studying Winnicott's notion of the absent mother, suddenly remembered how as a child, with a depressed mother, she had spent most of her early years smiling, in order to be seen by her emotionally absent mother as lovable.

Absence of the mother is particularly significant when the baby is tiny. However, clients often come to counselling who experienced the absence of a mother when they were much older, though the experience catapulted them back to being small, powerless and abandoned. They feel the sense of a self who is loved, and can love in return, was taken away, when the mother left them to their insecure selves.

Case Example | John: a client whose mother was absent

John had led an insecure life from being small to adolescence. His father's job had taken them to several countries and it seemed to John that just as he had begun to get used to one new environment, the family was whisked away to another. John said that his father was a rigid man whose relationship with his children was distant. His mother was warm but inconsistent. The children were aware of tensions between the parents. Then when John was thirteen his mother left the family to live with another man in another country. At a time when John was beginning to test himself as an embryonic adult, finding an identity for himself, discovering his sexuality, beginning to think about making relationships with girls, his mother disappears. This is a time when a mother is most needed, as a constant in the face of so much change. But John's mother had gone, leaving him to feel abandoned and rejected.

For a time John's father cared for the children, but then with little warning the children were sent home, to be looked after by their rather strait-laced grandparents. John started to behave badly and

ment. He was aware enough to know that his lack of secure

outside the baby. For example, a corner of soft cloth or wool is sucked alongside the baby's own flesh. Winnicott (1974) called these processes, 'transitional phenomena'. Later the child, as a defence against anxiety, to make himself feel safer, becomes attached to one object, which Winnicott calls the 'transitional object'. This may be a bit of old blanket or a toy or soft animal, but it has to be chosen by the child, and it cannot change. Bits of blanket cannot be washed, toys cannot be exchanged or they lose their meaning for the child. Many parents will know the agonizing search to replace a lost transitional object. It is doomed to failure. I remember when living in Central Africa a desperate quest to replace a lost panda. The only replacement available over hundreds of miles had a slight pink tinge and was instantly rejected.

The transitional object helps the baby make the journey from the breast, and identification with the mother, to a sense of a separate self, aided by an identification with an object. The object is 'not me', but is 'mine' and the baby feels he can control it. The transitional object eases the journey towards independence and lessens the child's anxiety.

Recognizing the use of transitional objects in counselling can be very illuminating for both counsellor and client. Transitional objects are bridges and can be utilised to ease transitions, whatever they may be.

Couple counsellors will be familiar with the partner who wants to leave a relationship, and uses some kind of affair, with another person, with an obsession with work, with overriding responsibilities to the family of origin, with commitments to a cause, to do it. Whatever the 'affair' it can be a transitional object, a stepping stone out of the relationship to a desired destination. It is a transitional object because it is only a temporary phenomenon and the final journey may have a completely different ending, perhaps, for the person leaving the relationship, to find the confidence to be able to live on their own. The capacity to be alone may need encouragement and may have to be strengthened by the security of the transitional object. Alternately another long-term relationship may come to fruition, via the 'safety' of a casual liaison with someone else.

Transitional objects have a function, though the user may not be fully aware of it. Probably the greater part of the use of transitional objects is unconscious. Counsellors are used as transitional objects when a client is moving from a secure position to an unknown one. The counsellor can be the bridge.

Student counsellors in further education colleges can attest to being used in this way. The student who is enmeshed with his family will use the counsellor to get away. Often this is to university, a prospect most students find daunting as well as exciting. The student from the enmeshed family, which sometimes he, himself, will term dysfunctional, finds the prospect almost impossible. He cannot contemplate the insecurity of the unfamiliar. Paradoxically, he longs to escape. The counsellor can provide stepping stones. He can test out on her what it means to be a young adult away from a parent. He can experience a good enough mother who is there for him, not all the time, but consistently at set times. If his own mother has been suffocating, this can be a liberating encounter.

Case Example | Frank: the counsellor used as a transitional object

As a student counsellor I saw Frank, a very bright student, who was preparing to go off to a prestigious university. His difficulty, he insisted in the first session, lay in his suffocating family, which he could not wait to escape from. He was the bright boy of the family and his two younger sisters joined the admiring family group, led by his mother, who boasted of his achievements. But this acclaim seemed to imprison him and he could take no pleasure in it. He just wanted to be away, he said.

Yet all his conversation hinged around the family – their awful rituals, their bizarre activities, their dreadful conversations and their prejudices. He railed against it, but was totally enmeshed in it.

At first he refused to acknowledge how enjoined he was with his family. How his life was entwined with theirs. How upset he was by family differences. Then he began to realize that his peers were more separated from their families than he was. Their families were more in the background. His peers had their own lives.

Over the weeks we explored his position in the family, his over-anxious parents wanting the best for their children, yet projecting their own fears of a hostile outside world, from which only the family offered protection. Frank admitted that he was frightened of the unknown. He was scared to go to university, though he longed for it. How could he ever make the move on his own?

But as time went on and as we got to know each other better, it seemed more of a possibility. He started to talk about the plans he had for university, the interests that he could pursue. He had never made friends easily, but now he began to think it might be easier at university. We talked about the sort of people he would be living with, other bright students, perhaps brighter than he was, so he would not stick out. He could be anonymous if he wanted to be. He would not have to feel on trial and suffocated.

But where would his family fit in? Frank had already begun to work out how often he would see them. He would go home often at first, if he could afford it. Then, gradually lessen the visits. He began to think further ahead. Perhaps he might marry eventually. Then he would have to let go of his family because he would have a wife and perhaps children. Though, of course, he would still see his family sometime.

It seemed as if Frank had used me as a transitional object, a bridge from his family to a more independent life at university. Ideas were tested out on me. I was there for him in the counselling room, but at no other time. Our relationship was boundaried. This was a revelation for Frank because he had only experienced the encompassing, ever-present relationship offered to the dependent child.

Frank went off to university, and though he contacted student services to report his progress, he did not contact me. I seemed to have served my purpose well as a transitional object.

The counsellor who accompanies a client on a journey can be used as a transitional object. It is usually a rewarding role because the client wants to get to the journey's end, but finds it difficult alone. The counsellor can be the bridge to the other side.

A place to play

Playing in our Western twenty-first-century world is firmly relegated to leisure or sport. The idea of play being part of education, beyond early years, is seen as an outdated concept belonging to the pejoratively named 'permissive sixties', where children of all ages learnt through play. In our corporate world play is prodigal. We are too busy to play.

Yet, for many of us, one of the most endearing aspects of Winnicottian theory is the idea of therapy as play. As the baby learns about himself by playing in a secure place, first with his mother, then on his own, so does the client. The counsellor's aim is to provide a safe therapeutic space, a place to play.

As Winnicott (1974) says, 'It is only in playing that the child or adult is free to be creative.' He believed that freedom was essential to creativity, and compliance was its enemy. The freedom to play lay on both sides of the therapeutic encounter.

In a game he played with his child patients, which he called the Squiggle game, Winnicott drew a squiggle and asked the child to develop it. Together they worked on the squiggle, developing something creative, which had a meaning for them both.

In the same way the therapist has to be able to be there for the client to play with. She has to be open to creative ways of working and eschew rigidity. Winnicott certainly did this with his patients, seeing them in places other than the psychoanalytic couch, seeing patients at irregular intervals if it suited them and generally breaking the rules, often to the dismay of his colleagues. His philosophy was that the potential for therapeutic play lay all around us, seeing in the institutions of the difficult boys he worked with, 'therapy in the walls'.

What Winnicott says of psychotherapy applies equally to counselling.

> Psychotherapy takes place in the overlap of two areas of playing, that of the patient and that of the therapist. Psychotherapy has to do with two people playing together. The corollary of this is that where playing is not possible then the work done by the therapist is directed towards bringing the patient from a state of not being able to play into a state of being able to play.
>
> (1974, p. 44)

Clients whose upbringing has been joyless, who have had critical parents and then become their own critical parents, and clients who are frozen through trauma will probably find it very difficult to play.

Case Example | Steve: the client who cannot play

Steve had experienced a joyless childhood. His parents were not unkind, but it seemed as if they lacked imagination, and could not begin to realize what a child needed. Both parents had been brought up in hard conditions and saw life as an exercise in survival. Any presents Steve had were strictly utilitarian. The family never had outings unless they served a clear purpose. Nothing was ever done on the spur of the moment or for fun. Fun was not a concept the parents recognized. As an only child there were no siblings to play with. But worst of all Steve's parents never hugged or kissed him. Sentiment was not a quality to be encouraged. In fact, emotion of any kind was suspect.

When Steve came to counselling he was depressed and anxious. The trigger for his arrival in the counselling room was ironically a game. It was a team game that his office had to take part in as part of a team-building exercise. Steve had made a fool of himself and felt humiliated. He had found it impossible to play, had alienated himself from his colleagues, as they had been furious with him because his section had come last. All Steve could say was that he could not see the point of it all.

In the sessions it became clear that Steve found it difficult to make relationships, could not relax with his colleagues and felt stressed and anxious most of the time. He did not really get on with anyone at work, but kept his job as a computer programmer because he was very good at it. He was happy working at his computer as it demanded nothing from him emotionally.

But yet he was aware that others got something out of life, which he did not. As a child he had been conscious of children in his class having a better time than he. He admitted that he was envious of the ease with which some of his workmates made relationships, and embarked on new experiences. It all seemed to pass him by. Steve wanted to learn to live.

In the counselling room the counsellor had to help Steve look at what he had lost in growing up in a family where affection was hidden and joy was absent. The counsellor had to stand in for the mother who was not able to live creatively, who had no capacity to play. Steve and the counsellor had to learn to play together.

For creativity and play are interwoven. Winnicott (1974, p. 83) said, 'We find that individuals live creatively and feel that life is worth living or else that they cannot live creatively and are doubtful about the value of living.' Winnicott went on to say that whether or not we have a capacity to live creatively depends on the experiences we have as infants. If we have had a nurturing environment, with a good enough mother who has offered us a place to play, we would have been given the foundations to live creatively. For those who have missed out, the counsellor can try to offer the adult a chance to learn to play. This could be the start of a life that feels more worth living.

The creative potential and the self

Unlike many psychoanalysts who wrote about the individual, Winnicott was fascinated by the person's sense of self and his creative potential. Maybe this was because Winnicott had a strong belief in the influence of the environment and saw individuals as people striving for development. This is very similar to the American schools of Neo-Freudian psychoanalytic thought with theorists like Otto Rank and Karen Horney who, like Winnicott, had a notion of a 'True Self'. And indeed the whole Human Potential Movement in the United States with its emphasis on wholeness, optimism and the potential of the self echoes Winnicott's ideas. Maslow, who put self-actualization at the top of his hierarchy of needs, and Rogers, with his sense of a true self, and his claim that the client is the expert in his own life, have strong affinity with Winnicott's thinking in this area. In fact many person-centred counsellors will feel a sense of agreement with much of Winnicott's work. Rogers was influenced by Otto Rank, but perhaps more by Alfred Adler, who broke away from Freud, partly because of his disagreement with Freud over the primacy of the unconscious. What Adler, Rank and Rogers shared with Winnicott was the significance of the environment on the development of the self.

Winnicott believed that the True Self is the creative self, while the False Self appears when the person tries to please, appease and be compliant. The creative potential in people, though, as the client Steve exemplifies, does depend on early experience.

In achievement of creative potential Winnicott believed that first a person has to experience potential space. It is first the space between mother and a baby, where the baby learns from the mother that he is separate. Whether or not the baby can learn this depends on the relationship with the mother, in which his needs are met, and the way in which the mother lets the baby use her. If the mother can withstand the baby's aggressive attacks as he searches for an identity of his own, then the baby does not need to be compliant. He can be free to be creative.

Potential space is not confined to mother and baby. As we grow through life, potential space can be experienced between friend and friend, husband and wife, and client and therapist. It is a place where something of import can grow, where something significant happens. A nurturing environment is cultivated where creative development can be established. And with the right conditions this can happen in the counselling room.

Cross identification

One of the conditions needed for growth is the capacity for both client and counsellor to have some sense of 'the other'. As the growing child interrelates through meetings in potential space, so he begins to relate to others through a process Winnicott calls, 'cross identification', the ability to stand in another's shoes. This is the realization and awareness of someone who is 'not me', who is different from me. This is learned through the infant's relationship with his mother, and its development. Where formerly she was there for him all the time, now his mother is helping him to be more independent. Although part of him wants this new independence, another part is angry with his mother for not being there for him all the time. The child responds to her withdrawing with fury and aggression. If the mother can withstand these attacks, understand them and not retaliate, the ground will be set for a creative separation. This is the acknowledgement of both 'me' and 'not me', mother as a different person from the child. The child can begin to have some concern for his mother. Eventually he may have some idea of what it is like to be her.

This quality, which person-centred counsellors would call empathy, is necessary for growth. The individual who can empathize with another has the capacity to make relationships through a strong sense of self. This is the development from a position of being able only to concentrate on 'me', to be able to imagine what it is like to be 'not me'. In Kleinian terms it would be moving from the narcissistic phase in the Paranoid Schizoid Position into the Depressive Position, or what Winnicott renamed, the 'Stage of Concern'.

For clients who have been severely traumatized, their main aim is to survive. They return to the stage of being the helpless baby whose whole being is focused on survival. So they remain in a narcissistic state until something changes so that they can begin to move on. This is where counselling can be very helpful.

Case Example | Susan: the client who is locked in self

A client, Susan, who had been subject to a severe sexual attack some years earlier, found it difficult to make relationships. The person who had attacked her was not a stranger, so she felt that it was her own fault for her lack of judgement. Had it been a stranger she felt she could have persuaded herself that it was bad luck, being in the wrong place at the wrong time. But, as it was, she was left with a sense of getting it all wrong, trusting someone she should not have trusted. And if she had got it wrong once, who was to say she would not continue to do so. So she defended herself from another possible attack by retreating into herself and refusing to relate in any meaningful way to anyone, except her immediate family. This meant that her life was lonely, she mistrusted everyone, but it was the only way she could feel safe.

In the counselling it became clear that she had divorced herself from everyone but her parents and sister and that she could not begin to imagine other people's lives. However, she had no hesitation in using other people, if they could be useful to her, but the transactions were without feeling on her part. She could be flirtatious and seductive if it served her purpose, leaving the recipients of her behaviour confused. She began to realize that she manipulated others so that she could be in control and feel secure.

Susan's family knew that something traumatic had happened to her but she refused to tell them any details. They were worried about her, but also rather impatient, because they felt she was doing nothing to help herself. They encouraged her to go out to meet people of her own age (she was in her late twenties), and generally to become the girl she used to be. Susan felt angry with them for their lack of understanding and felt even more alone.

When she came into the counselling she felt hostile towards the counsellor. She gave little of herself, was passive and silent, but the counsellor could feel Susan's aggression towards her. It made the counsellor feel that she had to do something for Susan, but she did not know what it was and felt useless. Because the counsellor was newly qualified she was convinced that it was her lack of experience which made her feel so deskilled.

However, in supervision the counsellor began to try to understand Susan's experience and with it how she defended herself from getting close to anyone. Susan's faith in her world had been shattered and she would have to relearn how to trust people again. It was as if Susan were a small child dependent on a parent to care for her and help her to take independent steps.

Although Susan was angry and hostile, she had come to the counselling, so part of her wanted to be different. She said that she hated her life and wanted it to change, but then attacked anyone who tried to help her. The counsellor talked with her supervisor about what she should do and the supervisor said, 'Nothing. Do nothing, but be there for her.' The counsellor was not sure what this meant, but after thinking hard about Susan and trying to put herself in Susan's shoes, realized that what Susan needed was someone to accept her, not try to change her, but be concerned about her. This holding of Susan in a nurturing environment, like a good mother eventually helped Susan to be able to think about taking hesitant steps towards relating to others. Susan had by now been able to talk about the attack with the counsellor and was beginning to feel that it was less raw. She began to think about the attack as something in her past, rather than a terrible event that she had to keep at a distance, as if it had not happened to her, and work hard at trying to blank it out.

Winnicott says the child who is secure in the relationship with his mother uses her as an 'object' to work through his aggressive feelings and destructive behaviour in order to develop (Davis and Wallbridge [1983]). In the same way the client can use the counsellor to develop.

As Susan's relationship with the counsellor grew and the counsellor withstood Susan's aggressive attacks, so Susan's confidence in her ability to be a lovable individual developed. Like the child seeking independence she could begin to contemplate taking risks. The biggest of these risks was to start to trust others and in doing so make herself vulnerable. The idea of making real relationships was now a possibility. This was mainly because instead of cynically using people as objects to do her bidding, she was beginning to see others as individuals, different from her and with needs different from her own. She was moving towards the notion of being able to stand in another's shoes.

Hate in the countertransference

Winnicott is often accused of being almost sentimental about the mother and baby relationship, seeing it in pastel tones whereas Klein saw it starkly in blacks and whites. However, this is untrue. Winnicott (1947) is firmly against sentimentality, saying that from the baby's point of view sentimentality in the mother is no good to him and 'sentimentality is useless for parents as it contains a denial of hate'. Whereas Klein thought the baby was envious of, and so hated, the mother, Winnicott saw the mother hating the baby, and he said, for good reason. In his 1947 paper on 'Hate In the Counter Transference', he lists the reasons why a mother hates her baby, even a boy!

The reasons range from:

- 'He is ruthless, treats her as scum, an unpaid servant, a slave.

- His excited love is cupboard love, so that having got what he wants he throws her away like orange peel.

- After an awful morning with him she goes out, and he smiles at a stranger who says, 'Isn't he sweet!'

- He excites her but frustrates—she mustn't eat him or trade in sex with him.' to the most frightening reason for the mother:

- 'If she fails him at the start she knows he will pay her out for ever.'

Other reasons for hate are that the baby interferes with the mother's private life and that she only had him to please her mother anyway.

This is an interesting perspective on Winicott's view of the mother–baby relationship. Even if it is ironic, it explains why he is so popular with mothers. Unlike Klein he appears firmly on their side. And it does highlight Winnicott's emphasis on the importance of the duo rather than the Oedipal triangle, Unlike Freud, Winnicott sees the hate and rivalry not between father and son, but between mother and baby.

Winnicott is comparing the mother–baby relationship to that of the analyst and patient, in particular the psychotic patient. He acknowledges that however much he loves his patient, at the same time he cannot but hate him. Winnicott looks for the roots of hate and finds it in the first relationship, the baby with his mother. 'I suggest that the mother hates the baby before the baby hates the mother, and before the baby can know his mother hates him' (1947, p. 200).

Winnicott has earlier said that his experience of working with children deprived of their parents convinced him that the child spends his time unconsciously looking for parents. If he is fostered or adopted he will test out his new parents in ways that ensure that they have to hate him. Winnicott suggested that a child can only believe in being loved after first having had the experience of being hated.

As a mother has to tolerate hating her baby without doing anything about it, so the analyst has to hold onto his feelings towards the patient. His hate must be objective. He must be aware that the hate comes from the encounter with the patient in the present, but has its origin in the past. The patient is transferring his hatred of his parents, particularly his mother, onto the analyst, and the analyst in the countertransference is taking on the position of the mother who hates her baby.

Winnnicott contended that hate is more evident when the patient is out of touch with reality. But Winnicott also maintained that it was always there, and that the analyst had to acknowledge the hate in himself, if he were to help the patient.

In the same way in the counselling room the counsellor has to be aware of her own feelings and constantly monitor them. She has to acknowledge that she is capable of hate and cruelty, and if she denies them she is more likely to use them against the client. Davis and Wallbridge (1983, p. 153) quote Winnicott's assertion that, 'The truly responsible people of the world are those who accept the fact of their own hate, nastiness, cruelty, things which co-exist with their capacity to love and to construct. Sometimes the sense of their own awfulness gets them down.' He maintained that sentimentality is a denial of personal awfulness.

In order to be whole as people and useful to our clients, we have to admit the darker side of ourselves. Winnicott suggested that we have to meet the client at a primal level. This seems particularly relevant if the client is traumatized. Then he has regressed to the dependent infant because he feels powerless. He has to be able to take good things from the counsellor, as the good enough mother, in order to feel secure. But he also needs to be able to get in touch with the whole of the counsellor, the bad as well as the good parts. If client and counsellor can meet at this level, which may not be conscious, the client can begin to grow, accepting the bad parts of himself. He is then on the way to feeling whole again.

Feeling whole for Winnicott is to feel alive. But this can include uncomfortable feelings attached to the primitive self. Integrating the creative self can help us manage our fear of madness, while keeping in touch with our primal feelings. Winnicott had a distrust of too much sanity, feeling that it could be an obstacle to the imagination and the creative process. A bland sterility could result.

Through artistic expression we can hope to keep in touch with our primitive selves whence the most intense feelings and even fearfully acute sensations derive, and we are poor indeed if we are only sane (1945, p. 150).

Comment

Winnicott's theories have much to say to counsellors. His work seems accessible and, perhaps because he tailored his message to different groups of professional workers, more easily understandable than those theorists who spoke solely to the psychoanalytic world.

Winnicott's ideas about the mother–child relationship within the context of a paediatrician who came across thousands of mothers and babies in his lifetime make his therapeutic concepts feel fitting to counsellors who work within ordinary settings, the GP's practice, the bereavement agency. It is away from what may seem the rarefied atmosphere of the psychoanalyst's couch.

Winnicott has been described as quintessentially English, with his life a stark contrast to the dramas and tragedies of Central Europeans like Melanie Klein. However, his life had its difficulties, not least his depression and anxiety when he first went into analysis at the beginning of his first marriage. Sometimes he seems overly cheerful and optimistic which suggests an unwillingness to acknowledge a darker side. He seems a paradox, in some respects egalitarian in his desire to work with parents and childcare professionals, seemingly modest in his writing, at other times omnipotent. Kahr cites Winnicott's letter to his colleague Michael Balint in which he says, 'even a Winnicott paper has to be thought out a little beforehand' (1996, p. 95). Kahr also cites Rycroft's description of Winnicott as 'a crypto prima donna' (1996, p. 111).

But he was very aware of the misuse of power. He knew that psychoanalytic theory could be used by 'unscrupulous people' to gain power over others. He asserted that the professional ethic for him meant, 'the patient is on equal terms with the doctor' (Davis and Wallbridge, 1983, p. 37). Whether his patient was an adult or child, he considered that he and they had equal status.

Winnicott was able to make immediate relationships with children. It was as if they recognized something in him that made them feel both safe and understood. He had a strong sense of fun and was generally described as 'impish'. But his spontaneous acceptance by the children he saw was more about his ability to stand in their shoes and have a genuine concern for their pain. This is a salutary lesson for counsellors for so often we are persuaded that good counselling is as much about strategies and skills as about relationships.

But Winnicott teaches otherwise. His approach, perhaps based on his Methodist upbringing, was always nonconformist. He offered his clients, children or adults, what he thought they needed, rather than offering a standard approach. In terms of standing in the client's shoes, it has to be a leather, rather than a plastic shoe. The plastic moulds the foot to the shoe, the leather shoe moves to accommodate the foot and let it breathe. Winnicott let his clients breathe and wiggle their toes around and as counsellors we can learn from this. Too often we hurry clients along at our pace rather than theirs, to meet our own agenda.

Winnicott talked about interpretations, the classic technique of psychotherapy, as often an unhelpful response, which stopped the patient from learning. Like a good teacher, instead of giving the answers, he felt that the patient should be given the space to reach the answer himself.

If only we can wait, the patient arrives at understanding creatively and with immense joy, and now I enjoy this joy more than I used to enjoy the sense of having been clever. I think I interpret mainly to let the patient know the limits of my understanding. The principle is that it is the patient and only the patient who has the answers (1974, p. 102).

Person-centred counsellors will see in this a similarity with Carl Rogers who always maintained the client is the expert on his life and has the answers. For both therapists their role was to provide a facilitating environment in which the client is free to grow. This involved for both of them a sense of empathy, the ability to 'stand in someone else's shoes', which Winnicott called 'cross-identification' (Davis and Wallbridge, 1983, p. 83). He believed that the baby brought up in a good enough environment will, through its nurturing mother, get a sense of being a separate person from the mother. This means that eventually he can relate to others because he is able to see them as 'different from me'. This also applies to the client who, through having a good nurturing experience with the therapist, may be able to improve his relationships with others. If he can feel confident enough to detach himself from the therapist and feel independent again, a separate individual, he may be able to develop the capacity to empathize with another. Clients who have gone through traumatic experiences can regress to a powerless, narcissistic state where they can feel like a child dependent on a 'mother'.

Although taking both Freud and Klein as his starting points, Winnicott came away with a very particular approach to development. Although he saw himself as a product of the Freudian School, he also thought that some things Freud believed were 'actually wrong'. It was the same with Klein. Winnicott saw Klein's view of normal development as pathological, believing that the norm is ordinary development at the hands of the good enough mother. He held a less harsh view of mothers than Klein, seeing the ordinary mother as usually good enough.

Winnicott's ideas were developed from theories of both Freud and Klein, integrating the two strands of their thinking. Like Freud, he was influenced by Darwin, and Darwin's theories of natural selection. Winnicott believed that the quality of the mother–child relationship is crucial, but he also was aware of the baby's innate instinct for survival, and the inborn behavioural patterns babies enlist to ensure maternal preoccupation. Mothers, in Winnicott's book, were normally 'good enough', a mixture of innate traits and learning. Like animal mothers they would groom their young towards independence. Winnicott was eager for his patients to meet their creative potential, qualities that were both a genetic inheritance and innate. The potential was aided by 'good enough' nurture.

In an age where, in some quarters, genes are heralded as the main determinant of our future, people can become fatalistic, feeling that they are powerless over their destiny. Although we have to be aware of this debate, our own experience tells us of the significance of nurture. It seems important, for counsellors, to help our clients to take both nature and nurture into account, exploring the relationship between them. As client and counsellor, we can work together on developing the client's unique personal resources.

The idea of the good enough mother can be a helpful concept, particularly to counsellors who think they must be perfect for their clients, never getting it wrong or making mistakes and always being available.

The developmental view of holding a baby to keep it secure, and extending the idea to the more independent toddler whom the mother keeps in mind, is so useful to the counsellor. Holding the client can be used, by counsellors, when the client needs a time to heal and feel secure, before he can begin to take the risks of trying to move on. It is necessary for clients who are in a state of extreme trauma, for example, devastating bereavement, rape, where it is enough for them to survive. They can be held by the counsellor and feel secure until such time as they can begin to work on the issues. But the holding, and holding in mind must be boundaried, so that the counsellor does not step out of counsellor role. If, out of misguided sympathy for the client's predicament, she offers something else, like friendship, or a totally accessible mother, this may meet the need of the counsellor, but not the client.

Criticism has been levelled at the theorists who, in using the analogy of the mother and baby for the therapist and client, licence practitioners to encourage helplessness and dependency. They say that unlike other therapies that see therapist and client as adults, mutually working together on the client's issues, the psychodynamic approach infantilizes the client.

Winnicott would disagree. He saw the mother holding the baby, both physically and in mind, but in doing so helping the infant to independence. When we feel helpless because of our distress we can feel like a dependent child. However, the good therapist, after an initial dependence, will wean us towards adulthood again. It is like being ill in hospital. Temporarily we put ourselves in the hands of the doctor and nurse, because at that time we need to be looked after. But we also want our autonomy back. As counsellors, our clients may need us while they are feeling powerless, and we can be the good-enough mother to them. But we are bad mothers if we hold on to clients when they are ready to fly the nest.

The mother–child relationship was the model for Winnicott's psychotherapeutic practice. As counsellors we can learn from the notion of the mother holding the baby, both in terms of offering security to the client and holding him in mind. Winnicott's ideas on play, and the therapeutic space as a place to play, can be extended to the counselling room and supervision. Our aim should be to provide that place to play, a facilitating environment, a therapeutic space.

Further reading

Davis, M. and Wallbridge, D. (1983) *Boundary and Space. An Introduction to the Work of D. W. Winnicott*. London: Penguin Books.

Jacobs, M. (1995) *D. W. Winnicott*. London: Sage Publications.

Kahr, B. (1996) *D. W. Winnicott. A Biographical Portrait*. London: Karnac Books, London.

Phillips, A. (1988) *Winnicott*. London: Fontana Paperbacks.

Winnicott, D. W. (1974) *Playing and Reality*. London: Penguin Books.

Winnicott, D. W. (1975) *Through Paediatrics to Psychoanalysis*. Collected Papers. London: Karnac Books.

5

Bion: knowing and not knowing

'Wilfred Bion was a giant. He was physically large and his influence remains immense' (Sayers, 2000, p. 113). Yet he is a theorist, who is little known in the counselling world. This is a pity as he offers valuable insights, which can be useful to counsellors. Most of his earlier work was with groups and, because of this specialism, he is often omitted from psychodynamic texts on individual therapy. He continued to be interested in group-dynamics throughout his life. However, after the 1940s he did not use his direct group experiences as the basis for his writing (Bleandou, 1994), so he has much to say to one-to-one therapists.

Like Winnicott, Bion used both Freud and Klein as the starting points for his new concepts, though he was more influenced by Klein. He continued to develop Klein's ideas on Object Relations, producing some revolutionary theories in the process. His life spanned the same epochs as Winnicott, they were both heavily involved in the two World Wars, with their different experiences in wartime having a profound effect on their ideas.

Life of Wilfred Bion

I am drawing on Bion's autobiography, *The Long Weekend, 1897–1919, Part of a Life* (1982) and *All My Sins Remembered and the Other Side of Genius* (1991), together with Gerard Bleandou's comprehensive biography, *Wilfred Bion. His Life and Works 1897–1979* (1994) and Janet Sayers, *Kleinians: Psychoanalysis Inside Out* (2000).

Early life

Wilfred Ruprecht Bion was born in colonial India, in 1897, in Muttra, in the Punjab (now Muthara, Uttar Pradesh). Generations of his family had served in India and there was an extended family living around him. His father's family was of Huguenot descent, and religion was still a significant element within the family. Some of the wider family were missionaries, his paternal grandfather, and others on his mother's side. All this meant that Bion was brought up in an atmosphere of strong religious principles.

When Bion was three, his sister Edna was born. It seems he was overcome with sibling rivalry. He also got the worst of any quarrels when they were older because his father assumed the elder child to be at fault. Looking back as an adult on these early years, he saw his father as having an image of an idyllic family, which the children could not live up to, whereas his mother could tolerate the children at times being two nasty brats. However, his mother was unpredictable, and moody. By contrast their ayah, like Bowlby's nanny, was a more consistent source of affection.

Bion's father was a civil engineer, but, unlike many expatriate government officers, he felt a moral responsibility to aid the indigenous community, so that they could have a say in the way that the country was governed. He worked part time as secretary to the Indian congress. On the other hand, he was noted for his prowess as a big game hunter. Bion was impressed by his father on all these counts, but he was also frightened of him. He had an inner image of his father with whom he had conversations in his head. This inner father he called, 'Arf, Arfer', an amalgam of the 'Our Father who art in heaven' of his Christian upbringing, the snorting shouts of laughter of his father's friends at the Gymkhana club and the fury of his father when dealing with Wilfred, his recalcitrant son.

At eight, Bion, like Bowlby, was sent to school, where Bion was not only much younger, but a continent away. He left India, which he now regarded as his spiritual home and never returned. When he was eighty-two, he was due to return at last to India, but in an ironic twist of fate, he died unexpectedly, 2 months before the planned trip.

He hated boarding school because he was homesick. He longed for India and the freedom of his earlier life. But he was not even able to see his mother for three years, so he was dependent on his own resources. He sought comfort in masturbation, but his Christian upbringing and the ethos of the school ensured that any consolation he gained was cancelled out by guilt and anxiety. We know about these episodes because Bion wrote about his miseries at prep school and his sense of alienation, from an adult perspective, in his autobiography.

Like Winnicott, Bion eventually became a proficient sportsman at school, and as such, something of a hero. School had become a place where he was not only accepted, but lionized. This made his disappointment at failing to get into Oxford all the greater, so, again like Winnicott, Bion volunteered to fight in the First World War.

Adult life

He became a tank commander. The tank was a new weapon, an impressive 40-ton sinister mass. Bion said it reminded him of the tiger traps, which had frightened him as a child, but this time it intimated something even more ominous and he would be in charge of it. He would also be in the terrifying position of standing outside on the tank, signalling to the driver through the front flap. He was possessed by the fear that he would fall off the front, wounded and then be driven over by his own tank.

When his battalion was sent overseas, Bion wished his mother could see him as a soldier rather than, in the way of all mothers, a child. But his mother was to be proud of him as a soldier, for he won the distinguished service order (DSO). Bion felt that he had been made into a hero and did not deserve it. He was haunted by the memories of those he had failed, who had died under his command. An incident when he was under fire, with one of his men dying in front of him, pleading with Bion for the help and reassurance he could not give, seemed to be the last straw. 'And then I think he died. Or perhaps it was only me' (1982, p. 249). The horrors of war, with the psychological trauma it wreaked stayed with him throughout his life and directed much of his subsequent work.

After the war Bion got a scholarship to Oxford, though he felt it was on the back of his DSO. He read history and also became interested in philosophy, particularly the work of Kant. Philosophy was to play a large part in Bion's later theories. He got his degree but did not feel he had done as well as he should have done. He left Oxford to teach at his old school, but was sacked after being accused by a mother of sexually propositioning her son. He felt too devastated by the charge to challenge it and afterwards hated himself for his submission. He later became engaged to a beautiful girl who sent him wild flowers, but this fairy-tale relationship was not to last and she soon jilted him for another.

All these incidents Bion saw as humiliating failures. He was consumed with rage and despair. This decided him to seek help in therapy. Bion at this time was a medical student, having decided to become both a doctor and a psychoanalyst. He had first read Freud after a school friend had brought it to a Boxing Day party. 'Bion seized and devoured one of Freud's works I had brought with me, and which may possibly have sown the seed for his eventual life interest' ('Anon', in Pines, 1985, p. 387). Bion went into therapy, with someone never named, hoping to manage his present difficulties. His therapist disappointed Bion, as after informing him that 12 sessions would be enough, he would not look at the current issues Bion was struggling with. Bion dubbed him, 'Mr Feel-it-in-the-past', as this was where the therapist kept returning.

At University College, where Bion studied medicine, was a doctor interested in psychoanalytic psychotherapy. He was J. A. Hadfield, who had been one of the original seven doctors to found the Tavistock Clinic, an out-patient clinic that offered psychoanalytic psychotherapy for patients unable to pay for it. Hadfield used his influence to get Bion a job there, as an assistant doctor. Bion at the Tavistock became a trainee in psychoanalysis, and one of the first patients referred to him for therapy, in 1934, was the playwright and novelist, Samuel Becket. Bion and Becket shared a number of similarities. Becket, like Bion, came from French Huguenot ancestors, who had fled religious persecution. Didier Anzieu, quoted in Bleandou (1994, p. 44), suggested that both saw the other as an imaginary twin. Bion had earlier said that 'the function of the imaginary twin is to deny a reality different from himself' (1967, p. 19). Anzieu claimed that both men had 'narcissistic and schizoid characteristics and both had turned to culture to contain this psychotic part of themselves'. An extra similarity seems to be the difficult relationships they both had with their mothers. Bion wanted Becket to acknowledge that he had 'an addictive relationship' with his mother, but maybe the same could be said of Bion. He appeared to long to see his mother, but was hostile to her when they were together. When they had met, when Bion was on leave during the First World War, he wrote: 'Relations with anyone I respected were intolerable, notably with my mother; I wanted nothing except to get back to the Front just to get away from England and from her' (1982, p. 266).

Bion saw Becket for nearly 2 years, although Becket, at times, seemed a reluctant patient. It has been suggested that Becket used their therapeutic encounter as the basis for his play, 'Waiting for Godot'. During the period of the therapy Bion (surprisingly in today's boundary terms) took Becket to a lecture given by Jung at the Tavistock Clinic. Becket was much impressed by Jung's ideas and saw them as relevant to his own work. Bleandou says that Becket was critical of his analysis with Bion (1994, p. 45). Sayers quotes Bion on his treatment of Becket, 'I don't know that I did him much good. But I don't think I did him much harm either' (2000, p. 117).

In 1937 Bion himself went into analysis. For 2 years Bion was analysed by John Rickman, a Quaker who was very influenced by Klein, but retained his own ideas and convictions. War terminated the analysis and brought Rickman and Bion together as colleagues. Bion's mother died a few months before the outbreak of the Second World War, so Bion was never able to work through his mourning in the analysis (1982, p. 266).

The work Bion and Rickman undertook was working with groups in the army. Groups were to be Bion's specialism and the subject of his first published essay, 'The neuroses of war', in 1940. His work was creative, controversial and not always appreciated by the army. He pioneered the idea of 'leaderless groups', which, perhaps not surprisingly, were regarded in some areas as suspect. Bion noted that he was the only psychiatrist, he knew, who had left the war at the same rank he had come into it. He was a Major when he went in and a Major when he came out. It sounds as if Bion contributed to his situation by refusing to compromise or play politics.

Apart from the death of his mother, Bion had suffered another personal loss, which devastated him. In 1940 he had married Betty Jardine, an actress he had first seen on the London Stage. In 1945 they had a daughter, Parthenope. Bion received the news in a letter from Betty, while he was working in Normandy. Tragically, 3 days later, he had a telephone call to say that Betty was dead.

Bion returned to civilian life, grieving and anxious. He bought a cottage outside London, where he installed his widowed father and the couple who were looking after his baby. He continued to work at the Tavistock, primarily with groups, he had his own patients and went into analysis with Melanie Klein.

But he says in his autobiography 'something was wrong'. He felt numbed and insensitive. This was brought to a head one day when his baby daughter was crawling towards him across the garden. She was waiting for him to pick her up. He ignored her and told the nurse to let her crawl. The baby doggedly persevered in her painful attempt to reach her father, by this time weeping bitterly. The nurse, astonished, ignored Bion and went to get the child. Bion writes, 'the spell snapped. I was released. The baby had stopped weeping and was being comforted by maternal arms. But I had lost my child' (1991, p. 70). Bion is horrified by this evidence of his pent-up anger and resentment. Most of all he is appalled at himself. 'It was a shock, a searing shock, to find such a depth of cruelty in myself' (1991, p. 70).

At fifty-three, when Parthenope was six, Bion met a researcher in the refectory at the Tavistock. Francesca was artistic and creative and like his first wife, a performer. Her world was singing. The couple married 3 months later. Francesca, too, had been widowed, but there were no children. A year after their marriage Francesca gave birth to a boy, Julian, and 2 years later, a girl, Nicola. It is clear from the letters Bion wrote to Francesca that he was immensely happy.

Bion had started to write during his 8-year analysis with Klein. He continued in the following years, chronicling his ideas on the mother–baby relationship and how it translated into the therapeutic relationship. He kept in contact with Klein, as a colleague, but, like the relationship with his own mother, seemed to find it difficult. Although admiring of her work he felt suffocated by her needy demands. During this time he was lecturing, seeing patients and enjoying family life. His papers continued to grow.

In 1968, in his seventies, Bion and Francesca moved to Santa Monica, California. Bion continued to give lectures and seminars, both in the States and in South America. In 1979 the couple returned to England to be nearer their children. They moved to Abingdon, near Oxford, and Bion was in the process of setting up a new private practice when he was diagnosed with leukaemia. Sayers describes the visit of Isabel Menzies Lyth, who had been particularly influential in applying Bion's Kleinian ideas in analysing groups and organisations, to arrange supervision with him. Instead she found him in hospital, but he did not disclose the diagnosis. He merely commented, 'Life is full of surprises, mostly unpleasant' (Sayers, 2000, p. 132). Bion died a week later on 8 November 1979. He was eighty-two.

Thinking and containment

Bion was influenced by Klein's view of the mother–baby relationship, but added compelling, revolutionary ideas of his own. Some of these ideas are complex, but worth struggling with, as they can throw light on the client–counsellor relationship. Bion posited an interesting answer to the question of how babies begin to think. He said that 'thinking is a development forced on the psyche by the pressure of thoughts and not the other way round' (1967, p. 111). Bion believed that the baby has a preconception, an inborn knowledge of the breast. He expects to find the breast waiting for him. Bion calls this 'an empty thought'. However, if the breast is there and the baby makes contact with it and is satisfied, Bion calls this a conception. When the baby expects to find a breast, but finds a no-breast, an absent breast, then he is frustrated. The mating of the preconception (I expect to find a breast) with the frustration (there is no breast there) can produce a thought in the baby. For the hungry baby it bridges the gap between wanting food and the arrival of the breast. This process depends on whether the baby can tolerate frustration. If he can tolerate frustration, the 'no-breast inside' becomes a thought and a means of thinking develops.

A baby who is unable to tolerate frustration can only see the internal 'no-breast' as a bad internal object to be got rid of as soon as possible. So possible thoughts are not allowed to develop. This evacuation means that the baby cannot learn from experience, the reality that the bad breast eventually becomes the good breast. He takes refuge in a false omnipotence.

Whether the baby can tolerate frustration and awful feelings depends on the relationship between mother and baby. Bion saw the baby putting into the mother, through projective identification, feelings that the baby finds intolerable. If the baby thinks it is dying, it can arouse fears that it is dying, in the mother. A mother in tune with her baby can take those fears and digest them for the baby, giving them back to the baby in a way in which the baby can take them in, in a manageable form. It is like the mother bird who finds food that the baby bird cannot digest. She chews it up herself, then gives the broken down, masticated result to the baby, who swallows it, and is nurtured.

In the human mother, Bion called this process of conversion 'alpha function'. Containment for the baby heralded the capacity to think which the mother had given to him, through her reverie. Bion saw the mother in a dreamy muse, taking in her baby's frightening sensations. She is identified with the infant, but able to be separate from him, manage his fears and contain him.

If the human mother is not capable of this metamorphosing, the baby is left with the intolerable fears, which he takes back into himself as a 'nameless dread'. This is a mother who is not capable of reverie. The result, Bion says, is a baby incapable of alpha functioning, but full of fearful unknown and unknowable 'beta elements'.

Therapeutic application

Bion related the mother–baby experience to therapeutic practice. Inability to tolerate frustration can obstruct the development of a capacity to think. Conversely a capacity to think would lessen the frustration for someone who cannot wait for a need to be satisfied. Bion gives numerous examples in his practice of his patients' lack of capacity to think.

This emphasis of Bion's on thinking is salutary, as often in the counselling room we emphasize feeling at the expense of thinking. How often do clients say, 'I can't think', when they feel out of control because their needs are not being satisfied and their lives seem worthless.

Sometimes a client will refuse to think and will just respond with 'I don't know' when asked to think about an issue. Presumably the possible thoughts are so disturbing that they have to be got rid of, so that the client has only a blank inside. But if a client can be helped to think, then the issues can take on a new perspective and some understanding can follow. If we are stuck in feeling alone, without being able to think alongside the feelings, we can seem paralyzed and powerless. There is no way out.

Case Example | Nasreen: feeling banishes thinking

A young Asian woman, Nasreen, born and brought up in Britain, came to counselling because she felt desperately unhappy. At seventeen, she had gone to Bangladesh for a holiday and returned, married, to a man she now hated. She felt she had been tricked. She had not given her consent and yet she had felt there was nothing she could do. 'I was just a walking passport', she said. Yet everyone else in the family had thought it a good marriage and could not understand her objections. No one listened because no one understood her position. They thought she was being spoiled and selfish. But Nasreen was comparing herself to her college friends and what she saw as their opportunities and freedoms. She said they had a life to look forward to, while she felt her life was over. 'What can I do?' she

Case Example | (Continued)

said. She felt helpless because nobody in the family supported her. 'They are all on his side', she said bitterly. 'There is no way out.'

The trainee counsellor who saw Nasreen was overcome by Nasreen's sadness. She listened carefully, was very concerned, but felt overwhelmed by the client's despair. It did feel helpless and that there was no way out. The counsellor felt helpless. Nasreen could not think and it was as if the counsellor had caught her paralysis. The counsellor could not think either. To make it more difficult the counsellor felt underconfident that she did not know enough about the cultural issues. It was as if her usual resources had deserted her.

The trainee counsellor took it to supervision and the supervisor helped the counsellor to think. The counsellor saw how she had not been able to separate herself from the client's feelings and so had been unable to contain her.

Now more able to think, the trainee counsellor felt more confident that she might have something to offer Nasreen. But Nasreen did not return for a second session. The trainee counsellor was left feeling that she had failed her.

Had the trainee counsellor been given the opportunity to work with Nasreen, Ryle's cognitive analytic approach might have been useful. With this the therapist uses psychodynamic concepts to understand the issues and a cognitive approach to changing the way of thinking about them, so that the issues may be resolved.

As the difference between the baby thinking and being unable to think lies primarily in the relationship between the baby and its mother, so the client being helped to think depends on a good relationship with the counsellor. As the mother takes in the baby's too-difficult-to-manage thoughts and feelings and returns them in a digestible form, so the client can give unmanageable thoughts to the counsellor to hold for him. If the counsellor is able to hold them for the client, which assumes that she is strong enough to do this, then she can eventually give back these dreadful thoughts and feelings in a way which makes the client feel contained.

The ability of the counsellor to contain the client will depend on the extent of her own containment. This will assume that she has worked through difficulties in her own therapy and is not likely to try to resolve issues of her own with the client in the counselling room.

Case Example | Anna: a client who cannot think

Anna came to counselling because she had episodes where at times she could not think. They were frightening episodes as they were accompanied by a feeling of panic that she wanted to die. Her life became constrained through a fear that an attack might happen at any time, so she started to cut her college classes and curtail her social life. She told her mother that she felt depressed, but her mother dismissed it as exam nerves. Anna had hoped that her mother would take her to the doctor but the subject was never raised; so, without telling her mother, she came to see me.

Anna was a bright, artistic student who said she 'lived in her head'. She had friends she saw at college, but rarely outside. This was partly through her fear of an attack coming on without warning, but also because her parents disapproved of drinking and night-clubs. The family, mother, father, elder brother and Anna, liked to do things as a family and would watch television together or play board games like monopoly. However, Alan, the elder brother was now away in his first year at university, so Anna said she felt like an only child.

As Anna talked over the weeks it became clear that she had an enmeshed relationship with her mother, where they did everything together. They talked of each other as 'best friends', went shopping together and even wore each other's clothes. Anna admitted that when her mother went out with her father, every Friday night, she felt lonely.

We talked about the attacks. How when she could feel them coming on she felt paralyzed, her mind seemed empty, but the feeling of wanting to die pervaded her. Anna had never tried to kill herself, she seemed shocked by the idea. She said after some thought that it was not exactly dying that she wanted to do. It was 'like not being here'.

At the beginning of our relationship I had felt very worried about the suicide fear. Anna was only seventeen and I felt that her mother should be involved in any referral. Anna felt that she could not

Case Example | (Continued)

tell her mother everything, as 'it would frighten her'. I then suggested that if Anna wanted to, we could ask her mother to join us for the sessions. Anna seemed pleased by this, while I wondered if I had, through anxiety, made an error of judgement and jeopardized the therapy for Anna.

In the event Anna's mother did not join us. She did, however, take Anna to her doctor, and Anna was prescribed antidepressants. I felt relieved, partly because I felt the responsibility shared, but also as I felt it cleared the way for us to be able to concentrate on Anna and her inability to think.

The attacks lessened but Anna was still having at least one attack a week. She had not been able to tell her mother the full details, although she had tried. It was clear to Anna that her mother could not bear to know, so Anna continued to protect her. The attacks usually happened when Anna was alone in the house while her mother was out. Friday nights, when Anna's mother was out with Anna's father, were the most likely time. All this was not lost on Anna who realized that it was something to do with the strong feelings she had for her mother, and their relationship.

Anna was expected to go to university like her brother and though this was an exciting prospect, it was also terrifying. She really did not know how she would manage without her mother. I pointed out that she managed the attacks without her mother and she seemed quite surprised as she acknowledged this to be true. Anna had started to ring her girlfriend from college after an attack. She did not tell the girlfriend why, but just let her chatter on, while Anna said little. But it steadied her. It was as if she got in touch with life, instead of death. Anna could not ring her mother at this time, although she wanted to. 'It would freak her out', said Anna.

Another thing, which we had talked about and Anna had herself decided to do, was to try to make some thoughts out of the blankness and terror of the attack. As soon as she could, she wrote down what she was felt was happening to her. The words often did not make sense, but sometimes they were satisfying and poetic and Anna felt rewarded by this piece of paper covered with writing that she hardly remembered doing.

During this time Anna had started to behave a bit more like a teenager. When I first met her she appeared very young and family oriented. Then she began to realize that her college friends had different lives from hers, and theirs were starting to look quite attractive to her. So she got herself a job at the weekend and enjoyed the feeling of not being dependent and of meeting new people. She arranged to meet her college friends in the evening at the pub. She never stayed long, but long enough to feel that she was accepted and normal. Anna had discovered that some of the boys at college had called her 'Weird' and was keen to lose this title.

Anna said that she felt less dependent on her mother. At times she was very angry and frustrated with her mother for not being there for her when she really needed her. At other times she said, 'I can manage.'

When it was time for Anna to go off to university she felt reasonably confident. Though she still had infrequent attacks, her writing during the attacks had become more coherent, which made her feel more in control. She had begun to replace emptiness with thought. Anna still rang friends when an attack was over, but she now had more friends to ring. This meant that there was less anxiety because someone would have a mobile turned on. Anna would be in contact with 'life'.

Knowing and not knowing

One of the most interesting of Bion's ideas, which are very pertinent to counsellors, is about 'not knowing'. Bion often quoted a letter, which John Keats wrote to his brothers George and Thomas, in 1817. In this letter Keats describes what he calls, 'negative capability'. Keats said that it had occurred to him that the great strength of Shakespeare was that he could tolerate mysteries and half-truths, without an irritable reaching for certainty.

'The important point about that', Bion wrote, 'is the "irritable reaching for certainty"'. Pressure is put on us as analysts to know what the problem is which is so obscure, so difficult to grasp and which is unfolding itself in front of our eyes' (2000, p. 61). The same can be said of counsellors. We feel we have to know. Not knowing makes us feel powerless and that is hard to tolerate. It is what makes us ask too many questions, the wrong sort of questions, the questions that are for our own benefit rather than the client's. Bion said, 'we hate being ignorant – it is most unpleasant. So we have an investment in knowing the answer, or we are pressurized from within to produce an answer and closure the discussion'.

(2000, p. 251)

The paradox is that those who think they know, who feel themselves to be the experts on the lives of others, 'don't know'. The counsellors who have doubts and are puzzled, but who let the client tell their story, who give the client the therapeutic space, are more likely 'to know'. The counsellor who stays with the client even if they both feel lost, the counsellor who has a healthy humility, the counsellor who respects her client and maintains the boundaries probably 'knows' her client. Like the mother who is the container for her child and lets him think, so the counsellor, like the mother, can be in reverie with her client. She can go alongside him, accept his painful sensations and thoughts, and give them back within a process that can make them both more aware.

This is redolent of Freud's free association, where the analyst accompanies the patient on the couch, alongside him, her unconscious meeting the unconscious of the patient. The analyst gives 'free floating attention', a term used by Freud, and reinforced by Bion. The patient is the one who plots the journey, who decides where they will go. The analyst gives meaning to the venture.

The counsellor in order to be in tune with the client has to go where the client goes. This means being able to tolerate uncertainty. Tolerating uncertainty makes us feel deskilled. It is much better to know and feel that we are the experts. But if we can go in tandem with the client's thoughts and feelings, unsure of the journey or the destination, we shall get there. Eventually we shall know.

So if 'not knowing' leads to 'knowing', how can we get an inkling that we 'know'? The seventeenth century Authorised Version of the Bible has an interesting use of the verb 'to know'. It is used to denote sexual intimacy. When a couple have a sexual encounter it is described as 'knowing'. 'And he lay with her and he knew her.' This suggests a coming together, a unity.

This kind of 'knowing' is more about understanding someone at a deeper level than facts and details. It is getting in touch with the essence of the person, what Freud would call the 'psyche', Winnicott the 'true self' and Bettelheim the 'soul'.

If counsellors come to counselling from areas of work where to 'not know' something is to be incompetent, it is particularly hard to work with the unknown. They are used to being the experts who categorize and respond to check lists and precedents. They have to know facts and details. Where knowledge is power, counsellors may be unwilling to 'not know' because it renders them powerless. This is where counsellors must be very aware of the ethical underpinning of the counselling encounter. There is an inherent power imbalance in the relationship between the client and counsellor, with possibilities for exploitation. When the client comes to counselling he feels vulnerable. He can be easily persuaded by the confident expert. This is most important for trainee counsellors to remember. The counsellor who is certain she 'knows' has to have the humility to realize she 'does not know'.

Case Example | Henry and Beryl: the counsellor who does not know

Some years ago, when I was in training as a couple counsellor, I saw a couple, Henry and Beryl. They were middle aged and this was a second marriage for both partners. Every session they started with a diatribe about the house they lived in.

Henry was furious because the house had dropped in value. Beryl was furious because she had nowhere to put her clothes. For Henry the house was his family house and had sentimental value for him. It had no sentimental value for Beryl and she felt conned that she had sold her bungalow to pool their assets. Henry said he could not sell until the market revived. Beryl said he had no intention of selling. Henry said he needed a house big enough for his son to live in, if he was down on his luck. Beryl said she needed a wardrobe.

I listened to all this and all I felt was frustration. They were avoiding the real issues. I refused to offer practical solutions, like, 'Buy a wardrobe!' but I was no less crass. I wanted them to talk about their relationship, their past, their fit, their dynamic. I had to know. I tried to introduce some of these issues, but to no avail. Back we went to the house. The windows leaked, the door refused to lock. Henry had not noticed Beryl's cleaning. Beryl did not understand Henry's worries about the roof.

I took the case to supervision and as I talked about it I began to realize what I had failed to understand in my need to know. If I had allowed myself to 'not know' I would have heard the

Case Example | (Continued)

couple talking about their anxieties about the relationship. Central was their commitment, or lack of commitment to each other, symbolized by ambivalent feelings and broken promises over house sales and money. Then there was the issue of security. How secure was this relationship? Was it like the unlocked door where external forces could come in and destroy the relationship? What about each partner's place in the relationship? If there was no room for their clothes, was there room in the relationship for two different personalities? What about responsibilities outside the relationship? Would there be a space for their children from another relationship? How did they fit together? Was it like the leaking windows that did not fit properly?

With my supervisor I saw that the house was a metaphor for the marriage. Had I really listened, by giving up my own thoughts and feelings to this couple and contained their anxieties, I would have 'known' earlier. I had missed the wood for the trees.

Curiosity

Curiosity plays a part in the urge to know. Presumably people who want to become counsellors are curious about what makes us what we are. But curiosity has to be boundaried. Unbridled curiosity has links with sensationalism and the client's story becomes a soap opera. It is essential that we have respect for our clients, which means respecting their right to silence, when curiosity demands we must know. 'Is this ethical?' we have to ask ourselves, and continue to monitor the reply.

Enduring the uncomfortable feelings of not knowing, feeling we are not sure of what is happening in the session is a challenge. Is this incompetence or ethically being with the client without directing? Where does the counsellor's responsibility lie?

Competence

As counsellors we have to realize the difference between 'legitimate not knowing' when we are working with a client, trying to be alongside him, still puzzled and uncertain, not yet really understanding, but at the same time recognizing the limits of our competence. Not knowing can never be a justification for incompetence. There are some things for ethical reasons, which we need to know. Being aware of 'not knowing' means keeping a check on limits of competence. This is particularly valuable in certain situations.

One of them is the position the trainee counsellor finds herself in when she is on placement in an agency and finds that what is expected of her is way beyond her competence. Often, a case, which presents itself within the bounds of the beginner's competence, can quickly be transformed into something that is too difficult, for example, a client who persistently threatens suicide. Supervision is crucial here, with the trainee able to be honest about the difficulties, seeing them as ethical issues, rather than personal failure. Referral may be necessary. Another arena in which we must monitor our competence is when working with cultural diversity. The counsellor may be making ethnocentric assumptions.

Case Example | Kwaku: the counsellor who misunderstands

A white middle-class counsellor working with a Ghanaian client, Kwaku, may completely misunderstand the importance of the wider family for her client. She may encourage Kwaku to look after his own interests when he tells her how difficult it is to remit money to Ghana, when he has so little. When he says that he has to offer free lodging to his nephew, who is studying at university in Britain, she talks about the difficulties to make ends meet which he, his wife and children suffer, and asks where does his responsibility lie. She does not understand the kinship ties and responsibilities, the acts of mutual aid, the paying back he is doing for help he has received, the expectations of his kin, the betrayal of their trust, the ostracism if he fails to deliver. All that this counsellor has communicated to her client is that she does not understand. Worse, she does not know that she does not understand.

Short-term work is another area where competence has to be monitored. Where time constraint limits the work that can be done it is important to tread carefully. It would be unethical to actively encourage a client to disclose something traumatic, like child abuse, when the agency only offers four sessions. If we do this we leave the client more vulnerable, having learnt more about the client, but offering little in return.

Sometimes the client will want to disclose, knowing the parameters. Whatever the circumstances, supervision is necessary and referral to an appropriate agency essential.

Being aware of 'Not Knowing' can help the trainee counsellor not to work so hard, and with that goes being directional. It is acceptable not to have all the answers and as a result to give one's whole attention to the client in the session.

Without memory or desire

Giving his whole attention to his patient in the session was very important to Bion. He claimed that the analyst should go into each session 'without memory or desire'. He explained that memory is misleading and can get in the way, as it is always influenced by unconscious processes. So memory of past sessions, which are necessarily 'false', can distort the truth of the present session. Similarly desire can be an obstacle to what is happening now, in the session, as it is concerned with what might happen. A desire for results, or for a cure, stops the psychoanalyst from giving whole attention to the patient. 'Every session attended by the psychoanalyst must have no history and no future. What is known about the patient is of no further consequence: it is either false or irrelevant' (1967, p. 17).

All this applies equally to counselling. We are too often hooked into what has happened in past sessions or what can be achieved in time. As Bion says this can prevent us from being in touch with what is happening in front of our eyes.

For Bion there is creativity in the 'not known'. 'The only point of importance in any session is the unknown' (1967, p. 17). Bion goes on to say 'in any session, evolution takes place. Out of the darkness and formlessness something evolves' (1967, p. 18).

Each session will be complete in itself because there is no going over old material already brought. There will be a 'quickened tempo' to each session. Progress is not measured by what has happened over a period of time, but the ideas, moods and attitudes, which will proliferate at each session. Bion suggested that at each session it should feel like a new patient. If the analyst feels he has seen the patient before, 'he is treating the wrong patient' (1967, p. 18).

All this was revolutionary when Bion first declared it. It still feels different from most psychodynamic thought on the therapeutic relationship. But it should make counsellors think about what is happening in the room and the process of the counselling.

I have found it enormously helpful when I am not sure what is happening, I cannot fully understand, I feel puzzled. It has helped me go with it, rather than anxiously scrabbling for a false certainty. If creativity is not present in the counselling we can so easily categorise people, 'this is a case of . . .' 'depressed clients always . . .' 'I'm expecting him to . . .' Already we have stopped listening to what the client is telling us. We already know better.

Comment

Depression and failure are a part of every life even the most happy and successful – I might say especially of the most happy and successful; it is the price you pay for joy and success if they come your way (1991, p. 180).

This was written by Bion, in a letter, to his children. But it could well be his epitaph. He suffered from depression because he felt failure; failure to live up to his own expectations, to live up to the expectations of others, those who depended on him, his family, the men under his command, even his patients. Yet this was only a part of his life. The other part was crowned with professional success and personal joy.

His life experiences shaped his theories. His life spanned the same eras as Winnicott's, two interesting English Protestant analysts working in their different ways with Jewish Central European ideas. Like Winnicott, as a boy, Bion both revered and feared his remote father and had a closer, if difficult, relationship with his mother. Like Winnicott, his war experiences influenced his work, though Bion shows greater evidence of the horrors staying with him. Much of Bion's work, both with individuals and groups was based on the frailty and vulnerability of the human spirit. His thinking was creative, revolutionary and startling. Like Winnicott, taking both Freud and Klein as his starting points, Bion uses his clinical work to produce theories, dazzling in their originality.

His writings on both theory and practice are robust and sure. Yet he had humility and in discussions with other professionals he was always prepared to look at others' views or even to 'not know'. Unlike Winnicott, Bion did not usually write for professionals other than those in the psychoanalytic field. However, what he has to say is pertinent for counsellors and we can reflect on what we can use to enrich our practice.

For counsellors working one to one, Bion's ideas about negative capability, taken from Keat's letter to his brother, are crucial. The notion that, paradoxically, those who think they know, the 'experts' who categorize their clients, responding to precedents in order to know, don't know. There should be no anxious scrabbling after facts and details.

This is important to counsellors who think they know. One of the leaps they have to make is in realizing they do not know. Because knowledge is power, counsellors may be unwilling to 'not know' because it renders them powerless. The power imbalance in relationship between client and counsellor needs to be carefully thought about, in particular the possibilities for exploitation. Being aware of 'not knowing' means keeping a check on the limits of counsellor competence.

Bion asserted that the therapist must go into each session without memory or desire, going alongside the client without knowing what's happening. She has to stay in the present session, not allow memories of past sessions to cloud what the client is bringing to this session now. Similarly desire for what is to happen in sessions to come; will the client change, will he feel more able to live his life more contentedly; all these hopes are obstacles to being with the client in the here and now. Bion posits that the therapist should be with his patient in the session, able to give his whole attention to that session. This has links with the person-centred use of empathy in the here and now. However, what may not be agreeable to the person-centred counsellor is Bion's assertion that the therapist needs to discipline her thoughts and the prerequisite is a thorough analysis. Counsellors working in a psychodynamic way would be expected to have had their own therapy, so that they could be more aware of transference and particularly countertransference issues. It highlights the position of being with the client, but keeping an objective stance.

Bion's other very useful ideas for the counsellor are about thinking and containment. Bion had a complex theory of thinking, but counsellors can use the theory in practice to help their clients who cannot think. Maybe it is too frightening to think, maybe thinking is denied and an enveloping emotionalism, which renders the client helpless, takes over. As Bion asserted that the mother can contain her baby and help him to think, so the counsellor can contain the client. She can take his dreadful thoughts and hold them for him and give them back in a manageable fashion when he is able to accept them. This means that the counsellor has to have the capacity to sustain the client's unmanageable thoughts, in order to help him.

'The idea that his patient may commit suicide is only one particular instance of the painful thoughts which the psychoanalyst must be capable of sustaining; otherwise he will be deflected from the work he exists to do and which no one else can do namely to analyse' (1967, p. 126). This applies equally to counselling, where counsellors often have to be able to hold on to the painful thoughts of both their clients and themselves. For the trainee counsellor this may be too much, too soon. It will need taking to supervision and perhaps referring.

Bion was an original thinker. His extension of Object Relations Theory gives us much to reflect on. But, more importantly, it gives us much to work with.

Further reading

Bion, W. R. (1967) *Second Thoughts*. Selected papers on Psycho-Analysis. New York: Jason Aronson.

Bion, W. R. (2000) *Clinical Seminars and Other Works*. London: Karnac Books.

Bion, W. R. (1991) *All My Sins Remembered and the Other Side of Genius*. London: Karnac Books.

Bleandou, G. (1994) *Wilfred Bion. His Life and Works 1897–1979*. London: Free Association Books.

6
Bowlby: attachment and separation

When I was a student at The Tavistock Centre in the late 1980s I was overawed by the presence of the man in the room next door but one to mine. His tall, patrician figure was commanding; in his eighties he was still tall and straight and I suspect I was not alone in feeling intimidated. For this was the great John Bowlby who had changed the course of social welfare history.

Bowlby's work on attachment and separation has had far-reaching consequences well outside the psychotherapeutic world. The fact that parents can stay with their children in hospital, that midwives encourage new mothers to bond with their babies, that children in care live in family units is in no small measure the result of his influence.

If you ask teachers, social workers and nurses today if they know of the work of Melanie Klein, some will have heard of her, but few will be able to describe her theories because Klein is not part of their training. It is a different story with Bowlby. His work has been so influential that most people in the caring professions, not only are familiar with his theories, but have been involved in their application.

I can personally chart the move away from huge residential establishments where it was more difficult for children to attach to one worker, to small family units set-up, specifically, so that the child could attach to substitute parents. In the early 1960s I was training as a child-care officer (soon to be renamed social worker) in Liverpool and visited children-in-care in large residential homes including Strawberry Fields, the inspiration for the Beatles' song of that name. Twenty years later I visited students in training for social work, on placement, working with small family groups of children-in-care, where the emphasis was on offering a substitute family. Critically, if it were possible, the unit's aim lay in keeping the child in touch with his original attachment figures, with the goal of eventually reuniting the family. Bowlby's ideas had been assimilated in such a way that no student could believe anyone could have doubted the validity of them.

Bowlby, like Klein, had changed the way people thought. In institutions in the 1950s it was believed that shelter, food and a warm, clean existence were all that was necessary to provide adequate care for children. Bowlby's work on attachment and separation was so powerful that it could not be ignored.

Today counsellors owe a huge debt to Bowlby, for his ideas, particularly on loss and grief, are used by all counsellors, not only by psychodynamic counsellors. Anyone working with loss and we could say that is all counsellors, if we interpret loss in its broadest sense, will have assimilated Bowlby's work, in their training, perhaps without knowing its source.

The losses clients bring are wide ranging. Experiences of bereavement, separation, divorce, rape, abuse, illness, empty nest, redundancy and retirement are all issues that counsellors work with. Clients also present more nebulous difficulties. Loss of confidence, loss of self-esteem, loss of purpose, loss of identity and loss of security are issues that counsellors and clients struggle with. To have some understanding of the processes of attachment, separation and loss, it is important to explore Bowlby's work.

Unlike most psychodynamic theorists he spent much time on research outside his clinical practice, believing, like Freud, that his theories needed to be scientifically justified. However, unlike Freud he offered evidence, which could easily be understood and utilized by diverse professionals. I believe counsellors can have a greater understanding of their own relationships, their clients' relationships, as well as the relationships they share with their clients by an examination of Bowlby's life and work.

John Bowlby was an idiosyncratic figure. He was a psychoanalyst who was also passionately interested in other areas and wanted to integrate them. He responded to ethology, the study of animal behaviour, in his quest to understand the human animal. This was regarded as heretical by the colleagues who were purist about the internal world, having little use for the external world of the individual, let alone the animal.

Bowlby's passion for the emotional care of children and social reform, on the one hand, and his objective scientific approach to his findings on the other, make him a controversial figure. If in the spirit of true psychodynamic research we look for the causes in his past, can we find their sources?

Life of John Bowlby

I am drawing on Jeremy Holmes's (1993) beautifully written account of Bowlby's life and work, 'John Bowlby and Attachment Theory', for biographical details.

Childhood

John Bowlby was born in 1907 into a well-known upper-class English family. His father was surgeon to the king. From such a background we might not expect a social reformer who worked in the public sector, and who for several years shared his family house with a labour government minister.

As in most upper-class families of the day, childcare was primarily left to the servants, with whom children often made strong attachments. Unfortunately servants can be hired and fired, can leave of their own volition. They are not necessarily a stable fixture in a child's young life, and are unlikely to provide a secure mother figure. Bowlby's own mother seems to have been typical of her class. She seems to have been a rather distant presence, preoccupied with her own affairs. She ensured that the children were well cared for through daily reports from Nanny, seeing the children formally each evening in the drawing room, for an hour, when she would read to them (see Holmes, 1993, p. 16). Both she and her husband seem to have had a more informal relationship with their children during their annual summer holidays in the Highlands of Scotland. Interestingly Bowlby had a house in Skye, and it was there that he died in 1990, on holiday with his wife and children. It seems those Scottish summers of his childhood, where he was able to have a closer relationship with his mother, were so important to him that for years he had recreated them with his own family.

In time-honoured tradition, when he was seven, John was sent off to boarding school with his brother Tony, 13 months his senior. If we think about Bowlby's passionate belief in the importance of a stable mother figure to securely attach to, it does not appear that he ever maintained that experience as a child. A distant mother, a remote father, changing hired carers and finally boarding school, noted more for 'making a man' out of a small boy than offering attachment figures, did not provide Bowlby with the secure base he sought for others.

It may be that having five siblings provided attachment figures, he might otherwise have lacked. It seems he was close to his brothers. In competition with Tony and protective of his brother Jim, who was left behind in this highly achieving family. Holmes suggests that this fierce protection of a disadvantaged brother may have been one of the catalysts for his later work with deprived children.

Anna Freud in her study of war-torn children concluded that children suffered disturbance as a result of separation from their mothers, temporarily or permanently, in the Second World War. However, she believed that the children showed less damage, in terms of being able to make relationships with others, if they had shared their, often horrific, experiences with brothers and sisters.

However, as Bowlby (1975, p. 438) notes, Anna Freud followed her father, Sigmund, in believing that humans are driven by biological needs. If these needs can be met by other than the mother, then the child will not suffer too much. The love attachment to the mother is secondary to the provision of food. She did not consider that separation from the mother could be the primary reason for anxiety and disturbance.

Early adult life

After leaving school, Bowlby briefly joined the navy, perhaps to please his father. However, he did not feel intellectually stimulated by the navy, so he persuaded his father to buy him out, so that he could go to Cambridge University to study medicine. When Bowlby was twenty-one, his father, in Bowlby's words, 'fortunately' died. So with no one to prevent his taking an unorthodox path for a year, he made a decision that was to have far-reaching consequences. Between leaving university to take up his clinical medicine studies, Bowlby went to teach at a school for maladjusted children, an offshoot of A. S. Neill's Summerhill school, still a progressive school today, and still controversial.

At the school Bowlby found he was able to communicate easily with the disturbed youngsters. He concluded that their difficulties could be attributed to their damaged childhoods.

Medicine had been something that both he and his father could agree on as an appropriate career choice, rather than a passion for Bowlby. With his experience with the disturbed children and influenced by a colleague, he saw a way forward, through medicine, that he could be passionate about. He decided to become both a psychiatrist and a psychoanalyst.

He trained for both at the same time, like Winnicott, going into analysis with Joan Riviere, of the glamorous hats, and associate of Melanie Klein. He qualified as an analyst in 1937 and immediately started training in child analysis. Melanie Klein was his supervisor and from the start there was disagreement. Bowlby thought that she, steeped in the internal world, did not take enough account of the influence of the external world, how environmental events and experiences shape our lives. He was however, grateful to Klein and to Joan Riviere for his psychoanalytic education in the object relations approach. In the preface to Attachment (1971, p. 17) he says:

Though my position has come to differ much from theirs, I remain deeply grateful to them for grounding me in the object relations approach to psychoanalysis, with its emphasis on early relationships and the pathogenic potential of loss.

Work

Unlike most analysts Bowlby's work was firmly in the public sector, working first in Child Guidance clinics, then, from after the Second World War at the Tavistock Clinic. He was a firm believer in the National Health Service (NHS) and fought for the place of psychoanalytic treatment within it. He retired from the NHS in 1972, but remained at the Tavistock clinic. He was honoured abroad but did not receive, in his supporters' eyes, the honours due to him at home, where he was still regarded with suspicion in some circles. The Kleinians could not forgive him for what they regarded as his scant attention to the internal world. Grosskurth (1986, p. 406) quotes Dr Susanna Issacs Elmhirst, 'He treats humans as though they were animals, which is just what they aren't. He ignores love and anguish, the real stuff of human life.' 'Bowlby?' exclaims another analyst. 'Give us Barabbas.'

Some commentators have suggested that Bowlby's upper-class Englishness, which was at odds with his mainly Central European Jewish colleagues, many of whom had suffered traumatic lives, made him appear remote and reserved from them.

But, of course, this was a part of his personality. His own children often found him a distant father, replicating his own father's behaviour with hard work and long holidays. Holmes (1993, p. 25) quotes Bowlby's 7-year-old son, 'Is Daddy a burglar? He always comes home after dark and never talks about his work.'

His work, for most professionals, including counsellors was immensely enriching. By linking together the disciplines of ethology, cognitive psychology, systems theory, developmental psychiatry with Object Relations theory, he produced comprehensible theories and models, which practitioners can easily understand and use.

Maternal deprivation

Bowlby was first known outside psychoanalytic circles through his passionate interest in maternal deprivation. He had written a report for the World Health Organisation (WHO) in 1951, on the experiences of homeless children after the Second World War and used it to throw light on what happens to any child who is deprived of his mother.

Earlier he had published in 1944, with additions in 1946, the results of his study into young offenders, entitled, 'Forty-four juvenile thieves'. Most of the 44 youngsters had been brought up in an orphanage or been separated from a mother figure for most of their lives. His findings had been used by the Labour government of the day to deter women from working outside the home. Their political decision was based on the premise that it is not sensible for any government to have a surplus of unemployed, disenchanted and formerly fighting men around competing for jobs with newly emancipated women. The message the women received was that if they cared for their children's mental health and future development they needed to be at home. If you deprive children of their mothers, they grow up to be delinquent was the stronger message.

Maternal deprivation is an issue that is often brought to counselling. Sometimes it is an overt issue, for example, the death of a mother when the child was growing up. Often, it is only after working with a client that the absent mother, a physical presence, but an emotional absence is revealed. Like John Bowlby, clients grow up with a mother who was never really 'there' for them. They may not even be aware of the loss. The deprivation for them was part of a family dynamic, which at the time they regarded as normal.

Case Example | Ken: maternal deprivation in a client's history

Ken was a young man who came to counselling because of a series of failures at work, not achieving promotions, failing the tests his

Case Example | (Continued)

colleagues sailed through. Over the weeks, as we talked, he became furious with me because I could not provide him with a solution. His work was scientific, so everything had a solution, if one could get the formula right. I did not have the right formula. As I am writing this I realise that the word 'formula' has another meaning, commercial baby milk. And of course here lay the key to his difficulties.

As we worked on the presenting problems, I tried to help Ken to look at his past. He could not remember anything of his childhood, he said. He clearly did not see the point of looking. But gradually a picture was built up of a sterile family life, a clean house, and an ordered routine, but little emotional interaction. He could only once remember his mother picking him up and holding him, when he had fallen heavily, in the back yard.

As an only child he was left to his own devices, while his mother and father separately carried out their own activities. In his family, he said, 'we just got on with things', much as he wanted me to do. Feelings were something he shied away from. They were too frightening.

As an adult, he still had a relationship with his mother; she did his washing. In this, it seems, the practical nature of his childhood attachment was reproduced. When I wondered if part of him would like a different relationship with his mother, he replied, 'Why?' Ken was attached to his mother and she to him, but the lack of an emotional base, which could not be acknowledged, had left him deprived.

One of the 'failures' he later brought to the counselling was his inability to form relationships. He said that he felt empty, that he had nothing to give. In his early life he had not had the experience of a close emotional attachment, and he had nothing on which to draw.

Attachment

Bowlby's work on maternal deprivation, being deprived of a mother, raised questions about the more usual situation of the child having a mother, with whom he can have a relationship. Bowlby's questions were about the nature of the relationship, the quality of the relationship, whether this kind of relationship can be reproduced throughout adult life, for example, with a spouse. He speculated that the desire to attach to a loved one was inborn, so began to look for evidence of this. And if we are programmed to attach, and obtain satisfaction from the relationship, what happens when we are separated, either temporarily or permanently from the loved one?

Bowlby believed that we are born with an instinct to attach ourselves to a loved person. This innate behaviour ensures our survival. Winnicott said something similar in his statement that there was no such thing as a baby. A mother figure has to be there to look after him, or he will die. But both theorists looked beyond mere survival, to a life of relationships, in which powerful emotions hold sway. These emotions mean that when someone is separated from the person they were attached to, the effect on their lives will be significant.

In his preface to the first of his three-volume treatise on 'Attachment and Loss', 'Attachment' (1971), Bowlby wrote of his struggle to make coherent sense of his findings and to present them in a way that they could be better understood by his colleagues. He starts by saying that he had no conception of what he was undertaking in 1956, when he and his colleague James Robertson prepared a book for publication. This was based on Robertson's observations on the responses of young children to the temporary loss of their mothers, and its theoretical implications. What started as a discrete study soon blossomed into something altogether more fundamental.

Bowlby realized he was grappling with the same issues of 'love and hate, anxiety and defence, and attachment and loss' that Freud had fought with 60 years ago, though they were coming at it from different corners.

Evidence in animal studies

Bowlby's corner included his ethological findings because the evidence he wanted to demonstrate, of an instinct to attachment, could be found in animal studies. He conceded that because animals acted instinctively it did not necessarily follow that humans would act in the same way, but he thought it was likely. Where was the proof that they did not?

Imprinting

He was impressed by the work of Konrad Lorenz, published in 1935, who believed that young birds and mammals are genetically programmed to imprint themselves onto a suitable object at birth. He experimented with ducks and geese, finding that a chick will attach itself and bond with the first thing it sees on hatching. Since this is usually the mother, the system works very well. However, Lorenz found that baby geese and baby ducks can be imprinted on a ball, a shaft of light or Lorenz himself. There are fascinating photographs of Lorenz swimming with baby ducks clinging all over him.

These are the origins of the work on imprinting and bonding which lead to the local maternity hospital, with the nursing staff's concern to ensure that new mothers have the opportunity to bond with their babies.

Tinbergen's work on attachment

Niko Tinbergen was another scientist whose findings influenced Bowlby. Tinbergen's work on birds and their territories led him to think that in order to defend their territories and therefore survive, birds must have instinctive behaviour, and he thought the instinct to attach was a fundamental key to survival. He observed birds not only warding off attackers who threaten their territory, but also saw birds attaching to each other through courtship rituals, together making nests, copulating, sitting on the eggs, feeding and caring for their offspring. These adolescent birds were eventually cast out of the nest to repeat the reproduction process. He concluded that attachment is a necessary instinct for survival of the species.

Harlow's work on attachment

Bowlby also utilized the work of Harry Harlow. Many counsellors will be familiar with, and maybe horrified by, Harlow's experiments with monkeys and in particular the experiment where a baby monkey was put into a cage with two 'mothers'. One mother was made of terry towelling, the other mother of wire. The wire mother provided milk. Experimenters may have been surprised by how much time the baby monkey spent with the cloth mother, only going to the wire mother when hungry. Within strict biological terms it would be expected that the baby would cling to the wire mother and milk, its source of survival. Instead it clung to the cloth mother, snuggling up to it and clearly getting comfort from this substitute mother.

If baby monkeys need to attach themselves to a warm, comforting object, obviously getting some satisfaction from being close to a mother figure, who appears to lessen their anxiety, how much more do human babies need a secure attachment figure.

The strange situation

Mary Ainsworth, a colleague of Bowlby, conducted short experiments with children, which she called, 'The Strange Situation'. The one-year-old child and his mother are taken into a playroom, strange to the child, with an experimenter present. The mother leaves the room for three minutes, leaving the child to play with the experimenter. After her return and reunion with her child, both mother and experimenter go out. Three minutes later they return and mother and child are again reunited. On the basis of the child's behaviour in response to the separation and reunion, all videotaped, the child is rated on his attachment to his mother.

Attachment anxiety

Much of counselling is about attachment. Because attachment, separation and loss are bound up together, it is often difficult to hang on to the attachment issue in what is often presented as a loss.

Case Example | Barbara: attachment – the key to present difficulties

Barbara, came to counselling because she was having panic attacks. Over the weeks it became clear that her panic attacks were tied to her thoughts about her grandmother's death. Barbara had felt guilty about her grandmother's dying, because although she had known that her grandmother was very ill, she could not bear to visit her. Barbara had realized this in the counselling. At the time she had given herself all sorts of reasons why it was not possible to visit. At the funeral she had felt 'nothing', gone back to work the same day and found herself saying to friends that it was 'all for the best', as her grandmother would have hated to be an invalid.

Although panic attacks happen in the present, it is usually important to go back to the past to discover their cause. Together we looked at Barbara's childhood and it became very clear what a significant role her grandmother had played. This seemed to have been

Case Example | (Continued)

forgotten by Barbara as the contact with her grandmother had been sporadic as Barbara had grown up, married and had two daughters.

As Barbara talked more about her childhood she began to talk about her younger sister. Barbara had been envious of her sister's relationship with her mother, whom she was convinced preferred her sister to Barbara. For this reason she was determined that she would keep her relationship with her grandmother for herself and forcefully persuaded her malleable younger sister that she was better off staying at home. At the same time Barbara managed to infer that she alone out of the daughters liked to stay with her grandmother; so a pattern emerged. Most weekends Barbara went to her grandmother's where she was showered with treats and fussed over. Occasionally she felt guilty about her sister's missing out but was quickly able to repress these thoughts.

In the counselling Barbara began to be very upset. She wept when she talked about her grandmother, whom she felt had been so good to her and whom Barbara felt she had abandoned when it suited her. She also wept over her younger sister whose life had been fraught with difficulties and whom Barbara felt she had deliberately disadvantaged. In adulthood Barbara had been able to see her mother's preoccupation with her fragile younger sister as protective, rather in the same way that she protected her younger daughter from a world that seemed too threatening to her. This was a link Barbara had hardly been aware of. It shocked her. Who was she grieving for? It felt frightening and confusing.

As Barbara allowed herself to acknowledge the attachment she had felt towards her grandmother and what it had meant to her, she also examined the attachment to her mother, her sister and her daughter. She acknowledged the guilt she felt, but she also began to accept that this guilt is an inevitable part of being attached to loved people whom one inevitably fails. All this was painful and difficult, but as she worked on it, so the panic attacks lessened and eventually disappeared.

Had Barbara had different treatment from psychodynamic counselling, she could have been rid of the panic attacks. But she felt that the counselling had given her something different. Barbara had gained an understanding of herself, which was very important to her. She had seen herself within the context of two generations of family attachments and seen how the present can have more meaning through an understanding of the past. Barbara felt more able to forgive herself for the past and work on the relationships with her daughters in the present.

As counsellors we may need to remind ourselves, and help our clients, to acknowledge the power of attachment figures on our lives. There is no escaping the other side of the coin, which is the consequence of separation from the loved figure.

Separation

Bowlby's studies of young children in separation from a loved person, usually the mother, or mother figure, backed up by his use of animal studies, started his work on separation and loss, which was to have such long-term effect. He used his own observations together with those of his colleagues; James Robertson, Mary Ainsworth, Christopher Heinicke and Ilse Westheimer.

Distress as a response to separation from the mother was not a new idea. Fifty years earlier than Bowlby's observations, even before Freud's comments, in 1905, on the anxiety demonstrated by children separated from their mothers, William James (brother of the writer Henry James) had said in 1890, 'The great source of terror in infancy is isolation' (Bowlby, 1975, p. 52).

Bowlby drew on the work of Freud. He also used the differing ideas of Klein, Winnicott, Fairbairn and Suttie to formulate his theory of attachment, separation and loss. Suttie, like Bowlby, had looked outside psychoanalysis to further his ideas. He too was interested by animal behaviour and also by social anthropology, in particular by the way other cultures organize their relationships. Suttie is not as was well known as he should be, possibly because he died on the eve of the first publication of his book, *The Origins of Love and Hate* (1960, p. 42). Suttie believed strongly in attachment that 'the infant brings the power and will to love with it'.

So it is clear that the notion of maternal separation and its consequences was not a new one. What Bowlby did, which was original, was to systematically collect together a body of knowledge, offering scientific evidence for his findings.

At the beginning children were observed within institutional settings 'and it was on the basis of these observations that the sequence of responses we term protest, despair, and detachment first came to be delineated' (Robertson and Bowlby, 1952).

The three-phase separation model

This three-phase separation model was to have long-ranging consequences. It was born out of observation, then used by observers as a template to match separation behaviour against. It later became utilized by workers trying to understand the separation issues they came across with their clients, and, later still, adapted to become a model of grief and mourning.

In the first phase, 'Protest', the child protests about the separation. This can take the form of crying, screaming and struggling against the separation, angry, hostile or even violent behaviour. The response will depend on different variables, the age of the child, his temperament and personality, the relationship with the person he has been separated from, together with the relationship, if any, he has with the people who have taken her place.

The second phase is 'Despair', which is characterized by depression, apathy and guilt.

The third phase Bowlby called 'Detachment'. In children in brief separation from their parents, the detachment is temporary. In nursery school, for example, the children will detach from a parent and attach, for the time they are at school, to the teacher.

We might think that because the original findings were confined to institutionalized children they would not apply to children within a 'normal' family setting. Yet later studies confirmed that children experience intense anxiety on separation, though because of circumstances like the length of the separation and the quality of the original attachment relationship, together with the quality of the substitute attachment relationship, the separations have different consequences.

Animal studies

Bowlby's separation work on humans was backed up by his animal studies. He was very influenced by the work of Charles Darwin, who was the subject of Bowlby's last book, before his death in 1990. In this book Bowlby pursues two strands of his own interests. One is maternal deprivation. In the preface (1991), Bowlby says that he has long wanted to pursue the idea that Darwin's chronic ill health had its origins in childhood bereavement, the death of his mother, when he was eight.

The other strand was the exploration of Darwin's concept of evolutionary biology. Bowlby felt indebted to Darwin for the light he had shed on emotions in animals, which were being developed by current scientists.

Separation from the mother in monkeys

Bowlby (1975, p. 85) quotes Jenson and Tolman (1962) on a study of pigtail monkeys, just removed briefly from their mothers.

'The mother struggles and attacks the separators', and later, 'the infant emits high pitched shrill screams intermittently and almost continuously for the period of separation'.

For experiments that go on no longer than 5 minutes the reunited mother and baby immediately remain in the closest of contacts. However, after longer periods of separation from 6 days to 4 weeks, all observers reported extreme, noisy distress up to a day after the separation followed by a period of a week or more in which the infants sat hunched and depressed.

The detailed description of the separation experiments make for distressing reading, particularly as Darwin's evolution thesis demonstrates the similarities between the young monkey and the young human.

I observed an incident when living in Tanzania, East Africa, which has stayed with me. Travelling along a dirt road I came across a baby monkey sitting in the middle of the road. I slammed on the brakes, and simultaneously the mother swung down from a tree. She slapped the baby's bottom hard and scooped up her terrified offspring. It clung desperately to her. Both were chattering wildly. Eventually she cuddled it. The incident had so many similarities to that which most people have witnessed, where a toddler tries to dash into the road, the mother in terror pulls him back, slaps him because he frightened her, and then eventually hugs him.

The animal studies, like the human studies, demonstrate to a greater or lesser degree Bowlby's three-phase model, Protest, Despair and Detachment. But the most graphic demonstration of the three-phase model is surely the Robertsons' films.

Children in brief separation

Many students may have seen the series of films made by John and Joyce Robertson in the 1960s on 'Young Children in Brief Separation'. When they were first shown by the Robertsons at professional gatherings, they produced extreme responses in professionals. Some were distraught. Others refused to accept that children do suffer such distress on separation from a mother figure. Sir James Spence, the distinguished Professor of Child Health at Newcastle University, who had given his name to the paediatric award Winnicott had won, said, 'What is wrong with emotional upset?' He went on to cite Wordsworth as an example of someone who 'suffered from emotional upset, yet look at the poems he produced' (Robertson J. and J., 1989, p. 20).

Today the films are used in several trainings, particularly social work, nursery teaching and nursery nursing to demonstrate the importance of a consistent figure for the child to attach to, when the mother figure is absent.

Four of the films show the Robertsons taking a young child into their own home while the mother is in hospital having a new baby. At that time in Britain mothers normally stayed in hospital for 10 days, an enormously long time for a small child to be without his mother. The Robertsons' fostercare was carefully planned so that the child knew them, and their home, before the mother was hospitalized. Even so the films show that the children still found the experience distressing because Joyce Robertson, though skilled, compassionate and affectionate was not their mother and the Robersons' home was not theirs. A poignant moment in the film on Jane (1968, 17 months, in fostercare for 10 days) whose home is in the same block as the Robertsons' is when she goes off on her own across the communal garden to stand wistfully at her own gate.

But the film that is most remembered by anyone who has seen this series is John (1969, 17 months, 9 days in a residential nursery). Here, there was no preparation, he is taken to the nursery in the middle of the night, when his mother has gone into labour. He wakes to a strange environment with no one he knows and with his mother disappeared into a vacuum. The phases of protest, despair and detachment are played out before us so painfully that many watchers cannot bear to see the disintegration of this little boy and become very angry. It raises, for many, experiences of their own, sometimes too difficult to contemplate, which may catapult them into their own personal counselling.

The three-phase model: Robertsons' film, 'John'

We see John at first in the nursery, willing to make a relationship with one of the nurses and find a substitute mother. But the timid John gets increasingly ignored and forgotten, as the nurses work with whoever is pushing for attention. Although John cannot yet talk, he makes his desires clear, half-hearted protests strengthening when his father, who visits daily, fails to take him home. He brings his outdoor shoes to his father, turning away when father refuses to respond. John is in the Protest stage.

But as time goes on he forgets the anger and becomes depressed and apathetic. He lies on the floor alone, his face buried in a giant teddy bear. He has reached the phase of Despair.

When the ordeal is finally over and his mother comes to claim him, John turns away from her. He is in the Detachment phase. Later he lets her cuddle him, though reluctantly. We know John is not returning to the place he had in his home, 9 days ago. There is a new baby who will need much attention, the ultimate rejection for John.

The Robertsons add a postscript to the film in their book, *Separation and the Very Young* (1989, p. 88). They report that on returning home, John had many temper tantrums and family life had to be reorganized to give John maximum attention. Seven weeks later Joyce Robertson visited John. Her association with the nursery induced extreme disturbance in John, which lasted for 5 days. This included aggression towards his mother. Three years later he was described as a lively boy but over fearful of losing his mother. He had days of provocative aggression towards her every few months.

So what can we as counsellors learn from this?

Remembering Klein's ideas on the mother–baby relationship transferred to the counselling room, we can try to integrate the Kleinian concept of the transference with Bowlby's theories on attachment and separation. This way we can hold together ideas of the internal world and the external world. Both seem important to learn more about the relationship between counsellor and client.

We can use experiences to learn more about our own and our clients' attachments and the separation anxiety, which results when the object of attachment is absent. Most mothers will be able to think of the agony for all concerned of the first day at school, or at the other end of the cycle, the leaving of the nest by the last child. Aunts, grandmothers and friends can provide anecdotal evidence, and perhaps because of the distance, can be more objective about their observations of separation from the loved person. They can see the despair of the child, separated from his mother. Mothers who have to cope with their children's pain all the time cannot dwell on it too much. It would be disabling. The scars of misery, disappointment and separation have to be integrated, so that the child can survive a world that is inevitably imperfect.

Separation from a loved person

Many trainee counsellors work in bereavement agencies. They are often fortunate, as it seems in an era of short-term counselling, in allowing their clients to have as many sessions as the client and the counsellor together decide is needed. After 20 or so sessions, the counselling couple will begin to know each other very well. This compares with Bowlby's observations, 'Attachment' (1969, p. 395) on 'the degree of fit that so many mothers and infants have achieved after 12 months of getting to know one another. During the process, it is evident, each has changed in very many ways, small and large.' Bowlby felt that each partner in the mother–baby relationship had shaped each other. In the same way this is true of the counselling dyad. As Patrick Casement says, in his writings, we learn from our patients (clients). This is sometimes forgotten. It can appear arrogance, though it is probably anxiety, which makes us feel so responsible for our clients and the counselling that it can feel a one-way process.

The trainee can have the mourning model in her head, but because she and the client are working more in tune with each other, as time progresses, the counsellor will not be trying to push the client to fit a particular stage in a predetermined model. She will also realize that grieving is not linear and that people's emotions go forward and back. Long after a separation most people will still be protesting at some level.

Case Example | Sarah: the three-phase model, separation

This example is about separation from a loved person. The client has lost her husband. But he is not dead, though he is lost to her. It is not an orthodox bereavement but a separation, leading to divorce.

For the client it can seem worse than a bereavement, for her husband, though alive, has rejected her. He may be living just down the road, but with someone else. The grief is complicated by her intense anger and his abandonment. The client often does not want to acknowledge the mourning part of the process as she is so angry and wants to deny what the relationship meant. She also may want to move on very quickly, perhaps getting a new partner to blot out the hurt, or to say, 'See I don't care.' But the grief must be acknowledged if the client is to eventually move on.

Sarah, after 10 years of marriage, had been left by her husband Alan. He had left her on her birthday. This seemed especially cruel to Sarah who felt utterly abandoned and bewildered. She also realized that, in his leaving, Alan had wanted to hurt and humiliate her.

In the counselling room Sarah recounted that day. She had lain in bed on her birthday, a Saturday, waiting for Alan to bring up her birthday presents, with a morning cup of tea, a birthday ritual. She had heard the car driving away and could not make sense of it. She only started to become anxious when her two daughters arrived in the bedroom and got in bed with her, another part of the birthday ritual, and her husband failed to return. Eventually she got up, made breakfast, and went through her usual Saturday morning routines, unsure of what to do. The children were watching television and did not seem alarmed when Sarah explained to them that their father had needed to go somewhere. 'But what about your birthday?' said 7-year-old Clare, the elder daughter. Sarah had told her, reassuringly, that they would have it later. But inside she felt a frightening chill. She had tried to ignore what she knew was Alan's growing away from her, convincing herself this was something all couples go through at some time.

As the day wore on Sarah's emotions see-sawed. There was no word from Alan. Should she ring his best friend? Or his mother? She felt foolish about contacting either. But perhaps there had been an accident. Ought she to ring the hospital? Anxiety and fear mixed with irritation, there was probably some reasonable explanation. Maybe Alan was arranging some big birthday treat for her that had not gone according to plan.

If we look at Bowlby's three-phase model, Sarah is going through the protest stage. She oscillates between denying the separation and

Case Example | (Continued)

potential loss, and feeling fearful and angry at what could be her husband's abandonment. She feels shock, tinged with incredulity. Jack could not have rejected her like this!

The day wears on for Sarah. She puts the children to bed, who are by now asking where Daddy is. Sarah says that he is probably at his friend's house watching a football match. Clare says nothing, but Sarah thinks she looks worried. Four-year-old Heather starts to cry, for what appears to be no reason and Sarah feels a stab of despair.

At ten o'clock the phone rings. It is Alan. His message is curt. He will not be coming back. He has found someone else who puts him first. She really cares for him. He was sick of being seen only as a father and provider. His solicitor will be in touch.

This is the situation when Sarah seeks counselling. She feels demoralized, depressed and despairing. Alan has refused to speak to her. She feels her world has fallen apart. She also feels some guilt. Perhaps she has neglected Alan in her determination to be a good mother to the children. Perhaps she did take him for granted. Perhaps it is her own fault that he left. Sarah is now mainly in the despair phase of Bowlby's separation model.

Yet sometimes she feels an overwhelming anger. How dare he do this to her? She has always supported him, been a good wife, put up with his mood swings and his unreasonable demands. Alan took her for granted, not the reverse. And what about the children? How could he bear to abandon his children? He could not really have cared for any of them. With these feelings Sarah is back in the protest phase of the separation.

The trainee counsellor who is working with Sarah knows about Bowlby's three-phase separation model. She also knows that people with losses do not work neatly through each phase but gravitate between the phases, according to both internal and external experiences. The counsellor is working with Sarah to help her accept the conflicting feelings she has, as a normal response to experiences of separation and loss.

Losses can trigger other losses. So the counsellor, in several sessions, finds herself working with Sarah on unresolved issues, left over from the death of a loved grandmother, when she, Sarah, was ten. Sarah's mother was so upset by the unexpected death of her mother that she could not bear to talk about it. Consequently for Sarah, her grandmother simply disappeared and was hardly spoken of subsequently. Sarah realized that 'Grandmother' was a taboo subject and so coped with her grief alone, as best, she could.

The counsellor sees that it is important for Sarah to return to the past and try to manage this unresolved grief. She does not hurry Sarah back to the present and what was 'the presenting issue'. The counsellor is learning that people cope with grief in their own ways and the worst thing the counsellor can do is have her own agenda, which she urges the client towards.

Sarah has also spent much of the time in the sessions going over the early years of her relationship with Alan and become very upset by these early memories. She has wondered endlessly where it all started to go wrong. The counsellor has held her through these difficult sessions, not falling into the trap of trying to find answers, but just being there for her. For new counsellors, sometimes the pain of sad sessions, connected to the past, is too difficult to hold on to, and clients are encouraged to move on. This counsellor has resisted that temptation and has tried to stay with the pain. It has not been easy.

As the work moves on Sarah starts to begin to concentrate more on the present and then the future. She is reaching the detachment phase, the last phase of the three-phase model. Of course, there will be times when she goes back to the despair phase; birthdays, anniversaries, Christmas are all classic times to feel despair. It is important for the counsellor not to see this as regression. It is part of the process.

Feelings of protest can also return at any time, however 'detached' we feel from our loss. Waves of anger, fury and disbelief can still sweep over Sarah, taking her by surprise. It is necessary for the counsellor to stay with these feelings and help Sarah to accept them. It is all part of integrating the experience so that it becomes less raw and more manageable. The aim is not to make it go away, however attractive that can seem to both client and counsellor. The experience has happened. By denying it, pushing it away or burying it, we ensure its power. It will continue to exert a force on our behaviour, that we are unaware of, where depression is the most likely result. Many of us can recall friends or family who everyone complimented

Case Example | (Continued)

on 'getting over' their loss so quickly, and who months or years later experience severe depression.

Over the time they work together with the counsellor providing a safe therapeutic space in which Sarah can express her fury, her sadness, her fears and eventually her hopes, the client will begin to feel attached to the counsellor. It is important for the counsellor to acknowledge this and to manage it. Holiday breaks, referrals, if they are appropriate, for example Sarah might decide she needs some career counselling, now that her financial position is changed, all need to be carefully handled. Otherwise the client can experience the separation as another rejection. Most difficult of all is the situation where the counsellor has to leave the agency, for whatever reason, before the counselling has finished. If the counsellor is leaving because of illness, the client may feel personally responsible. 'My counsellor could not tolerate what I brought to her and it has made her ill.' Where rejection is a large component of what the client brings, the counsellor has to monitor herself, and take to supervision, any actions that could add to the client's feelings of rejection and abandonment.

Loss

Bowlby's work on loss was founded in his work on separation, in particular the separation of the young child from his mother. He found that the three-phase model, originally formulated after observation of children in brief separation from a loved object, usually the mother, could equally apply to permanent separation and to adult loss.

Transitions include loss, and transitions are often brought to counselling. The transition to widow or widower clearly involves traumatic emotions. And there are other transitions, which involve painful conflicting feelings. These include divorce, parenthood, retirement, redundancy, the so-called empty nest, changing jobs, changing houses, going to university, a child going to nursery, the last child going to school, separation from an attachment figure, or secure attachment to a role or place is involved in all these changes.

Losses do not have to involve another person. They can be felt as losing a part of oneself. This often happens after an experience, which is perceived by the individual as traumatising. It is our reaction to the experience, which is important, not the experience itself.

Most of us have lost an object of value or had it stolen from us. In teaching about loss I always encourage students to begin thinking about loss by recalling a time when they lost something, an inanimate object, not a person, or something momentous or life changing, but something of value, a personal possession like a handbag, or a car. Then we go through all the feelings involved in the loss and associate them with Bowlby's three-phase separation model, 'Protest', 'Despair' and 'Detachment'. We usually find that the feelings are the same as for life-changing losses. It is the degree of emotion and depth of feeling, which is different.

Case Example | Loss of an inanimate object

Some time ago my car was stolen, ironically during a seminar discussing psychoanalytic theories on Object Relations. Finding it gone, I immediately doubted myself, I must have parked somewhere else. I toured the car park and walked up and down the road.

Then with fury I recalled that the boot was full. For once, trying to be efficient, 2 weeks before Christmas, I had been to the supermarket, rather than leave everything to Christmas Eve. I began to rail at myself for trying to be someone else. Why could I not acknowledge that I do things at the last minute? It had always worked before. Why could I not accept myself? My feelings are of doubt and insecurity.

Then I thought about my nice little red car. It had been such a faithful friend, never let me down. More fury as I remembered I had had it serviced that day. After work I had paid a large bill at the garage. What a waste! I had brought the service forward because of a strange engine noise which turned out to be nothing. Had I known more about cars I could have waited for the usual service. It was my own fault. But how dare someone take my car? If I could get my hands on them . . .

You will note I am at the protest stage of Bowlby's model. Unbelieving about its loss, I think it will turn up. It is not irreparable. I have hope. I am angry as well, for part of me, the reality part, knows it has been stolen and I am unlikely to get it back. I hate the people who have stolen it. Not only have they hurt me, but by taking the Christmas bonanza, have attacked my family.

Case Example | (Continued)

Yet at the same time I blame myself. Knowing more about cars I would not have wasted money on the service. And, again, why buy those Christmas things so early? What a fool. I have started to feel guilty about my behaviour.

I might also perhaps have castigated myself for becoming a counsellor. Had I not been, I would never have been at a psychoanalytic seminar. Perhaps I could not bear to contemplate this, as it is now so much part of me. Yet I am attacking myself. 'Why can I not accept myself as I am?' was one of my questions and this hit at a central part of me.

I become unsettled, disturbed. I doubt myself. Maybe I hate myself. Already I have passed to the despair stage still not properly acknowledging the loss. Eventually I concede the car is stolen, and ring the police.

A day later, in an awful parody, the police take me to identify 'the body' – burnt out remains on waste-land, next to a stigmatized housing estate. I feel sad for it, remembering when it was 'almost new' and shining. But my head is already full of its replacement. I have moved towards detachment, currently scanning the Used Car section in the local paper.

Later, quite a bit later, I can visualize the kick that disaffected kids probably had in 'twoccing' it, dancing on it, crowing as Christmas treasures are revealed. Finally it is a funeral pyre. By this time I am the owner of a really cool old car, in which, I convince myself, I cut quite a dash. I have successfully detached myself from its predecessor, and the experience is no longer painful.

If most people consider their inanimate object losses I am sure they will find they go through similar processes, in which quite strong feelings are employed, if only temporarily. How much more so when we consider the loss of a loved person?

Bereavement

Mourning is an activity, which is all encompassing. People who are bereaved cannot understand why they feel so tired and exhausted and why they cannot concentrate on anything other than their loss. Bowlby disagreed with Klein that in times of bereavement we regress to an infantile position, which can become pathological. He considered that because throughout life we attach ourselves to significant others, when we are separated from them permanently, it is natural for us to grieve.

Bowlby took his three-phase separation model and extended it to incorporate the first, usually brief phase of mourning.

> Phase of numbing that usually lasts from a few hours to a week and may be interrupted by outbursts of extremely intense distress or anger.
> Phase of yearning and searching for the lost figure lasting some months and sometimes years.
> Phase of disorganization and despair.
> Phase of greater or lesser degree of reorganization (1998, p. 85).

In bereavement we lose so much and at the time of death most of the losses are not apparent. They come later. Both Murray Parkes, who worked with Bowlby, and Peter Marris, a sociologist, carried out surveys into the state of widows after their husbands had died, finding them struggling to come to terms with their myriad losses. Widows usually lose out financially. Those whose husbands have died unexpectedly may find themselves almost penniless. Certainly widows lose status. They may in the process lose friends and social activities. 'No-one wants an odd woman at the dinner table', said one lonely widow. 'They invite you for a time after the death, then it stops.' An elderly woman on her own is a pariah. A widow may lose her best friend, her sexual partner, the person who has known her longest, the father of her children and there is no replacement. Trainee counsellors working with bereavement agencies increasingly seem to be working with elderly widows looking for a new role and a new purpose in life to replace the aching loneliness.

Murray Parkes' fourth edition of his classic book, *Bereavement, Studies of Grief in Adult Life*, co-authored with Prigerson, was published in 2010. They quote the Yale Bereavement Study (Maciejewski et al., 2007). This involved a sample of 200 people in Connecticut who had lost a family member to natural causes and who were not suffering from complicated grief. Questions aimed at identifying the phases of grief – disbelief, yearning, anger, depression and acceptance of death. They were interviewed at 6, 11 and 20 months after bereavement.

Changes in the indicators of grief changed over time since the death. But there was no reason to believe that one phase must end before the next could begin. In fact 'acceptance' was the most commonly reported characteristic from the outset and 'yearning' the most prominent painful feature throughout the first two years. Features of all phases were often present at the same time.

In other theories of grief Stroebe and Schut (1999) demonstrate a Duel Process model. In this they suggest that grief is not always useful. Avoiding grief can be helpful in allowing the bereaved person to do the practical things that have to be done after a death and focusing on the future, like getting back to work (restoration orientation). Grieving for the dead has to have a time and place to be useful (loss orientation). Sometimes coping with grief is so disabling that the person has to take time off from the pain and loss so that they can manage to carry on living. Alternating grief work and restoration work enables some people to cope with daily life.

Klass et al. (1996) challenged the view that grieving was necessary so that individuals could make a new life for themselves after they had mourned the dead person. Klass suggests that the function of grieving is to continue the bonds with the dead so that the relationship is not lost, but can continue alongside new relationships. Klein had a similar idea that the dead person continued to live with you. In her view this was a part of one's internal world peopled by internalized figures, some of whom would not be living.

These are interesting ideas and may complement the ideas of Bowlby and Murray Parkes in some circumstances. However I think it true to say that Bowlby's theory of attachment and separation have stood the test of time and are very useful to practitioners.

Bereavement always triggers difficult and painful emotions. Deaths are particularly hard to come to terms with if they seem untimely, unexpected or unnecessary. An example of what is usually seen, by those bereaved, as an unnecessary death is suicide.

Suicide

Guilt is a common feeling for those who have been bereaved, but where the death is a deliberate act, it leaves the survivors with intense feelings of having let the dead person down. 'Why did I not notice something was wrong?' 'Am I so bad that he had to escape me by dying?' These are all questions to which the bereaved person can get no reply.

Other questions centre around the survivors' anger. 'Why did he do it?' 'How could he leave us all like this?' Anger, another common grief feeling, is intense where suicide is concerned. Although the woman, whose husband has died of a terminal illness is angry at being left, the rational part of her knows he could not help it. It is a different case with suicide, where not only has the dead person taken his own life, he has usually not given those around him a chance to stop him. Trying to understand can become obsessive and trying to forgive can feel impossible. Where a father has committed suicide, his children may have a strong urge to copy. Bowlby suggests this is a need for identification with the lost attachment figure.

Case Example | Mavis: a father's suicide

Mavis was the eldest daughter of a family of three whose father had committed suicide. She was an extremely competent high-flier in a much sought after corporate organization, used to being in control, with a particular talent for problem-solving. But she could not solve the problem of her father's death. It seemed inexplicable. He appeared to have everything to live for. The question she lived with was, 'Why?' Because the 'why' haunted her, she found it difficult to move on from the anger. Whenever she allowed herself to move into sadness and despair the anger pulled her back. 'But he didn't need to do it? How could he put us all through this?'

When we talked about the loss she said that was what she felt, lost, bewildered and lost and she hated it. It was as if she had lost her identity, the efficient corporate woman had disappeared and she could not bear the lost child who had taken her place. Over the months she worked to accept what had happened, she allowed herself to feel the pain and desolation. She began to acknowledge she would never know 'Why', why he never told anyone how he felt, why he put the family through so much suffering, why he felt so despairing, why he killed himself. Eventually she left the counselling knowing that she had to live without answers, that the way forward was to go on with what she had begun, to continue to integrate the uncertainty.

Some time after the counselling had ended, I bumped into Mavis in a multistorey car park. 'You look lost', she said. I confessed that I was looking for my car, as I had stupidly not made a note of the number of the bay. Mavis, who would never have been so foolish,

Case Example | (Continued)

wished me well. She said that her life was fine, she felt 'sad but grounded' and left with a cheery wave.

Reflecting on the encounter I wondered if her choice of words, 'You look lost' was conscious or unconscious. Being lost had been so much part of the therapy. I felt that our roles were reversed, which pleased me, as it meant that Mavis was in control again, not bewildered or lost as she had been. I drove home, when I had eventually tracked down the car, feeling rewarded by the outcome and also amused at Mavis's transparent and rather accurate view of the counsellor who cannot properly manage her own life.

Recurring losses

When we suffer a loss it invariably brings back other losses. It seems that even past losses, we thought we had integrated, can be reactivated by a current loss. Counsellors need to remember that they will not be only working with the loss presented to them currently, but a past history of losses, partly accepted or defended against.

Case Example | Rosemary: a reactivated loss

A client, Rosemary, who was held up at gunpoint in the course of her work at a bank, found that in the counselling sessions she was spending much of the time talking about her divorce, rather than the holdup. She came to see that the loss of security she had suffered at gunpoint reminded her of the awful loss of security she had suffered when her husband told her he wanted a divorce. Rosemary realized that she had never properly looked at these feelings, having pushed them away in the business of trying to make a new life for herself and the children. They were surfacing again now, when she felt so vulnerable, and without the emotional energy that it had taken to keep them firmly at bay.

Bowlby's work on loss is a reminder to counsellors that so much of our work, too, relates to client loss and in particular the loss of a close attachment figure. Sometimes the losses are hidden in other issues and we must try to be attuned to hidden pain. We also need to have an awareness that most of us prefer to be angry than sad, so that we can help the client to move on from a stuck position of bitterness. We also have to remember how we are shaped by the messages from our past experiences.

'Indeed, in preparing this volume nothing has impressed me more deeply than the evidence showing the pervasive influence at all ages of the pattern of a human being's family life on the way he responds to loss' (Bowlby, 1998, p. 439).

Comment

John Bowlby's work on attachment theory has had long-ranging institutional consequences, as he was unusual in the psychotherapeutic world in being more a researcher than a practitioner. Some critics said that his attachment theory was so at odds with orthodox concepts, that it could not be considered part of psychoanalytic thought. Bowlby's ideas were often met with hostility, but he was so passionate about children and families, with the role which disadvantage plays, that he was determined to be heard.

Critics suggest that students of object relations psychodynamic thought, in particular followers of Klein, are so obsessed with nurture that they do not take into account innate traits and genetic disposition. They say that Klein saw an individual's entire personality as the result of the relationship between the mother and the baby. Like John Stuart Mill earlier, Klein saw the baby as a 'tabula rasa', a blank slate on to which the mother writes the child's script for life.

However, this is not a fair criticism of the Object Relations school. There is a strong tradition from Freud onwards of examining biological drives and instincts. Bowlby is an example of a theorist, who, influenced by both Freud and Darwin, based his theory of relationships on the innate need to attach to another. In fact he was heavily criticized by Kleinian followers for being influenced by the findings of animal studies, anathema to his critics. Lorenz, Tinbergen and Harlow, with their diverse research on animals and birds, made their contribution to Bowlby's attachment theory.

Bowlby's ideas on attachment and separation had their genesis in ethological findings. If animals bond with mother for security and affiliation, how much more must human infants. As a baby attaches to his mother in the hope of belonging in a loving relationship, so humans repeat this process in relationships throughout life. Because of the emotional investment in attaching, when the relationship is severed for whatever reason, grief and mourning ensue.

Unlike Klein, who thought that mourning was a regression to an infantile stage and if prolonged could become pathological, Bowlby believed that the whole process of grief and mourning was a natural, healthy, adult response to separation and loss.

These ideas are very useful for counsellors working with separation and loss, which do not apply only to bereavement counsellors. If loss is regarded in broad terms it is relevant to virtually any counsellor, as most clients bring issues of loss. These include loss of marriage in divorce, work in redundancy, health in illness, children as they fly the nest. There are other more impenetrable losses of security, identity, status, self-respect and hope. There are many recent theoretical developments on loss and bereavement.

Bowlby was accused of caring only for the external world, and refusing to see the interrelationship between it and the internal world of the individual. This seems an unfair criticism. Reading Bowlby's three volumes on attachment there is passionate empathy for the inner despair of the child, separated from his attachment figure.

Maybe Bowlby is a good antidote to Klein who often disregarded the external world, because he did not see everything in phantasy terms. Bowlby described how in 1952 when he and James Robertson presented the film, 'A Two Year old Goes to Hospital', Anna Freud was very enthusiastic about it, but the Kleinians criticised it, refusing to see the child's distress as despair at separation from the parents. Instead they suggested it was a reaction to the mother being pregnant. Counsellors can learn from an integration of both inner and outer worlds. Certainly we owe a debt to Bowlby.

Further reading

Bowlby, J. (1971) *Attachment and Loss*. Volume 1. Attachment. London: Penguin Books.

Bowlby, J. (1975) *Attachment and Loss*. Volume 2. Separation: Anxiety and Anger. London: Penguin Books.

Bowlby, J. (1998) *Attachment and Loss*. Volume 3. Loss. Sadness and Depression. London: Pimlico.

Holmes, J. (1993) *John Bowlby and Attachment Theory*. London and New York: Routledge.

7
Legacies I: from Freud to feminism

The preceding chapters looked at the work of five classic theorists, which shaped the British School of Object Relations. For those, not closely acquainted with psychodynamic theory, it would be easy to believe that these ideas stopped with Bowlby's death in 1990. In fact so many interesting developments have been spawned from the theories, both alongside the lives of the theorists and since their deaths. This chapter will explore some of the developments that have particular relevance to relationships and understanding in counselling practice.

As we have seen in the examination of these theorists, they took their starting point from Freud, rather than Jung. Freud's ideas of the 'personal unconscious', Jung found 'banal and uninteresting'. 'All those personal things like incestuous tendencies and other childish tunes are mere surface; what the unconscious really contains are the great collective events of the time' (Jung, 1968, p. 182). Freud's very different ideas on conflict within the person and the importance of infantile development resonated strongly with the Object Relations theorists.

Though she diverted sharply from many key concepts, Klein had always called herself a Freudian. Freud had been a strong influence on Winnicott, Bion and Bowlby, though their evolved theories were diverse. Where the Object Relations School differed from Freud was in placing relationships, with oneself and others, at its core. This is why it is so pertinent to counselling.

The strengths these theorists brought to their work have been explored.

In this chapter, and the next, their influences are examined. Following the pattern of the preceding chapters I have arranged the developments under the name of the theorist most closely connected with the ideas.

This chapter examines the legacies of the two giants, Freud and Klein.

The legacy of Freud: neo-Freudians

In 1909 Freud went to America to give lectures at Clark University. He had been reluctant to leave his practice and only agreed to go when the honorarium was upped to $750 (a substantial sum, worth around $20,000 dollars today). Freud was accompanied by Jung, though the visit was to provoke the dissent that ended in a vituperative split.

Freud spoke off the cuff, and his lectures were well received, though they were in German, without translation. William James, the psychologist (brother of the writer Henry James), came over from Harvard to join the eminent audience.

In spite of the plaudits Freud gathered, he did not enjoy the States and never returned. He regarded America as 'a gigantic mistake'.

But although Freud disliked America, America took to Freud and to his daughter, Anna. The Neo-Freudian movement, which adapted Freudian theories away from the biology Freud emphasized, towards social and cultural factors was the result.

Anna Freud was lauded in the States as a Neo-Freudian. She spent much time there, especially for the last 30 years of her life. She lectured and taught the principles of her ego psychology.

Anna Freud (1895–1982) and ego psychology

As we have seen Anna Freud was groomed by her father to take on his mantle. From the start she had enjoyed a close relationship with him, in contrast to that with her mother, Martha. As the last child, 'it seems that by this time Martha, who had borne five children in 8 years, had had enough of infants'. 'Anna was bottle-fed and remembered her childhood as unhappy, left out by her siblings and envious of her mother's overt favouritism of her sister Sophie' (Appignanesi and Forrester, 1992). According to her father, she carried 'an age old jealousy' for her attractive sister (Gay, 1988). So when Sophie died in 1920, a devastating blow for Freud, whatever were Anna's feelings about her sibling's death, it meant for her exclusive access to her father.

Maybe Anna's experience of childhood ensured her empathy with children. She was successful in child psychoanalysis, which her father said, had received a powerful impetus 'through the work of Frau Melanie Klein and my daughter Anna Freud' (Gay, 1988).

Freud was proud of his clever daughter, who seemed happy to live vicariously in the shadow of her father. But her self-surrender served the Freud family well. In 1938, Anna was rounded up by the Gestapo. Armed with the Veronal (a barbiturate, which could be used as a suicide drug) which she always carried, she insisted on being seen by someone in authority. There she gave such a cool description of the work of the International Association that she was released. On her return her father was seen to weep for the first time. He at last announced that the family would leave Vienna (Appignanesi and Forrester, 1992).

Freud's relationship with Anna seems to have been both needy and authoritarian. Freud could not tolerate dissent so it is interesting to speculate on how he felt about the publication in 1937, 2 years before his death, of her influential book, *The Ego and Mechanisms of Defence.* This took a very different approach to the Ego, and challenged Freud's emphasis on the Id.

Anna Freud said that a much greater importance should be attached to the ego, or the conscious mind. 'Of the analysis of dream-symbolism she writes, "by translating symbols we may reveal the contents of the Id without really gaining any deeper understanding of the individual with whom we are dealing". It is therefore by the analysis of the ego's unconscious defence mechanisms that we can understand the transformations which the instincts have undergone' (Brown, 1961).

So the concept of the Id takes a second place in relation to the importance of the ego. The Id, the wild untameable part of ourselves is seen by Anna Freud as less useful to concentrate on, and to work with, than the rational thinking part. Anna Freud, unlike her father, worked with children, 'where negotiations with the here- and-now reality are central and where enhancing an individual's ability to cope with a destructive environment is often the only viable aim for therapy' (Frosh, 1999). (It could be said that this is also true of short-term counselling.)

While Anna Freud sees the study of the ego as the primary aim of therapy, there are some disadvantages. Frosh (1999) says the assumption is that the appropriate direction for development is always towards ego strength and adaptation to the environment. This is at the price of neglecting the irrationality of mental life. Anna Freud is less attuned to the unconscious factors, which disrupt even achieved positions.

Relevance to counselling

For long-term counselling, psychodynamic theory is invaluable in looking at the client's unconscious and working with its needs and desires.

For most short-term counselling, working with the conscious in the here and now is vital to meet the needs of the client. This is equally true for person-centred counsellors and CBT counsellors. However, this does not mean we must forget the client's past, particularly his infant past; or that we ignore themes and patterns in the client's life. And we are still aware of the unconscious processes, in particular the irrational thoughts and desires, which get in the way of rational conscious plans.

Case Example | Derek: wanting to please a dead father

Derek came to counselling for the contracted six sessions. He was a gay man in his thirties who said he was comfortable with his sexuality. He consequently could not understand why he felt unable to commit himself to his partner, Harry, who wanted them to live together in a stable relationship. Derek admitted that part of him wanted that too, but then felt 'panicky at the thought'.

The counsellor asked more about the 'panicky' feelings. Did he have them often? Derek replied, 'Not really, though they had been a feature of my adolescence.'

The counsellor asked Derek more about his adolescence. He replied that he had struggled with feelings about his sexuality then. The counsellor asked about support from his family and Derek replied that he had not told his parents and in any case his father had died suddenly of a heart attack when Derek was seventeen.

When the counsellor asked about the relationship that Derek had with his father it became clear that it was quite distant, with Derek respecting his father but being rather frightened of him. 'I hope you are not going to be one of those queers,' his father had said when Derek did not have a girl friend. 'Did that make you feel panicky?' asked the counsellor. 'I'll say!' replied Derek.

Over the remaining sessions Derek explored and began to understand what he had repressed about his father. He knew that his father would have disapproved of his being gay, and in particular his 'setting up house with another man'. Although he had not been conscious of it, he now realized that his father's approval had meant much to him. Though his father was long dead, Derek irrationally still wanted to please him. When Derek understood this he was more able to make a rational decision about his future.

Erik H. Erikson (1902–1994) and ego psychology

Erik Erikson met Anna Freud in Vienna, was analysed by her, and so began his passion for ego psychology. He became an ego psychologist who is primarily remembered for his adaptation of Sigmund Freud's five psychosexual stages of development and his interest in the question of identity.

Most commentators have suggested the link between his theoretical search for identity and his early life experience.

He was born in Frankfurt, of a Danish Jewish mother. There is some mystery about his biological father, who was probably Danish, but he took the name of his stepfather, whom his mother married when Erik was three. He became Erik Homburger.

He was a tall blonde blue-eyed boy, who was mocked for being Nordic by his Jewish peers, and for being Jewish by his classmates.

His Jewishness forced him to leave Germany on the rise to power of Hitler, and he settled in North America. Then he became an American citizen. He changed his name to Erik Erikson.

The twin perplexities about his parentage and his race seem to have driven him towards the search for identity.

Erikson's eight ages of man

Erikson (1965, p. 238) says, 'we must now recognise the place of identity in the human life cycle'.

He wrote the book, *Childhood and Society* in 1950. It has become a classic, not only for the psychological world but also for parents and carers. Erikson's interest in anthropology and sociology led him to study child-rearing practices across the world. He examines the balance between physical, emotional and social influences on the identity of the child.

Stage 1: Basic trust v. basic mistrust

This is the first stage of the eight ages of man and applies to the infant. As Winnicott famously said, 'There is no such thing as a baby.' The baby has to trust its carers that he will be safe. The amount of trust, says Erickson, relies on the quality of the maternal relationship. 'This forms the basis in the child for the sense of identity which will later combine the sense of "being all right", of being oneself, and of becoming what other people trust one will become' (1965). Parents must have faith in their ability to do the right thing by their child.

Stage 2: Autonomy v. shame and doubt

This is the stage of the toddler. Freud termed it the anal stage and Erikson also sees this as the stage of holding on and letting go, but he is not only speaking of toilet training. He sees the parents holding on to the child too tightly as repressive, too loosely as frightening for the child. Letting go can become an untethering of destructive forces, or a relaxed 'let it be'.

This stage, therefore, becomes decisive for the ratio of love and hate, cooperation and wilfulness, freedom of self-expression and its suppression. From a sense of self-control without loss of self-esteem comes a lasting sense of good will and pride; from a sense of loss of self-control and foreign over control comes a lasting propensity for doubt and shame. (Erikson, 1965, p. 245).

Stage 3: Initiative v. guilt

This is Freud's oedipal period and Erikson too thinks it can be a time of guilt. He sees the guilt as the child feeling he is failing to live up to his sense of his newly found morality. This can be experienced when he acts manipulatively and aggressively, or his jealous rages can lead to attacks on his siblings. This is against the pleasure he derives from wielding tools, manipulating toys and his emergent feelings of responsibility in caring for younger children.

Stage 4: Industry v. inferiority

This is the school stage for children in industrialized societies and in all cultures children receive some systematic instruction. (Erikson had studied simple societies.) It is Freud's latency period, and like Freud, Erikson thought this was the period where peer group affiliations and pressures are most important. Erikson sees this as a time when children can feel a strong sense of inadequacy and inferiority.

Erikson, unlike Freud, holds the view that all of childhood is a preparation for parenthood. He says of this stage, 'For before the child, psychologically already a rudimentary parent, can become a biological parent, he must begin to be a worker and potential provider' (1965, p. 250).

Stage 5: Identity v. role confusion

This is the stage of adolescence, a stage generally associated with role confusion and questions of identity. Childhood has come to an end: the young person has to cope with puberty, its body growth and genital maturity.

Erikson sees adolescent love as an attempt to arrive at identity through the projection of one's image of self on to another, and seeing it reflected and clarified. He says this is why so much of young love is conversation.

Stage 6: Intimacy v. isolation

The young adult, insisting on his search for identity, is eager and willing to fuse his identity with that of others. 'He is ready for intimacy, that is the capacity to commit himself to concrete affiliations and partnerships and to develop the ethical strength to abide by such commitments, even though they may call for significant sacrifices and compromises' (1965, p. 255).

The successful adult has to be able to face the fear of losing the ego in situations that call for self-abandonment, chiefly in the orgasms of sexual intercourse. Erikson says that the avoidance of such experiences, through the terror of the Id taking control, may lead to a deep sense of isolation and consequent self-absorption.

Stage 7: Generativity v. stagnation

This is the stage of mature adulthood, where marriage, having children and stabilizing one's situation in terms of job, and shelter are basic goals. The aspirational goals are a good career, a desirable house and the children being successful.

Erikson uses the term generativity to describe the tasks of the mature adult in establishing and guiding the next generation. The concept is meant to include, though not be replaced by, productivity and creativity. Mature man needs to be needed, and maturity needs guidance as well as encouragement from the younger generation, 'from what has been produced and must be taken care of' (1965, p. 258).

Stage 8: Integrity v. despair

This is the stage of late adulthood where children are grown, and the time when economic activity is being relinquished.

Only in him who in some ways has taken care of things and people and has adapted himself to the triumphs and disappointments adherent to being, the originator of others or the generator of products and ideas – only in him may gradually ripen the fruit of these seven stages. I know no better word for it than ego integrity.

(Erikson, 1965, p. 259)

In order to remain integrated the individual has to accept the reality of his life without regret or remorse. There are no second chances. The good parts should be remembered with pleasure.

The loss of the accrued ego integration is signified by the fear of death. Despair expresses the feeling that life is too short and there is no time to try out alternate ways to reach integration. In order to remain integrated the individual has to accept the reality of death without the fear or disgust, which can mar the adoption of the notion that this is the end of life as it has been lived.

Relevance to counselling

Erikson's eight stages are useful to the counsellor, particularly for those counsellors working with clients having difficulties with developmental stages. Erikson's emphasis on all stages of development, away from Freud's preponderance on the infantile is useful, particularly for clients with identity issues. Also the idea of building on stages in order to feel integrated is helpful. The adult client who behaves like a child may need help in working on the stages he has 'missed out'. He may need to work on his feelings of inferiority in the presence of his peers or take more responsibility and initiate actions.

However it must be remembered that Erikson, in spite of the experience gained in studying other cultures, was writing primarily for a North American market. Words such as autonomy, initiative, industry, role confusion, isolation connect with industrialized nations and in particular the attainment of the 'American Dream'. The Sioux indigenous Americans, whom Erikson studied, with their emphasis on family and people rather than individualism, would not recognize autonomy or isolation.

For Erikson it does seem that the individual's meeting the mores of the culture suggests good mental health. But as Frosh says, 'Erikson's concern with society actually drifts into a legitimation of it: the problems that individuals experience occur because they are dislocated from their culture, not that the culture itself may be disturbed' (1999).

Perhaps the counsellor should bear this in mind, being aware of the importance of cultural influences while recognizing that not all are benign.

Developments of the Oedipus complex

We have seen in the work of Erikson his adaptation of Freud's psychosocial stages including the Oedipus complex, which Freud put at the heart of his theory. You will remember that Freud, steeped in his classical education, took the narrative from the Greek myth of Oedipus, a man destined to murder his father and marry his mother. Freud used it to symbolize the rivalry between the growing boy for the love of his mother and the resentment, even hatred of his father. In therapy it can be a metaphor, for example, illustrating the frustration and envy of the employee locked out of the decisions of his bosses. Power as well as sexuality is a significant factor. It is useful to see how this original notion of Freud's has been developed by others to provide material for different interpretations of triangular relationships. We shall next look at how Fairbairn highlights the consequences and alternatives to parental abandonment, while Britton looks at how the oedipal threesome can offer the child the challenge of an integrated self.

Ronald Fairbairn and the relationship between parents and children

Ronald Fairbairn (1889–1964) was an Object Relations theorist, heavily influenced by Freud, but dissenting from many of his theories. He was a Scot from a strict Calvinist background who spent most of his life in Edinburgh, training first as a doctor then a psychoanalyst.

His private life was difficult, a conflicted relationship with his wife, together with the trauma of twins who died at birth. Gomez (1997) suggests that their youngest son, Nicholas, who became 'an eccentric and cynical Conservative politician' suffered particularly badly from his parents' disintegrating relationship during his formative years.

Fairbairn was at first a lone figure, with little support either personally or professionally. He was a shy man, tortured by the same neurotic symptom that his father had, an inability to urinate when others were nearby. His anxiety in this situation could reach suicidal proportions (Gomez, 1997).

Fairbairn (1952) had a different perspective on the Oedipal myth, which contrasted with that of Freud. He said that the significance of the myth was not, as Freud said, about avoiding patricide and incest, but the abandonment of Oedipus, by his parents on the hillside, which was intended to lead to infanticide. For Fairbairn the meaning of the legend was not about sexual rivalry within the family, but about the relationship between parents and children. On the one hand, there is the opportunity for hate and cruelty, and on the other, love and security.

This interpretation may reflect Fairbairn's own feelings of isolation and abandonment. The work he carried out was primarily with people who were in many ways abandoned to their fate – traumatized soldiers, sexually abused children and psychotic patients and offenders.

Relevance to counselling

For counsellors, Fairbairn's most useful idea based on the relationship of parents and children and its replication in the consulting room is his notion of a 'real relationship'.

Fairbairn was adamant that change could only come about if the patient and therapist met in reality, rather than in the phantasy of the transference relationship which Freud pursued. For Fairbairn a successful outcome to therapy was the result of a real, meaningful relationship.

This suggests that the client can be angry with the counsellor, and like a good parent the counsellor can hold him emotionally. Challenging the client, which may be uncomfortable for both parties, is necessary if the client is to work through difficult material. As Casement 1990 says, it is not enough to be a 'better parent'. The client does not need to experience an idealized counsellor but a real person, warts and all, who is doing her best to be with the client and will sometimes get it wrong. Then the client can find it helpful to test out his feelings of anger from the past relationship with his father, with a counsellor who can both accept his anger and contain it.

Ronald Britton and the observer in the triangular relationship

Ronald Britton is a practising post Kleinian theorist who emphasizes the depth of loss we experience in being excluded from our parent's sexual relationship, within the oedipal triangle.

Britton was born in 1932 to a large extended family in Cumbria, not far from Wordsworth's birthplace. He became a doctor, then a psychiatrist and finally trained to be a psychoanalyst, where he was supervised by Hannah Segal. He worked at the Tavistock Clinic with children and parents and in his writings stressed the role of fathers, which Freud had done, as well as mothers, on whom Kleinians had placed their emphasis. (You will remember Klein's daughter's challenge to her mother, 'Where is the father in your work?') Britton's theoretical writings included examples from poetry, in particular his fellow countryman, Wordsworth (Sayers, 2000).

To guard against the voyeurism of others, particularly as he still sees patients, Britton publicly says little about himself. He is also scrupulous in protecting patients' anonymity (Sayers, 2000). This is always an important consideration for counsellors: to be assiduous in preserving the trust and confidentiality of the client.

Britton was particularly interested in the clinical implications of the oedipal complex. As a Kleinian he examined the effect on the self and its relationship with others. He argued that the child begins to recognize the difference between the parents' genital and procreative relationship, and the parent–child relationship. 'This recognition produces a sense of loss and envy, which, if not tolerated, may become a sense of grievance and self denigration' (1989). However if is able to be tolerated, it can lead to a way of thinking about self-knowledge and insight. He suggests that if the child can hold in his mind the link between the parents 'perceived in love and hate', it provides him with a 'prototype for an object relationship' in which he is the observer. This also means that he can imagine himself being observed. It suggests that we have the capacity to be able to observe how others see us and be able to hold both our own points of view as well as theirs, 'for reflecting on ourselves whilst being ourselves' (Britton, 1989).

Sometimes the oedipal relationship is viewed as a stalemate. Intergenerational parents and children have no means of communicating their adult feelings, other than falling back on the needy child intruding on the sexual exclusion of the parents. Britton's notion of toleration of the conflicting feelings of the child can change this view. If the child or adolescent can hold the loss and envy he carries for the genital relationship of his parents on the one hand, while accepting the loving feelings his parents offer on the other, he can achieve some integration.

This makes the child in the triangle an active participant in a situation, which could lead him to greater independence and a stronger sense of self.

Relevance to counselling

For practitioners the idea of the Oedipal triangle is a useful one. In couple counselling, the couple make a threesome with the counsellor. Couple counsellors are trained to look at the collusion they may be entering into with one of the partners, perhaps joining with one to become new parents, and leaving the other, the locked out child.

Counsellors, working with an individual client, who brings an absent partner 'into the room', can also learn from the Oedipal triangle. Whether the partner is dead, separated, or the object of the client's fury, anxiety or wroth, it is important for the counsellor to be aware of this hidden dynamic and not be seduced into collusion or affiliation. Criticism, reassurance or approval could be the unwary counsellor's response.

Case Example | Clive: return to the Oedipal stage

Clive came to counselling because he found it difficult to maintain relationships with women. The beginning of the relationship would be, 'Wonderful, then it would go downhill'. The counsellor discovered that Clive idealized his girl friends to start with, then began to feel they had 'things wrong with them'. The counsellor probed and found that most of the 'things wrong with them' were connected to their relationships with ex-boyfriends. The counsellor worked psychodynamically, so she suspected that Clive's difficulties might be connected to the oedipal period. When she asked about his relationships with his parents Clive, an only child, said he always wanted to be with his mother but his mother often 'fobbed me off. She wanted to be with my dad.' When the counsellor asked Clive to remember his feelings about this he replied, 'I was mad with my dad. And with my mum. I felt left out.'

The counsellor acknowledged Clive's sadness, but was careful not to collude and criticize his parents. Over the time of the counselling Clive came to understand that he was transferring his fury and envy from his frustration at being excluded from the parental relationship, to the girlfriends' relationships with their ex-boyfriends. He admitted, 'I can't bear to think of them together having sex.'

When the counsellor asked who 'them' was, 'parents or girlfriends', Clive thought for a long time and then said, 'Both.'

With the understanding came some tolerance. Clive is trying to work through his frustration and envy, while acknowledging the love and care his parents gave him. He does not want a life consumed with bitterness.

Siblings and the Oedipus complex

The Oedipus complex posits a threesome: yet does this suppose an only child or serial threesomes with the current youngest child in the family? What about the siblings?

It seems that this phantasy only-child relationship has not been fully explored until now and it is two mothers who have considered it important enough to do so. Recent works by Juliet Mitchell and Prophecy Coles have highlighted the place of siblings. They both agree that the role siblings play within the dynamics of families have been underplayed within psychoanalytic theory.

As we have seen Klein, Winnicott, Bion and Bowlby stressed the dyad of the mother–child relationship, with both fathers and siblings alienated from it. If we look at the Oedipus triangle, the father is present, but the siblings are absent.

> My mother and father and I were always three, and we were always happy . . . . 'A perfect trinity of love'.
> (Iris Murdoch, quoted by Conradi in Coles, 2003, p. 33)

The oedipal triangle is rarely depicted in such glowing terms, but in Iris Murdoch's case, it was exclusive. Coles says, 'If we give Oedipus the central role in psychic development we do not need siblings' (Coles, 2003, p. 2). She holds the view that we cannot understand our psychic life without the presence of others. As an object relationship theorist she, like Fairbairn with his emphasis on 'real relationships', perceives siblings as 'real events', placing less importance on siblings as internal phantasy objects. She contends that they play a significant part in our development. 'The feelings we have towards our siblings have an important place in the complexity of our emotional life, and to dismiss their significance is to impoverish our internal world' (2003, p. 2).

Maybe theorists see the place of siblings in terms of their own experience. Freud's view was that all sibling relationships are based upon 'primal hatred'. As a child he did not seem to have much connection with his siblings; perhaps he suspected they resented his being the golden boy. His sister Anna may not have forgiven the banishing of her piano when it interfered with his studies. Freud's 'partner in crime' (Wollheim, 1971) was John, a year older, but in fact Freud's nephew. In *The Interpretation of Dreams* Freud referred to all his friends being 'reincarnations' of the 'first figure (John)' in the 'phantasied childhood scene' (1900).

Coles cites Melanie Klein as an example of someone who had 'deep passionate love' for her siblings. As we have seen earlier this was certainly true of her brother Emmanuel whom Grosskurth describes as Klein's 'phantom lover' (1986, p. 39). Coles cites Klein's writing in 1932 that 'the existence of sexual relations between children, especially between brothers and sisters . . . may influence the child's general development favourably' as rooted in her own experience (2003, p. 4). Whether it was 'favourable' is debatable. Klein suffered cruelly under Emmanuel's manipulative influence, yet was devastated when he died.

Many of us will have observed the primal hatred when the elder child is dethroned, 'Lock her in a cupboard', 'Don't feed him' and the physical attacks of pinches and slaps. But the other side of the hate coin seems to quickly establish itself, with a proprietary protection and later collaborative relationships: love and hate alternate.

Relevance to counselling

For counsellors it is important to hold the client's siblings in mind. First because where the client is placed in relation to siblings is pertinent. When a sibling arrives how the first child is able to manage the transition has long-lasting consequences. Clients can come to counselling in midlife, never having resolved their resentment as the elder child being displaced, or the envy of the heir, by the second born. The eldest child is often given responsibility beyond his years, which he finds hard to throw off; the youngest may be indulged as the last child from the parent's loins and feels he has a charmed life, so finding obstacles impossible; the middle child may have felt he has to fight for a place. Counsellors will have clients who are stuck in an infantile battle with a sibling and cannot own adulthood. Other clients may make great sacrifices for siblings, which can cause fractured marital relationships. Siblings hold the memory. They are the persons who will have known you longest. When parents die they are the only link to the childhood past.

Mitchell and an anthropological perspective on siblings

Professor Juliet Mitchell is a psychoanalyst, feminist and specialist in gender studies. In emphasizing the importance of siblings, she highlights the lateral relationships within families, that is sibling to sibling, as against the usual 'vertificalization' of parent and child. The latter, she says, is normally associated with male dominance and patriarchy.

It is also associated with the Oedipus complex, which concerns two parents and a child. A question long raised is whether the Oedipus complex is a world wide or ethnocentric concept.

In the 1920s, the anthropologist, Bronislaw Malinowski, argued with the Freudian, Ernest Jones, against the universality of the Oedipal complex. Malinowski maintained that the incest taboo between brothers and sisters can be stronger than that between parent and child (Mitchell, 2003, preface).

Malinowski had studied the Trobriand Islanders, a matrilineal people in whom the line is traced through the mother. In such societies the woman marries a man outside the family, but usually stays within her family of origin, under the protection of her brother. Her husband stays with his own family, offering protection to his sister. The married couple meet to eat and sleep with each other. When they have a child, the responsibility for the child rests with the uncle, the social father.

(I observed this when I taught in Ghana in the 1970s, female students from matrilineal Ashanti villages said that their uncles paid their school fees, sometimes reluctantly. This still happens today, particularly in rural areas.)

Does the child whose uncle is his 'father', who may rarely meet his biological father and not together with his mother, experience an oedipal conflict? If the Oedipus conflict is universal perhaps he must experience it wholly at an unconscious level with no conscious reinforcement.

Malinowski argued that in a matrilineal society the boy feels hostility to his uncle, so the Oedipal conflict cannot exist in its classic form. Henrietta Moore (2007, p. 139) says that many anthropologists took the view that Malinowski made a major contribution, by showing the existence of an alternative Oedipus conflict. However, she says that others believed Malinowski understood little of psychoanalytic theory. Their view was that developed hostility to the uncle, as father, and incestuous desires for his sister, as mother, is evidence for a strong Oedipus complex. In effect Malinowski had confirmed its basic principles.

(I imagine a similar case could be made for adoptive parents in a Western society.)

Moore contends that 'the general position on the Oedipus complex in anthropology now is a loose consensus that a "family romance" in some sense must be universal, but that its content is cross-culturally variable and open to empirical investigation' (p. 140).

Mitchell (2003) says that Freud argued that in order to marry a wife, a man needs to know in childhood that he cannot marry his mother. She suggests that he also needs to know he cannot marry his sister, if he is to eventually marry his sister's psychological successor. But do we marry someone who resembles our sister or brother?

This is perhaps the ideal situation, says Mitchell. To marry someone who is like the prohibited sibling whom we may have had childhood incestuous desires towards, but is also like ourselves, though not too alike. People say, 'he's married his mother'; maybe he has married his sister.

Mitchell believes that siblings are essential in any social structure and psychically in social relationships, including parents and children, but she maintains that siblings have been left out of the picture in our preoccupation with vertical interaction. She asks why we have not considered that lateral relations in love and sexuality, and hate and war have needed a theoretical paradigm. 'Siblings and femininity have a similar overlooked destiny' (2003, p. 4).

Relevance to counselling

When clients come to counselling and complain of a spouse's behaviour, it is often because the spouse is not enough like them. At the beginning of a relationship couples can revel in the fact that they are so different. There is an excitement that one desires a lover who is dissimilar. 'We're like chalk and cheese', the couple may say wonderingly. But as the relationship grows and they make a commitment to each other, there is also a desire to be one.

The wife who rails against her husband because he does not talk, when she wants to talk, is really saying, 'I want him to be so much part of me that he would know what I want, and give it to me, without my having to ask.' This hoped for symbiosis has to be understood by the couple, and its yearning for fusion tested against the reality of a coupling of two different people.

Feminism and psychoanalysis

Mitchell is lauded for her work on feminism. In 1974 she offered a major challenge to the feminist position on Freud with her book, *Psychoanalysis and Feminism*.

Freudian theory had been criticized for its assumptions that women are inferior and that they can only be defined through men. The theory of penis envy renders women perpetually lacking and subordinate. But the theory of penis envy can also be read in a more general way, as a resentment against powerlessness. For Freud was writing against a backdrop of women subservient to men in all walks of life, together with an almost universal assumption that they should be. Viewed in this light Freud looks positively liberal. When the subject of whether women could be elected to the Vienna Psychoanalytical Society was raised in 1910, Freud said he would 'see it as a serious inconsistency if we were to exclude women on principle' (Appignanesi and Forrester, 1992, p. 194).

To his credit Freud did encourage woman to become analysts and could be supportive to the chosen ones. However, it seems he would have no truck with Melanie Klein, perhaps because he thought her too much a threat. In contrast to Klein who became so powerful, he thought highly of Hermine Hug-Hellmuth, the 'forgotten' first child analyst. In 1911 Freud recommended a paper of hers to Jung, 'I have received a splendid, really illuminating paper about colour audition from an intelligent lady PhD. It solves the riddle with the help of our psychoanalysis.' It seems Hermine Hug-Hellmuth was regarded as creating a scandal through being murdered by her nephew in 1924, and so was lost to obscurity in a psychoanalytic movement looking for respectability (Appignanesi and Forrester, 1992, p. 196).

However, the women who became analysts, and his rich, interesting women patients were a breed apart. Freud's ideal of womanhood was a woman who was passive and feminine. 'A robust woman who in case of need can single-handed throw her husband and servant out of doors was never my ideal, however much there is to be said for a woman being in perfect health. What I have always found attractive is someone delicate whom I could take care of' (quoted in Appegnanesi and Forrester, 1992, p. 53). Freud's wife Martha wore the mantle of Freud's ideal of womanhood apparently happily. It seems that Freud's patients did not fit the mould so willingly.

Critics also castigate psychoanalytic theorists for reducing women to a one-role relationship, that of mother. Women have no identity other than being defined by children. They also bear the responsibility for child rearing and are to blame if the child turns out badly. Both Klein and Winnicott stressed women's role as mother, to the exclusion of any other. Yet paradoxically Winnicott had two wives who never became mothers and Klein, who had three children, found the role of mother difficult and was unhappy within it.

Counteracting classic notions, some of the most recent advances in psychodynamic thought have come from feminist theorists. There has been a redefinition of women's identity by writers such as Mitchell and Chodorow. Feminist writers have also explored gender issues, as well as the question of sexual orientation, topics never fully examined in classic psychoanalytic thought.

Feminists in the mid-twentieth century were mainly hostile to Freud seeing the spread of psychoanalytic theory as a major factor in the oppression of women. Simone de Beauvoir in her book *The Second Sex* (1949) was heavily critical. She believed that Freud saw women not as subjects with their own rational desires, but as objects dependent on the whims of men. She says witheringly, 'Freud never showed much concern with the destiny of woman; it is clear that he simply adapted his account from that of the destiny of man, with slight modifications' (1949).

Betty Friedan in *The Feminine Mystique* (1963) although praising Freud for his genius, criticized him for being a prisoner of his time. 'Much of what Freud described as characteristic of human nature was merely characteristic of certain middle class European men and women at the end of the nineteenth century.'

But Mitchell (2000), controversially, contends that these feminists missed the significance of the unconscious, narcissism and the different female experience of the Oedipus conflict. She sees psychoanalysis as imperative in the understanding and challenging of female oppression, with Freud's writings as acute observations and comprehension of the status of women in a patriarchal society.

From her psychoanalytic reading, alongside anthropology, Mitchell suggests that because women had to marry outside the family in order to avoid incest, patriarchy and capitalism were upheld in the establishment of the nuclear family. The man entered 'class dominated structures' while the woman stayed bound by family and children.

Mitchell says that Freud in his investigation of the Viennese bourgeoisie found that although limited to place and class, and specific to the psychic make-up of man under capitalism it was generalizable to human culture. Freud had examined the eternal structure of patriarchy and its effect on the family

> Instead of lamenting the specifics of Freud's milieu, we should rejoice – nothing could be more useful.
>
> (Mitchell, 2000)

Relevance to counselling

Case Example | Susi: the counsellor learns about diversity

June was a trainee counsellor who had just joined a women's organization. She was thirty, married to a man from the same office she worked in, saving up for a house and a baby.

One of her first clients was Susi, a lesbian woman, anxious about her long-term relationship, as she wanted a baby and her partner was reluctant.

June felt very anxious as Susi told her story. She had never met anyone who called herself lesbian before, and immediately felt out of her depth.

But she listened carefully to Susi's story and began to see that Susi wanted the same thing as she did, a baby; but it seemed that Susi's path to motherhood looked as if it could be more difficult than her own.

Susi also talked about feminism, and the place of women, and how significant it was; something June had never really thought about.

But again June listened very carefully and realized that she was learning something important. Susi saw that June was struggling to get into a world new to her, and appreciated her efforts.

As the counselling continued June was able to offer the support and understanding, which Susi needed.

Case Example | (Continued)

June felt she must learn more about the things in which Susi had educated her. She realized that the role women played was crucial, particularly for the women she saw grappling with little money, children and no supportive partner. To be a good counsellor she saw you had to understand and be available to people who were not just like you. This meant an awareness and understanding of diversity – race, class, religion, sexual orientation and colour. 'Can't believe I've had my head in the sand so long,' said June.

The legacy of Klein on child development theory and practice

Melanie Klein started the move away from Freud's emphasis on the older child, 3 to 5 years, within the Oedipus complex, as the bedrock of future development. She relocated the seminal relationship to a much earlier stage, the newborn baby. Klein, Winnicott and Bion and Bowlby all fix the mother–baby interaction as the harbinger of future relationships. This is particularly useful for counsellors as it can aid understanding of the adult client. It can also be a metaphor for, or replicate the counsellor – client relationship.

Infant observation: The Tavistock model

Esther Bick (1902–1983) was a disciple of Klein. When she introduced Infant Observation at the Tavistock Clinic in 1948, she devised a method for studying babies, which is now used all over the world.

(Reid, 1997)

The observations take place in the baby's home. Ideally the observer meets the parents before the baby is born, and as soon after birth as possible, visits the baby for an hour each week, on the same day at the same time, replicating the analytic frame. The observer is told not to take notes during the hour, but afterwards to record as much detail as she can remember. The emphasis is on what is seen and felt, and not to hypothesize.

The student is encouraged and supported to see what is there to be seen and not to look for what they think should be there.

(Reid, 1997, p. 1)

It is surprising how dismaying it is to be required only to see and feel. One is so used to attaching premature meanings to any observation and almost feels negligent for not doing so. When I was a student at the Tavistock Clinic, I found beginning the baby observation the most testing part of the programme. Without the usual markers and guidelines I realized that I relied on, I felt naked. In the study group where we discussed our sense of the observations, I saw I was not alone. Group members were knowledgeable professionals, and to 'not know' was a salutary experience for us all.

However, the learning was immense. Apart from getting in touch with a baby beginning to make sense of his world, one inevitably made contact with the infantile part of oneself. I found this both frightening and enlightening.

As this method of infant observation has spread, although it was developed for training purposes, it is now beginning to be used for research. This is particularly useful for as Reid says, 'the method of writing up these observations has required observational and narrative description, largely uncontaminated, at the data collection and recording stage, by theoretical conceptualisation' (1977, p. 177).

Briggs (in Reid, 1997, p. 207) has carried out research on infants at potential risk. This demonstrates how effective this method could be to the wider caring professions.

Participant observation

Participant observation is necessarily less objective because of the observer's relationship with the observed. However, the following is enlightening as a detailed personal account, which highlights the influence of object relations' ideas on child development theory.

Charles Fernyhough, a developmental psychologist, charted the journey of his daughter Athena from birth to three, using his own observations and matching them against current developmental science.

He describes Athena at 4 months old:

People come and go. There is a tall person whose clothes open at the front at mealtimes and an even taller one who has no such talent . . . . The breast one is in a hurry. Athena watches with one eyebrow curled in puzzlement as the breast one leaves and then immediately comes back in .... Not-Breast is sitting at the desk ... Breast finds what she has mislaid and goes out through the door. Athena is almost completely immobile, her limbs made useless by incoherent routings from motor cortex to musculature.

(p. 49)

Athena lifts up the rattle in her hand and roots at it shaking her head rapidly from side to side before contact, like an attacking Rottweiler. She gets no comfort from it, and tries instead to suckle at the cushion she is propped against. The cushion is dry and rough. She looks at the door. The vanishing of Breast is associated with it somehow ... Associations that she couldn't have made, even a few weeks ago are now marking paths through the chaos. At a hundred and twenty days of age, she has the necessary tools: vastly improved perception of space and depth, greater visual acuity and colour vision that is as good as any adult's. Her neonatal synaesthesia has receded, and things are starting to appear as they really are.

(p. 50)

These observations are intriguing to the lay parent. For the professional, the mix of intimate detail and neuroscience is an arresting combination.

Jealousy in infants

My analytic work has shown me that envy (alternating with feelings of love and gratification) is first directed to the feeding breast. To this primary envy jealousy is added when the Oedipus situation arises.

(Klein, 1957, p. 79)

Recent research confirms Klein's contention of the infant's jealousy of another, who has captured the mother's attention. Klein was primarily seeing the father as the object of jealousy, but this research suggests that the baby's jealousy is directed at anyone who threatens the exclusivity of the mother–child relationship.

Riccardo Draghi-Lorenz of the University of Surrey has studied the emotional development of babies in their first 12 months. Speaking at an international conference he said that some parents reported observing jealousy in babies as young as 4 months. 'Video recordings of babies showed that as soon as they can control their bodies they may, for example squeeze in between the mother and another person, pushing away and sometimes even hitting the latter.'

He asked mothers of 5-month-old babies to show affection towards another baby in front of their own child. 'This was usually watched intently. Within five minutes more than half of their babies were so upset they cried. This did not happen when the mother simply spent five minutes chatting to another adult' (Simon Bowers, The Guardian, 18 July 2000).

This was widely reported in the media, a good example of how psychodynamic theory can be useful to the general public.

The first relationship

Daniel Stern, in 2002, wrote a new introduction to a book published in 1977, based on his research, in the late 1960s, observing mothers and babies. He said, 'I was astonished to find in it almost all the ideas that have guided my work in the subsequent decades.' These ideas were first, to view the mother and baby in natural surroundings; second, find new methods, scaled down and adjusted to the split-second, nonverbal interaction of mother and baby; and third, monitor 'mutual regulation', attempts by both mother and baby to regulate the baby's momentary state, for example hunger, excitement. For this he used portable television and movie cameras, so that he could freeze frame, look in slow motion, and review (2002, pp. 1–2).

Stern proposed that the internal world of the infant was made up of the basic units of repeated interactive sequences with the caregiver, which was generalized to form RIGS (representations of interactions that have been generalized). John Bowlby (1971) called them 'internal working models'. These, of course, are profoundly different perspectives from those of Klein.

Stern disagreed with Freud and Klein who 'described the phases of psychological development in terms of some later form of psychopathology'. He thought they were 'wrong headed'. 'A young infant in the proposed "normal" phase of primary narcissism should, according to that theory, be largely uninterested in and inattentive to the external world and minimally attracted and related to other human beings. But quite the opposite is true when you observe real babies. They seek external stimulation. They have clear preferences for certain stimuli. They attend carefully. This is especially true when the external stimulus is human. They engage their caregivers fiercely, avidly' (2002, p. 8).

Depressed mothers

Sue Gerhardt, a psychoanalytical psychotherapist, agrees with Stern that the babies of normal mothers, experience very few negative states. She too questions Kleinian theory that babies are innately full of greed and envy, but thinks it more likely that negative emotions are associated with abnormal experience of the mother–baby relationship; interesting because Klein herself found her own babies difficult. One wonders how much her personal experience coloured her theories. She did admit to feeling depressed, particularly after her daughter's, Melinda, birth, and we know they never had a good relationship.

Gerhardt says of babies of depressed mothers:

> They don't have the normal left hemisphere predominance that other babies have, even at times when they look quite happy playing. These babies with less left frontal activity have been described as less affectionate and less likely to approach their mother whilst playing. It may be because the mother's own left frontal brain is less active, she cannot stimulate her baby's left frontal brain.
>
> (2004, p. 122)

A study (Cohn et al., 1990) cited by Gerhardt found that depressed mothers offer few positive interactions. About 40 per cent of the time they are unresponsive or disengaged, while much of the remaining time they are angry, intrusive and rough with their babies. When the mother is being overtly or covertly angry the babies look away a lot. Babies make the most protest when their mother's attention is switched off, as if this is more unbearable than maltreatment (2004, p. 124).

Gerhardt develops Bowlby's notion of internal working models.

> They are models of one's self *with* another person; models of interaction between people, not static internal mages of 'mother' or 'father'. This means that the inner pictures that we draw on to guide our behaviour are images that conjure up how it *feels* to be with another person.
>
> (2004, p. 148)

Because babies have to rely on their parents for an internal working model, how they feel about themselves will depend on how they are treated. Critical or emotionally absent parents will result in babies feeling themselves to be bad.

Using different concepts, Klein would agree with the result, a damaged child.

Comment

As we have seen the trajectory of some of Freud's legacies was away from his biological focus, moving into cultural and social arenas. His daughter started the process with her rejection of the primacy of the unconscious Id, in favour of the rational ego.

This led to the search for identity, a project that was seized on in the United States with theorists, for example, Erikson, offering a template for life.

Meanwhile in Britain, Fairbairn was abandoning the biological heart of the Oedipus complex in favour of a social and cultural explanation of the relationship between parents and children. Opportunities for love and security vie with hate and cruelty. How they are resolved has a lasting influence on the child's future.

Whether the Oedipus complex is a universal phenomenon has long been the source of disagreement. Ten years before Freud's death anthropologists and psychoanalysts were arguing over it. Anthropologists today suggest that a family romance in some sense must be universal, though it is cross-culturally variable.

The Oedipal triangle posts a threesome, but where are the siblings? The role of siblings has been underplayed within the psychoanalytic literature. Freud seems to have had little to do with his own siblings and wrote that all sibling relationships are based on primal hatred. Today Mitchell and Coles in their different examinations of sibling relationships contend that there are other complex emotions and behaviours. Siblings play an influential part in our social patterns and emotional lives.

Mitchell offers a feminist perspective on psychoanalysis, which is at odds with earlier feminists in the mid-twentieth century. Writers such as Simone de Beauvoir thought that the spread of psychoanalytic theory was a major factor in the oppression of women. In antithesis, Mitchell maintains that psychoanalysis is imperative in the understanding and challenging of female oppression.

Critics have also castigated psychoanalytic theorists for reducing women to a one-role identity. Klein stressed women's role as mother, to the exclusion of any other. Yet paradoxically Klein, who had three children, found the role of mother difficult and was unhappy within it.

But what Klein achieved in theoretical terms was to start the move away from Freud's emphasis on the older child within the Oedipus complex, as the bedrock of future development. She relocated the seminal relationship to a much earlier stage, the newborn baby, fixing the mother–baby interaction as the harbinger of future relationships. For therapists, this insight into how the past may inform the present can aid understanding of the adult client. It can also be a metaphor for the therapist–client relationship.

Since Klein, observations of babies' emotional behaviour have become more sophisticated. From the Tavistock method of an observer watching a baby without any intervention, to filming actions and responses and realizing brain imagery. Gerhardt and Stern disagree with Klein that normal babies are full of envy and greed. They think that it is more likely that negative feelings are connected to abnormal experiences in the mother–child relationship.

Further reading

Erikson, E. H. (1965) *Childhood and Society*. Harmondsworth: Penguin Books.

Mitchell, J. (2000) *Psychoanalysis and Feminism: A Radical Reassessment of Freudian Psychoanalysis*. New York: Basic Books.

Mitchell, J. (2003) *Siblings*. Cambridge: Polity Press.

Reid, S. (ed.) (1997) *Developments in Infant Observation. The Tavistock Model*. Hove: Routledge.

Stern, D. N. (2002) *The First Relationship*. Cambridge, MA: Harvard University Press.

8
Legacies II: developments in attachment theory

This chapter examines the legacies of Winnicott, Bion and Bowlby. All three drew on the work of Freud and Klein, whose influence is discussed in more detail in the previous chapter. Their influences have particular relevance to counsellors in the demonstration of the practical application of the theory.

The legacy of Winnicott

Too-good mothering

Winnicott was adamant that most mothers were 'good enough'. He believed that too-well-adapted mothering was detrimental to the baby. 'The mother who persists in anticipating her baby's needs before he even recognizes them himself, may be experienced as a witch' (1965).

Juliet Hopkins, in the 1990s, using the Tavistock infant observation method, studied Louise, from 6 days old to 18 months. For comparison she observed Janet, when she and Louise were both 50 weeks old. A follow-up visit was made to Louise when she was 6 years old.

At 6 days Hopkins observed Louise, contented and in perfect harmony with her mother. This was the period of primary maternal preoccupation, which Winnicott says is essential for the baby to feel secure through the mother's identification; an extreme state, which lasts a few weeks. What Hopkins observed, though, was that for Louise's mother the state went on indefinitely. When Louise was 15 weeks and indicating attempts at separation, pulling away from mother, and to the observer making a clear bid for independence, it was thwarted. Mother picked up the cue that

Louise wanted to lie kicking, on the carpet, and immediately got down beside her to play.

This was to be the pattern. As Hopkins says, 'She seemed to want Louise's life to be an idyll in which there was no room for conflict, dissatisfaction or anger' (1996). It was up to Louise to assert herself. She would wake screaming in the night, perhaps an indication of the rage at her mother's intrusions and over identification. Her mother said she was not resentful as she shared Louise's distress. Louise refused the breast and weaned herself at seven months. Her mother found it painful, but felt she must always respond to Louise's lead.

Hopkins wanted to evaluate Louise's development, so observed her in parallel with a second baby, Janet, a child whose mother could be 'termed good enough'. Both at 50 weeks were greeting their mothers after a brief separation.

Janet was a child brought up in a family where she had an older sibling and was no stranger to frustration. In contrast to Louise she enthusiastically greeted her mother's return with a wet kiss, although her sister got there first. Louise in contrast turned her head away when her mother made to pick her up in greeting. Later, she sat passively waiting for her mother's initiative. While acknowledging innate differences in temperament, it does seem that the too-good mothering Louise received resulted in her being developmentally behind.

Hopkins says, 'Unlike Janet, she had not yet begun to give affection.' When the observation finished at 18 months, although Louise enjoyed receiving cuddles she still did not initiate them.

Hopkins cites (Demos 1986), a developmental psychologist. 'Demos points out that a baby who is comforted at once has no chance to become aware of what has upset her, or of the intention and desire to mend it, and no means to discover how to put it right.'

This passivity, though not valued in Western culture, is valued in other cultures. I have observed that some African cultures feel it important not to let a baby cry and encourage them to be passive. This is where family and dependence are valued as against individualism and independence. Particularly where polygynous marriages are the norm, compliant, nonrebellious children ease the difficulties that might otherwise arise between competitive wives.

Louise's mother continued to adapt to her. Unlike Janet, who had been told 'No' at an early age, Louise's mother continued to second-guess Louise's needs, so that rebellion was nigh impossible. However, at the age of 15 months Louise refused for 3 weeks to eat anything except milk and bananas. Her mother complied with this new diet without a fuss.

Louise then refused to eat anything, which had been on her mother's plate. Hopkins reports the mother saying, 'she seems to think I'm a witch who's poisoning her'. When Louise hurt herself, she cried with outrage as though the world was out to get her.

Hopkins cites Enid Balint (Balint 1993, p. 65), 'who has described how a paranoid attitude can develop in children like Louise, who are reared on a theory that only their own needs matter, that children create the laws and mothers have to obey them'. Balint says, 'According to this theory any increase in tension is felt as an injustice and therefore an attack on the individual by the world and intolerable.'

Hopkins speculates that a mother like Louise's who is so self-effacing and eager to please must have repressed her own hostility. Perhaps Louise's paranoid feelings developed partly in response to her mother's unconscious hostility.

In contrast Janet, in her situation, with a mother who showed anger towards her, had plenty of opportunity to manage her aggression and also to show empathy and make reparation.

Louise had been presented with a sister when she was nearly three. Hopkins says;

> There had been no major difficulties until Louise's sister was born, when Louise amply confirmed Dunn's finding (1984, p. 143) that 'in families with an intense relationship between mother and first-born daughter, the siblings are likely to be hostile'. Soon after her sister's arrival she became extremely oppositional and negativistic. She refused to accept affection from either parent and persistently wished her sister dead. She appeared to have no sense of concern for anyone who was ill or unhappy at home or at school, and she refused to say 'please', 'thankyou', 'sorry', 'hello' and goodbye.

Her mother's conviction that Louise thought she was 'a bad person' together with her behaviour, Hopkins says, 'suggested Louise had fulfilled Winnicott's prediction by rejecting her parents'.

The stage of concern

I have already written of Winnicott's renaming of Klein's depressive position as the stage of concern. This centres on the acknowledgement of 'the other' and with it the ability to stand in another's shoes (p. 128). Louise was deprived of opportunities to do this by a 'too-good' mothering, which meant she could not comprehend 'not me'. She had never been allowed to separate and make reparation for the guilt of her aggression, so had never reached the stage of concern. Winnnicott says, 'temporarily the mother has put herself out for the child, she has at the beginning put herself in the child's pocket' (1964, p. 91). The significance is the word temporarily. For Louise's mother it was not temporary. Nor had she done what Winnicott refers to, as the later 'job of disillusioning' that what is needed and wanted does not happen automatically. It is a step towards independence.

Hopkins warns of the dangers of too-good mothering and of 'the benefits of conflict, anger and hate in infant development that are needed to balance the present emphasis in much clinical thinking on the unalloyed benefits of sensitive and responsive maternal care'.

Juliet Hopkins wrote this paper in 1996. Today there is much media emphasis on parenting and the debate at all levels continues on whether parental response to children's needs is balanced. Parents are accused of not setting boundaries, being frightened of angering their children and of over indulging them in the 'quality time' they snatch from their busy lives. The debate is polarized from 'spare the rod and spoil the child' to 'little princess on board'.

Parents do seem anxious and confused by conflicting professional and not so professional advice. Winnicott's book, *The Child, the Family and the Outside World*, was written for parents, based on his radio talks. It was published in 1964, but is as relevant today.

The overstimulating mother

A different sort of intrusive mother is described by Stern.

> Controlling and intrusive behaviours by the caregiver are among the most common causes of over stimulation. When viewed blow by blow or instant by instant, most controlling behaviours involve interfering with the infant's self-regulatory behaviours.
>
> (2002, p. 134)

Stern describes the observation of a baby, Jenny at three months old. 'Her mother was an animated woman who would clearly be categorized as intrusive, controlling, and overstimulating by most standards' (1977, p. 135).

Stern observed the mother indulging in high-gear stimulating behaviour, which Jenny could not tolerate. When mother started her determinedly engaging moves, Jenny would rapidly look away. Undeterred mother would chase Jenny's gaze, adding other excited behaviours such as tickling, which Jenny wriggled to avoid and closed her eyes. Stern called it, 'the chase-dodge pattern'.

> The blatant nature of this kind of intrusive behaviour makes it difficult not to infer some unconscious maternal hostility toward the infant or the caregiving role.
>
> (Stern, 1977, p. 136)

Stern, like Hopkins, worried about the effect of this on the child. Stern wrote that he was 'positively alarmed' after several weeks to observe that the dyad 'seemed to have given up on the other a little'. Jenny avoided eye contact with her mother and the mother interacted less, spending more time sitting. Stern was afraid he was watching the early onset of autism (1977, p. 138).

Stern went back to the home with his camera to observe a now 4-month-old Jenny. He went as a clinician ready to intervene, unless things had changed considerably. They had. Jenny and her mother were now achieving and maintaining more mutual gaze and there were some smiles. The interaction continued to improve.

Stern was never sure why. The mother had lowered her level of stimulation. However, Stern pondered whether the change had mainly occurred through Jenny's maturation. Stern cites Burton White (1971) who showed that infants become increasingly able to tolerate larger doses of stimulation. Stern suggests that Jenny's more positive feedback to her mother, allowed the mother to alter her behaviour.

Winnicott's legacy stretches into the theory and practice of health care professionals today. Much of the work of health visitors, for example, is influenced by Winnicott's position on the needs of a baby. Older readers may remember the consequences of the legacy of New Zealander Child Care Expert, Truby King, who advocated feeding four hourly, on the hour, and nothing though the night: otherwise baby would become 'spoilt'. Truby King died in 1938, but even 30 years later mothers would feel guilty at giving in to a crying baby before the appointed time. Women, breast milk soaking their blouses, told of waiting outside the nursery door, until the clock struck the hour; if it could be heard against the screams of the hungry baby inside.

The legacy of Bion: the psychodynamic theory of organizations

While Winnicott's work had focused on the dyad of the mother and baby, as we saw in Chapter 5, Bion's legacy was his interesting work with groups. His ideas have been particularly useful for psychoanalytic thinkers looking at organizations.

The hospital

Isabel Menzies Lyth (1917–2008) a psychoanalyst working in the Tavistock Institute of Human Relations, was very much influenced by Bion. He was her mentor and she felt that his startling ideas made sense of the dysfunctions of the organizations she studied.

Her paper written in 1959 (published in 1988), on the nursing service of a general hospital, which explored reasons for the high turnover of nursing staff, still has relevance today.

Menzies Lyth says,

> Nurses are in constant contact with people who are physically ill or injured, often seriously. Nurses are confronted with the threat and the reality of suffering and death, as few lay people are. Their work involves carrying out tasks, which by ordinary standards are distasteful, disgusting and frightening. Intimate physical contact with patients arouses strong libidinal and erotic wishes and impulses that may be difficult to control.
>
> (1988, p. 46)

These lead to strong feelings, pity compassion and love on the one hand, guilt, hatred and resentment on the other. For nurses who have come into nursing because at an unconscious level they want care for themselves, envy of the patient.

She found primal levels of anxiety that the institution could not contain. She believed these were unconscious infantile responses to the fears and horrors surrounding illness and death. These were so overwhelming that the nurses and the organization defended against them in ways, which proved to be dysfunctional.

Nurses who came into the profession to care for patients and make them better felt cheated. First the patients did not always get better and nurses found their pain and suffering hard to bear. They dealt with it by splitting. The compassion and emotions felt were so painful that the only way to deal with it was to 'switch off'. This was done through depersonalization, categorization; 'the liver in bed 10 or the pneumonia in bed 15' (Menzies, 1988, p. 52). There was a general denial of feelings and of the significance of the individual.

In the hospital the organization colluded in this, moving nurses around from ward to ward so they could not get attached to patients. Work was task oriented so that again nurses would be emotionally disconnected from patients. The roles and tasks were hierarchical and the military style uniforms reinforced this. Perhaps the nurses did feel they were on a battlefield. Patients were not seen as whole people, but damaged body parts.

The retreat into part objects is one of the features of Bion's basic assumption groups. A basic assumption group forms when a work group is overtaken by uncontainable anxiety and people start to behave in a primal way. Two of the three emotional states these groups get into are played out in the hospital. One state is dependency where everyone is looking for an omnipotent leader to save them from taking responsibility. The second is fight and flight, where the group seems to want to escape from a common enemy – presumably the patient who threatens the hospital order.

Although in 2010, hospitals may have learnt much from the time Menzies Lyth was writing, with attempts to personalize patients using strategies like 'named nurse', perhaps there are other defences in their place. The fact that nurses now have to hold degrees may be an intellectual defence against being too physically and emotionally near to the patient.

Another defence may be the institution's function to categorize its staff; doctors belong to firms, nurses have a station, people have a place. This makes for a feeling of security and belonging. It is significant that film and television series about hospitals concentrate on the relationships of the staff, particularly their personal connections. The patients become the wallpaper to their interactions.

Patients can feel the outsider. As they walk to the outpatients department they see hospital staff greet each other, refer to social events that exclude the patient. They clearly belong to a club where the patients are not members.

Perhaps this is necessary. In order that they do not look only to the patient to give them validation, nurses need a satisfying life outside the hospital doors. As with the counsellor, the nurse who lives vicariously through her patients in order to have a 'place' and a strong sense of self will not be the integrated person the patients need.

So it seems some defences are essential. However, it seems important that the defences are not so impregnable that they provide a barrier to emotional accessibility to the patient.

The day nursery

Menzies Lyth carried out a study in 1970 (published in1989), to establish a picture of day care for the under fives. In 1970 the picture of day care was very different from that of today. Then, Menzies Lyth writes, 'the clientele was in trouble. This arose not only because the intake system gave priority to children from families in trouble, but also because normal healthy families, well integrated in their communities were less likely to put their children into the day-care system' (1989, p. 216).

Today 'normal healthy families' routinely put their children into day care. However, as in 1970, this does not necessarily mean that their children have not experienced, 'some kind of breakdown in the quality and amount of mothering available to the child' (1989, p. 216). The reasons may be different; the chief one being parents pressurized to work long hours outside the home.

In 1970 Menzies Lyth wrote:

> In the day nursery the staff wished to deploy their skill and concern for the children in their care but had to do so under conditions which made it essential for them to erect personal and communal barriers against the pain of real awareness of the situations they were working with: of the tragedies in many of the families, the needs and disturbance of the children and the damage that day nursery-care itself might do. The fact that these barriers had to be erected unfortunately increased the likelihood that care would be defective.
>
> (p. 224)

Menzies Lyth described many of the staff as coming from deprived or disturbed backgrounds and overidentified with the children. They hoped to overcome their own deprivation by caring for others and did not understand their own experiences. They often denied they had suffered from these and failed to recognize the suffering of the children. In particular young nursery nurses said they chose the job because they loved children. 'The "love" was genuine, but it was indiscriminate; it was not based on a real relationship with real children, not all of whom is lovable all the time. It gave no place to the hatred children can arouse, which must be coped with by everyone who looks after them. It allowed for no confrontation with the child's or their own hatred, an important maturational experience for both.'

As in the hospital, emotions were defended against in different ways. One was to escape into constant activity with the children, or from the children into chores.

Menzies Lyth observed that the staff did not seem able to distinguish between the normal and abnormal. Normal distress was treated as a nuisance and the child as difficult. Detached, indiscriminate relationships with staff were treated as helpful. Aggressively disturbed children got attention because they were troublesome and had to be controlled. Withdrawn isolated, disturbed children were neglected because they were quiet.

Menzies Lyth found it striking that observers sitting still and quiet in the room would attract quiet, disturbed and distressed children to them. The children would start by tentatively touching, then climbing into laps and even talking. The need was painful to the adult who tried to meet it. Little wonder the staff unconsciously avoided distressing confrontation by devices like overactivity (p. 228).

Splitting took place at all levels. Observers noted how the staff split off the child from its family and had minimal contact with the mother. Sometimes mothers were denigrated, and there was a decided climate that the nursery knows best. This was something that the mothers colluded with, perhaps to assuage their guilt at 'abandoning' their children. Nursery staff did not encourage mothers to stay and help settle in their children to the new environment, believing that 'a clean break' was best. 'Reunions in the evening took place fairly rapidly and not very affectionately when a tired and perhaps irritable parent met a tired child who might well have spent the last hour or so aimlessly waiting to be picked up' (p. 230).

Menzies Lyth says,

> In conclusion, one can only say again that while staff in nurseries worked hard and often devotedly to care for the children, the attitudes they had developed over time to their work and to children did in fact only too often interfere with the real effectiveness of the care they gave in terms of the children's psychological and social development.
>
> (p. 229)

In both the hospital and the day nursery, staff, who had been drawn to the work because they wanted to help and care for others, found that they were prevented from doing this effectively. They had no understanding of unconscious processes, and could not find meaning in the painful environments they encountered. Any emotional response was overwhelming, so, had to be defended against.

The staff who 'survived', and found the job rewarding, were those people who could recognize and acknowledge pain and distress, and, importantly, were able to contain it. This is as true of counsellors as others in the caring professions. The desire to help others does not necessarily include the capacity to do so.

The legacy of Bowlby: attachment theory and research

Evidence-based research

Psychodynamic theory is often lambasted, by its critics, for its lack of evidence-based research. This is patently not true, as illustrated by the examples below.

However, there is a conflict in the psychoanalytic world between those who believe that integrating psychoanalytic thought and scientific principles strengthens the theory and those who feel it dilutes it.

As we saw in an earlier chapter Bowlby's attachment theory was influenced by ethological findings. Lorenz with his work on imprinting; Tinbergen who concluded that attachment was necessary for survival in birds; and Harlow who showed that monkeys will cuddle up to a warm soft cloth as a substitute mother, to lessen anxiety. All produced evidence for attachment in birds and animals, which strengthened Bowlby's ideas on human attachment.

Because Bowlby had seen the effectiveness of an evidence base he utilized this way of working to prove his theories. At the time it was not popular and Bowlby was heavily criticized for bringing science into an area within which psychoanalysis did not fit.

Attachment theory

Within the tradition of attachment theory, methodologies have been developed, especially the 'Strange Situation Test', which have enabled standardized observations to be made of large numbers of infants.

A conference in 1994, initiated by Professor Michael Rustin, a sociologist, with a particular interest in psychoanalysis, brought together the attachment theorists, Mary Main and Eric Hesse, with Tavistock trained infant observers. Comparison of the two methodologies proved stimulating. The attachment theory tradition has developed powerful empirical tools, invaluable in clinical research, but it is acknowledged that in so doing the complex and differentiated descriptions of infant development and family interactions yielded by the psychoanalytic method has of necessity, been sacrificed.

(Reid, 1997, p. 177)

However, Rustin contends that there is the opportunity to use infant observation as a method of research. Current clinical trainings are making links with academic institutions. Clinicians are more likely also to be trained researchers (Reid, 1997).

Attachment figure as regulator

Allan Schore has been dubbed 'The American Bowlby'. He is a neuropsychoanalyst and a pioneer in integrating social, biological, psychological and psychoanalytic theory. Using Bowlby's attachment theory as the overarching model he has drawn extensively on psychoanalytic theory including object relations theory. He maintains that insecure attachments, often associated with early abuse, predict an inability to cope with stressful situations. Early abuse negatively impacts on the development trajectory of the right brain, which is dominant for attachment affect regulation and stress management.

Schore heralded Bowlby as the theorist who developed Freud's project to integrate neurobiology with psychology. Freud had been forced to abandon attempts to correlate psychological functions with the physical brain and body, because the scientific models, then, were not sufficiently advanced. Schore asserts that research, and clinical evidence, show that the early developing emotion processing right brain represents the psychobiological substrata of Freud's unconscious. Because the span of attachment theory now includes not only psychoanalysis but also developmental psychology, psychiatry and the biological sciences, these other fields are now talking about unconscious representations.

Schore claims that because Bowlby was a psychoanalyst, he was in touch with the inner world. However, Bowlby argued with Klein that the relationship between mother and child was not a phantasy relationship, but a real relationship with real events. These were indelibly and permanently in place and in a way that would affect personality over the life span. Bowlby perceived that the mother shapes the infant's coping system. This has been taken up by psychiatry. Psychiatry has looked at early positive and negative interactions and how they affect the brain's coping systems. The information has been used to predict the predispositions to later psychiatric disorders. In the psychobiology of attachment, the attachment figure is seen as the regulator of all forms of cognition, affect and behaviour. In psychiatry regulation is seen as the work of mother and infant. The loss of the ability to regulate feelings is seen as the most far-reaching effect of trauma.

Schore, in his insistence on the importance of early attachment has made stringent comments on maternity leave. He said that in the USA this is only 6 weeks, the very time that 'the face to face joy interactions just begin'. He contends that society should feel shame at how much money is spent on defence budgets and how little on what are the real investments in the future, the security of early human life.

Mentalization

Peter Fonaghy is one of the most important researchers in the field of attachment and places much emphasis on mentalization. This is the ability to make and use mental representations of one's own and others' emotional states.

We apply a philosophy-of-mind approach in order to capture and specify the process by which infants fathom the minds of others and eventually their own minds.

What differentiates our approach is the attention we give not just to cognition, but also to affects. In this regard we rely on attachment theory, which provides empirical support for the notion that an infant's sense of self emerges through the affective quality of relationship with the primary care giver (Fonagy et al., 2004).

Fonagy reinforces the observations of Winnicott and Lacan about the way in which a baby sees itself in its mother's face. For the securely attached infant, he sees as if in a mirror, the love and concern for him. He knows he is lovable.

> The securely attached child perceives in the caregiver's reflective stance an image of himself as desiring and believing.
>
> (Fonagy et al., 2004)

Affect regulation, being able to adjust one's emotional response to different situations, is closely related to mentalization. It plays a key part in the building of a sense of self, and the recognition of what other people may be thinking and feeling. What Winnicott called 'cross identification, the ability to stand in another's shoes'.

Fonagy and Gerhardt both agree with Bowlby that the relationship between the primary care giver and the infant is crucial to development. What is alarming about the learning from neuroscience is that the capacities for empathy and self-control are not present at birth. These qualities, not just far reaching for the individual, but also for society, have to be nurtured. If the nurture is not appropriate, a damaged individual is the result.

We have already seen the dangers of too-good mothering. Winnicott believes that the mother only needs to provide a facilitating environment for the child to be able to develop his creative potential. Frosh (1999) notes that Winnicott sees the mother's ability to aid the development of the child's 'true self' as rooted in biology. It is something that develops in pregnancy, it is intuitive and a naturally occurring basis for all human development. All it requires is a supportive, nonintrusive environment. However, although Winnicott lays stress on the biological programme, Frosh argues that it is a thoroughly social theory. This is because it is written in terms of the relationship, the infant existing in the context of the mother. (There is no such thing as a baby!)

> It should be noted that the extremely influential nonpsychoanalytic theory of attachment, derived from the work of John Bowlby, shares exactly this characteristic of being a biologically oriented theory in which mentally healthy development is held to depend on good-quality interpersonal experiences. It is the mother's capacity to create a 'nonintrusive' interpersonal environment that determines the infant's developmental outcome; at its best, there is a kind of 'collaboration between mother and child which promotes the psychological well being of each of them.
>
> (Frosh, 1999, p. 110)

It is interesting to note that Frosh sees Bowlby's theory of attachment as nonpsychoanalytic, whereas Schore claims that because Bowlby was a psychoanalyst he was in touch with the inner world. You may remember, from the chapter on Bowlby, that Kleinians could not forgive him for what they saw as his scant attention to the internal world. 'Bowlby!' exclaims one analyst. 'Give us Barabbas.'

Maternal deprivation

Bowlby's work on attachment and loss has been invaluable to counsellors, not just those working with bereavement. His stress on the absence of the mother, with its deleterious effect on the child, has helped us, as counsellors, to understand the adult client who still feels like an abandoned child.

But critics of Bowlby have suggested that his insistence on the absence of the primary care giver inevitably resulting in maternal deprivation is both fatalistic and nihilistic, not allowing for growth and reparation. Michael Rutter (1991), while agreeing with Bowlby's thesis that maternal absence can cause deprivation, also provides research evidence to demonstrate that it is not inevitable. He cites other factors – the resilience of the child, support outside the home and the reciprocal nature of parent–child relationships – which can mitigate deprivation. Bowlby's stress on exclusivity of the maternal relationship, that the mothering has to be done by one person, was challenged when research suggested that multiple caretakers can be enhancing rather than restricting to the child's security.

It must also be acknowledged that the pattern of the nuclear family, where a baby is looked after exclusively, by the mother, is statistically an abnormal pattern, reflecting the values of Western industrialized societies of the 1950s.

Though even then, the extended family was still important in some sections of the community, particularly in rural areas and within less affluent socioeconomic groups. In world terms, particularly in the Third World nations, babies are cared for by a number of caretakers within a family group. The natural mother has a special relationship with the child as she normally feeds him at the breast. However, the baby will also make relationships with other 'mothers'. In some African societies, particularly matrilineal societies where the line goes through the mother, an individual will call all close relatives of his mother's age, 'Mother'.

Counsellors should remember that Bowlby later acknowledged that his initial position on maternal deprivation had been rigid, and he had been too adamant in declaring that lasting damage would be the inevitable result of an absent mother. Counsellors might bear this in mind when working with clients, particularly those with absent mothers. It may be that others, who could include the counsellor, might be able to be mother substitutes.

The social brain

We need emotions other than fear and anger to create our families and societies.

Sue Gerhardt cites Jonathon Turner (2000) who suggests that sadness, shame and guilt help us to control our behaviour and meet social goals.

As the emotional brain developed we were more able to make choices in our interactions with others. This required a capacity to think and reflect on our emotions, which led to the development of the cortex, in particular the prefrontal cortex. The first part of the prefrontal cortex is the orbitofrontal part, which is found behind the eyes. If this part is damaged, social life is undermined. People with this damage cannot relate to others sensitively. They become oblivious to social and emotional cues and may even be sociopathic.

The capacity to empathize requires a developed orbitofrontal cortex, which is particularly linked to the right side of the brain. Gerhardt cites Schore (2003) who asserts it is the controller for the entire right brain, which is dominant throughout infancy (Gerhardt, 2004, p. 36).

Gerhardt says that the ability to hold back and defer immediate impulses and desires is the basis for willpower, self-control and our capacity for empathy. She was surprised to discover that we are not born with these capacities. It is no good trying to 'discipline' a baby or to expect a baby to control its behaviour since the brain capacity to do so does not yet exist. His social capacities are only potential at birth. This part of the brain develops after birth and does not begin to mature until toddlerhood (2004, p. 37).

The baby does not develop an orbitofrontal cortex as a matter of course. The kind of brain a baby develops is the brain that comes from his experiences with people. When we are babies, our brains are socially programmed by the older members of the particular social group we must live in.

> Rather than holding up flashcards to a baby, it would be more appropriate to simply hold him and enjoy him. Without the appropriate one to one social experience with a caring adult, the baby's orbitofrontal cortex is unlikely to develop well.
>
> (2004, p. 38)

When the mother–baby relationship is dominated by pleasurable interactions they are building up the baby's prefrontal cortex and developing his capacities for self-regulation and complex social interactions.

Relevance to counselling

Sue Gerhardt's book should be very useful to counsellors. We all know how insecure attachment, in infancy, can lead to the consulting room. After reading this book, even counsellors who do not normally ask about the client's childhood may have pause for thought, when confronted with a client with low self-esteem, little empathy and an inability to make relationships.

Gerhardt spelt out so clearly the lasting consequences of the interactions between mothers and babies that it would be easy to feel hopeless. However she says, and we know, that counselling can help to repair some damage. Having the experience of being heard, being taken seriously, acknowledged as someone with worth, are new and important experiences for a client who missed out in babyhood. As the client–therapist alliance develops, more startling interactions can take place. The client can be angry and yet the embryonic relationship does not crumble. The client refuses to talk and that is tolerated. The client starts to make reparations, by engaging in the therapy. A relationship is developing. For counsellors working in a psychodynamic way they will see this as 'the counsellor as mother'. Their job is to help the client towards a healthy independence, as an adult.

Psychoanalytic theory as science

The theorists explored in this chapter have made new and interesting discoveries by integrating psychoanalytic theory with the biological sciences.

Freud laid emphasis on his theory being scientific, but met criticism. Unlike Bowlby, who was a researcher and published his findings, Freud, who had been a scientist at the start of his career, claimed that psychoanalysis was a science, but offered little in evidence. He wrote up his clinical work, which was naturally based on his observations and opinions, so consequently subjective. The other source of his theoretical concepts was his 30-minute daily self-analysis, no less subjective. Put this with Freud's assertion that only those who have been analysed are fit to criticise psychoanalysis, and we arrive at a position that says, 'Trust me!'

Today the counselling fraternity has acknowledged that in terms of accountability, research into the efficacy and ethical underpinning of counselling is essential. Although research into the effects of psychodynamic theory is more difficult to quantify than, for example, behavioural therapy, it is being undertaken. What also must be taken into account is the fact that psychodynamic thought has not stood still. It has been modified, adapted and extended by other theoreticians, and Freud's original concepts have been subject to intense scrutiny by those who came after. Winnicott thought that some Freudian theory was just plain wrong. Klein believed that the early mother–child relationship, virtually ignored by Freud, was the bedrock of all relationships. Bowlby, with his emphasis on attachment figures, developed the idea of the importance of relationships, away from the primacy of instinctual drives.

But all do not agree with the integrating of psychoanalytic thought and scientific principles. Chief among these is Andre Green, a French psychoanalyst, who has castigated those who would 'reduce emotional conflict and the psyche to cognitive and neuroscientific constructs'. He and Daniel Stern are on opposite sides of the fence and Green has written extensively of the differences between them.

When they were to debate at University College, London, Green asked Peter Fonagy and Joseph Sandler to send some references on Infant Observation.

> They sportingly communicated to me Peter H. Wolff's uncompromising paper, The Irrelevance of Infant Observation for Psychoanalysis (1996). It was fair to send me a work that was supportive of my point of view.
> (Green, 2000, p. 42)

Green feels that in all this integration, psychoanalytic thought has been diluted and trivialized. He compares it to the French love of skylark pate, which, because there is not enough to go round, is mixed with horse-meat!

Green says that the results of the integration are misleading. The main point that science is about the conscious: psychoanalysis is about the unconscious is overlooked. Green thinks all the key theories have been well worked out by the theorists and do not need to be verified further. In essence psychoanalysis is more about thinking than doing.

Relevance to counselling

Counsellors might wonder if this last sentence is true of counselling. Is there too much doing at the expense of not enough thinking? Thinking is a very important part of psychodynamic theory. Casement in his books on learning from the patient (1985, 1990) places thinking, by both therapist and patient, at the heart of the therapy. In how the therapist manages to think about what the patient is saying, consciously or unconsciously, lies the key to a creative therapeutic relationship. In my view too many counsellors get out their 'tool box' when the counselling seems difficult, instead of listening, thinking and containing. Myriad techniques are no substitute for staying with the relationship and learning together.

Respecting the lack of evidence for evidence-based practice

> There is irony in the fact that although there is an increasing require-
> ment for practice to be based on evidence, we are not aware of systematic
> evidence demonstrating the benefit of this process.
>
> (Roth and Fonagy, 2005, p. 503)

The authors claim that guidelines imposed on the basis of evidence
alone, without the continued support of clinical judgement, are problem-
atic. The result could be some treatments falsely identified as effective
and the chance of misclassifying an effective treatment as ineffective.

They argue that method only accounts for a small proportion of the
outcome. More important is the therapist skill and judgement.

> Implementing the science of evidence-based practice while ignoring the
> 'art' of therapy risks reducing creativity, and with it, potential advances in
> technique.
>
> (Roth and Fonagy, 2005)

That, this was written by the authors of the most comprehensive tome on a
critical review of therapy research, is significant. It reminds us that whatever our modality, the most critical element of the therapy is ourselves.
A good outcome relies on our skill and judgment and our ability to make
a therapeutic relationship. This is boundaried by the ethics of our practice. The most effective therapies are conducted by the most effective
therapists.

Comment

Winnicott's legacy has been his monumental work on the mother and
baby dyad. As a paediatrician, estimated to have seen sixty thou-
sand patients over his lifetime, he believed that most mothers are
'good enough'. However, he also felt that mothers could be 'too good'.
The mother who invasively anticipates her baby's every need 'can be
experienced as a witch' (1965).

Both Hopkins (1996), who observed the 'too well adapted mothering',
and Stern (1977), who recorded 'the over stimulated mothering', speculate that unconscious maternal hostility to the child or the care-giving
role could be the root of the mothers' intrusive behaviour. Like Winnicott,
they found the encroachment detrimental to the child's development.

Hopkins suggests that a mother who is able to show anger towards the child enables him to be more able to manage aggression.

Healthcare professionals still cite Winnicott not only as a man who could empathize with the needs of mothers and children, but also as one whose writings have been immensely helpful in comprehending the complexities of human interaction.

Bion's work with groups has been similarly useful, particularly to the understanding of organizations. His protégé, Isobel Menzies Lyth, in analysing the ways both hospitals and nurseries defend themselves against overwhelming emotional responses to distress, threw new light on behaviour which in rational terms often seems counterproductive. She realized that coping with the results of the frailty of the human condition cannot always be directly addressed, as it is too unbearable. Organizations escape from this too close emotional contact by erecting barriers, be they uniforms, bureaucracy or a group collusion that insists on professional distance. Institutional safeguards become a bar to the investigation of emotional affliction.

In contrast, Bowlby was eager to explore and document emotional distress. He believed this led the way to understanding and better practice. Having begun by examining ethological findings, and concluding that the results were illuminating, he moved from animals to people. Bowlby's work produced some of the first evidence-based research. His studies on attachment and separation were extended by other theorists, such as Main, Rustin and Rutter. They produced further evidence-based research.

Schore, dubbed 'The American Bowlby', contends that Bowlby developed Freud's project to integrate neurobiology with psychology. Schore, using Bowlby's attachment theory as the overarching model, has integrated social, biological, psychological and psychoanalytic theory. He maintains that insecure attachments, often related to early abuse, portend an inability to cope with stressful situations. Early abuse negatively impacts on the development of the right brain, dominant for attachment affect regulation and stress management.

Fonaghy is one of the most important researchers in the field of attachment and places much emphasis on mentalization. This is the ability to make and use mental representations of one's own and others' emotional states.

He maintains that attachment theory provides empirical support for the idea that an infant's sense of self emerges through the affective quality of relationship with the primary care giver.

Affect regulation, being able to adjust one's emotional response to different situations is closely related to mentalization. It plays a key part in the building of a sense of self, and the recognition of what other people may be thinking and feeling.

Fonagy and Gerhardt both agree with Bowlby that the relationship between the primary care giver and the infant is crucial to development. What is alarming about the learning from neuroscience is that the capacities for empathy and self-control are not present at birth. These qualities, far reaching not just for the individual, but also for society, have to be nurtured. If the nurture is not appropriate, a damaged individual is the result.

Gerhardt says that the ability to hold back and defer immediate impulses and desires is the basis for willpower, self-control and our capacity for empathy. She was surprised to discover that we are not born with these capacities. The kind of brain a baby develops is the brain that comes from his experiences with people. The earliest relationship shapes the baby's nervous system. That is why love matters.

Evidence-based research is crucial to our learning. However, Fonagy and Roth dispute the notion that the increasing requirement for practice to be based on evidence produces more-effective practice. They argue that method only accounts for a small proportion of the outcome. More important is the therapist skill and judgement. They claim that the 'art' of therapy is more significant in effecting creative practice.

Further reading

Fonagy, P., Target, M., Gergely, G. and Jurist, E. (2004) *Affect Regulation, Mentalization and the Development of Self.* London: H. Karnac (Books) Ltd.

Gerhardt, S. (2004) *Why Love Matters: How Affection Shapes a Baby's Brain.* Hove: Routledge.

Menzies, I.E.P. (1988) *Containing Anxiety in Institutions.* Selected Essays (Volume 1). London: Free Association Books.

Menzies, I.E.P. (1989) *The Dynamics of the Social.* Selected Essays (Volume 11). London: Free Association Books.

9

Practice

Practice has been referred to throughout the text, within the context of the application of the particular theorist's concepts.

In this chapter I want to look at the psychodynamic ideas, which underpin the building, using and understanding of the therapeutic relationship, primarily through case study material.

Much of this way of working has echoes of other practice. Some is different. Trainee counsellors and counsellors from other trainings should find aspects of psychodynamic practice that can be safely incorporated into their existing way of working.

Links

The first example describes a trainee counsellor beginning work with a client.

The case material is interspersed by ideas on how a counsellor might respond in a psychodynamic way.

One of the most useful concepts psychodynamic theory has to offer is the understanding and use of links. Being able to identify what seem diverse episodes, behaviour, thoughts and feelings, and bringing them together for both client and counsellor to reflect on, can help to make better sense of the experience of the client.

Case Example | Penny: using links

Session 1

Marjorie was a trainee counsellor on placement with an organization, which supported single mothers. Her new client, Penny, was

Case Example | (Continued)

a 25-year-old woman, whose partner had left the relationship when she announced that she was pregnant and wanted to keep the baby. Penny had been devastated by the break-up, as the couple, who had met at university, had been in what she considered to be a stable relationship.

Penny had come to ask for help saying that she felt overwhelmed by her feelings of panic for the safety of her daughter. Zoe was 6 months old, but since her birth, Penny had been terrified that Zoe would die. Zoe would be struck by a deadly virus; a lorry would mount the pavement and crush the buggy; burglars would break into the flat and murder Zoe.

Penny realized that her fear would harm Zoe. Penny could not bear anyone else to look after Zoe. 'I hate leaving the flat,' said Penny. 'I feel safe there. But I know it's unhealthy. And all this is bad for Zoe.'

Marjorie, who was in her forties, had three teenage children and worked in the health service, decided to take a practical approach. First she asked Penny where Zoe was today as Penny had come alone. Marjorie wrote in her subsequent notes that "Penny pulled a face at this question" but then answered that Zoe was with her grandmother, Penny's mother. 'It's the first time I've left her.'

Marjorie asked if Penny got on with her mother and Penny said, 'OK. We're not close.'

Marjorie said that in her experience it was normal to be worried about a first baby. She could see that Penny was anxious, but she was sure that as Zoe got older Penny would feel more able to let her go – to a child minder, to nursery, perhaps to her grandmother.

Penny said, 'But I won't! I feel sick at the thought. And I have to return to work in 6 months time. I don't know what to do.'

Marjorie listened and felt herself wanting to help. She had often helped worried mothers in the past. She suggested ways in which Penny could gradually get Zoe to have new experiences; perhaps increase visits to her grandmother; meet other mothers and invite them with their babies over to play; show Zoe the shops in town; take her to the park to watch other children.

Penny was silent. Marjorie said it was time to finish. Penny said, 'Thank you for listening.'

Responding in a psychodynamic way

How would a counsellor working psychodynamically have used that first session. From the start she would have been aware of the sense of foreboding in Penny. She would have picked up on the words Penny used; 'struck by a deadly virus, crushed to death in her buggy, murdered by burglars'. Penny had voiced her feelings of panic and being overwhelmed. The counsellor would acknowledge them, while keeping part of herself apart, so that she, the counsellor, was not panicky or overwhelmed. This containment of emotion should mean that the counsellor was able to put her energy into understanding, rather than precipitous problem solving.

Something the counsellor might be thinking about, though at this stage would probably not share with the client, were the unexpressed negative feelings about Zoe. There could be resentment. Zoe was the reason that Penny's partner had left her. Zoe was the reason that Penny's life had become unmanageable. Maybe Penny was terrified that she might be the one to hurt Zoe. The thought would be so unbearable that Penny's defence mechanisms would ensure that the threat was externalized. In this situation Penny could not trust anyone, but herself, to look after Zoe safely. This must make Penny feel encapsulated, and perhaps fuel any resentment.

The counsellor would also realize that Penny's relationship with her own mother was central to her experience of parenting. Perhaps feelings of rejection and abandonment were at the root of the more anodyne 'we're not close' response; emotions that had been replicated when Penny's partner deserted her.

The counsellor in building a relationship with Penny would be aware that in the transference Penny could see her as the good mother or the bad mother. The validating of Penny's terrifying feelings would be the core of the session. The counsellor would not reassure, but would communicate her desire to understand and find meaning in what Penny had brought.

Case Example | (Continued)

Session 2

At the second session Penny arrived with Zoe. Marjorie was taken aback by this and clearly showed it, as Penny said, 'Sorry. I had to bring her.'

Penny started off by saying that she had a dream last night about Zoe drowning in a swimming pool. Marjorie said that must have been frightening, but Penny was not likely to be taking Zoe swimming. 'One dreams strange things when anxious.'

'But there is a basis of truth in this dream', said Penny. 'I know it can happen.'

Penny then told Marjorie the story of what happened when she was five. She was staying on holiday with her parents at a hotel in Greece and had just learnt to swim. She went swimming in the hotel pool every day, until one day the pool was empty. She asked her parents why this was and her mother said 'they've drained it to clean it'.

Penny was at first merely disappointed but then began to hear hotel guests murmuring about 'the tragedy'; 'those poor parents'; 'such a sweet little boy', and frightened asked her parents what it all meant. Her father said nothing. 'He always left things to my mother.' And her mother said that there had been 'an accident in the pool and a little boy had got hurt'. When Penny said, 'Did he die?' her mother had told her not to worry about it.

But Penny had worried and after pestering her mother for an answer had been told that the boy did drown, but 'these things happen'.

Penny wanted to know more, but her mother refused to discuss it. Penny had nightmares about the drowning, but when she tried to talk about them, her mother responded that 'it was very sad, but nothing to do with you, so forget about it'.

Penny went on to talk about her mother's relationship with her throughout her childhood. When Penny was bullied at school her mother had told her not to make a fuss, 'these things happen' and 'I'm sure you can sort it yourself.'

Penny had learnt in this and in subsequent episodes where she needed support that she would get little emotional help from her mother, so 'I do sort things myself'. There was a pause as she turned Zoe to face Marjorie; then she said, 'But I can't sort this.'

Responding in a psychodynamic way

The counsellor working psychodynamically would think hard about the meaning of bringing Zoe to the session. Was Penny offering Zoe to her because she wanted the counsellor as a good mother for herself, and a grandmother for Zoe. Or did Penny want to display Zoe as a child she competently cared for, in spite of the chaos that rattled around, inside Penny's head.

Perhaps both! Certainly when Penny left, making it clear she needed help, Zoe was symbolically turned, to face the counsellor. Maybe Penny was saying, 'Help us both'. Or more alarmingly, 'If you can't help me, I may hurt her.' An aggressive 'on your own head be it' message to the counsellor.

Penny had started the session by bringing a dream, in Freudian terms, 'the royal road to the unconscious'. The dream equated Zoe with the 'sweet little boy' who drowned. This could be the time to reflect to Penny that she seemed terrified that she could not keep Zoe safe. It would open a space for Penny to voice her anxieties about safety and perhaps be able to speak about fears of hurting Zoe.

The counsellor would realize the full horror of the drowning incident to 5-year-old Penny. There were many strands to it. One of them was the realization that children could die. Therefore Penny could die. She was old enough to have some ideas about death, including its finality. The way Penny's mother had told her to forget about the boy's death raised further disquiet. If Penny died would she, too, be forgotten? Penny's mother's handling of a traumatic situation was a foretaste of how she would fail to manage difficulties throughout Penny's life.

The counsellor would give Penny the space to mourn the lack of an emotionally present mother. Also, it would seem, an emotionally absent father. The notion that her parents had done their best, though it was not good enough, could be raised. Perhaps Penny, being able to forgive her parents for their inadequacies, might help strengthen a relationship Penny sorely needed.

The counsellor would realize that Penny, seeing her as the good mother, would have an idealized view of what she could offer. Penny

Case Example | (Continued)

would no doubt be disappointed. However, what Penny would experience was a counsellor who took her seriously. This would not just embody Penny's relationship with Zoe, but Penny's inner relationship with herself. The sessions would focus on understanding and finding meaning.

Supervision

Marjorie took the case to supervision. Her supervisor, Nancy, was an integrative counsellor who was aware of psychodynamic concepts and found them useful in helping to make sense of clients' narratives.

Nancy asked Marjorie what were her feelings about the case. 'I feel out of my depth', said Marjorie. 'I've suggested lots of things she could do, but Penny doesn't seem able to do any of them. In fact I don't think she was really listening to me.'

'Were you listening to her?' asked the supervisor.

'Of course', Marjorie said indignantly. Penny thanked me for listening at the end of the first session.

'So why do you think Penny couldn't hear you when you were trying to help her', asked Nancy. Marjorie thought for a while and said, 'Well, I suppose she was frightened.'

'What was she frightened about?'

'That something could happen to her baby; most young mothers are. But this was extreme.'

'What about the story of the dream and the swimming pool death? Would that begin to explain her fear?'

Marjorie said quickly, 'Oh, not really. It was one incident and a long time ago.'

Nancy said, 'You sound like Penny's mother. She couldn't understand how significant that was to Penny.'

'So you think it's so important,' said Marjorie.

'Well, let's look at it.' When Penny is five, old enough to want to understand about difficult things, she stumbles on the death of a child younger than she is. She asks her mother to explain it but she gets fobbed off with platitudes, which trivialize her very real anxiety. Worse, her mother puts an end to any discussion with the very significant phrase: 'These things happen.'

'Well, they do', said Marjorie.

'But to me that suggests that people have no control over their lives', said the supervisor. It is a phrase you say that Penny said her mother used whenever there was a frightening episode and Penny appealed to her mother for help. The message seemed to be that there is no-one to help you. You are left alone with fate. Abandoned!'

Marjorie said, 'I hadn't thought of it like that. I suppose she could feel abandoned by her mother. And when I think of it her partner left her when she was pregnant. I suppose that was another abandonment.'

'I'm sure you're right', said Nancy. Does it start to make more sense to you?

'Yes', said Marjorie. She feels alone and powerless. My mother was a great support when I had my three children, But Penny's mother hasn't really been there for her.'

'Maybe she isn't able to be; but you are.'

'What, be her mother?'

'Why do you think she brought Zoe to the session?'

'Well, she had no one to look after her.'

'She left her with her mother before. I think she believes you are a better bet. She knows you want to help her'.

'So what should I do?'

Nancy thought for a minute. 'Penny needs to be able to think that someone understands her. For that you have to really listen for the meaning behind the words; and for what is not said.'

'I will try. But how will that get her to feel less worried about Zoe?'

'Penny seems already to see you in a maternal role. If she also begins to feel you understand her fears and take them seriously, that will be a new experience for her. She will not be alone.'

'So I can start suggesting things, like taking Zoe to the park.'

'I would hope that awareness of your support will give her confidence in herself. She will probably make her own decisions about how she manages Zoe, but want to come and talk to you about it.'

'So she will use me as a mother if she wants to. I quite like that idea.'

Case Example | (Continued)

'But remember you must stay in the counsellor role. To be useful, you must remain professional. You aren't her mother. But she may be angry with you as if you were.'

'I think I can put up with that. She's gone through a lot. I do want to help her.'

Comment

Of course this was but the beginning of the counselling and the sessions were not easy. However, Marjorie learned that counselling is not necessarily about solving problems. This is what she had learnt to do in the health service where she had to be the expert. It was hard to be there, trying to understand Penny, trying to imagine what she was feeling, rather than what she Marjorie would do in similar circumstances. A person-centred counsellor would know she must use empathy to be with the client. In supervision Marjorie was being stimulated to do this. As well, she was encouraged to use the psychodynamic ideas of looking for links, linking the past and the present to see a way forward.

Building the therapeutic relationship

There are many facets to the building of a good therapeutic relationship in psychodynamic terms and counsellors need to be aware of them all.

This applies equally to trainees and to those who have been counselling a long time. It is easy for us to become complacent, so we need to continually monitor ourselves.

Power and authority

We have to constantly remind ourselves of our privileged position in being privy to the inner worlds of others. Part of the process of the counselling is for the counsellor to be idealized in the transference. We can bask in the glory, or use the experience to learn more about the client. Have we become the mother the client never had, or are we the omnipotent healer, with magical powers?.

Conversely we may become demonized. Can we learn not to take this personally, accept the client's anger and use it to understand more about the client?

We have the power to damage the client. We need to take authority to keep the client safe.

The setting

Because of the transference and the exposed emotions of the client, his imaginings can encourage him to misread the evidence around him. For the counsellor this means that she has to think carefully about making a safe, therapeutic space. If it is in her home, perhaps she will have to confine her counselling to the evenings when the small children are in bed, or counsel during the day if teenagers are going to play their music loudly in the evenings. Ordinary family activities can feel very excluding to clients, who should be able to rely on peace and calm. The counsellor has to free her mind and cannot do this, if she is anxious about what is happening elsewhere in the house.

Within the counselling room it should feel calm and safe. Clients feel more comfortable if the chairs are comfortable, and if the counsellor's chair does not tower over the client's. When sitting in his chair, what the client looks at will become part of the therapy. A friend said that he used to escape to the pattern of rooftops outside, when the therapy became too painful. Another talked of losing herself in a picture on the wall. For this reason pictures on the wall need to be thought about quite carefully. I have agonized over pictures in case they could be construed as disturbing. But I also know that if clients feel very anxious, even anodyne pictures can perturb.

I had a coal fire in my counselling room, and clients used to say that the counselling became twinned with the fire, in their memory. Of course the obvious symbolism with fire is warmth, but the other element is danger. And counselling can feel very dangerous. To open ourselves to someone, whom we know little about, though hope we can trust, is exposing and makes us vulnerable. As counsellors, who have also been clients, we should always keep this in mind when assessing the safety of our settings.

For trainee counsellors, working in agencies, they will tend to have less control over space and time. I know that many trainee counsellors working in agencies, where they feel the space is inappropriate, work incredibly hard to change it, if they can, and worry over it, if they cannot. Some know first hand how lack of appropriate space in their training facilities inhibits confidence and trust. They have had the experience of being the client in role-play, who is withholding because the setting is not safe.

The frame

Psychodynamic counselling, because of its awareness of unconscious processes, emphasizes a consistent frame to work within. The purpose of this is for clients to know where they are, so that they feel held and safe and any opportunities for misunderstanding are lessened. The frame includes time, the orthodox 50-minute hour, or an agreed 60-minute hour, which is strictly adhered to. If boundaries are continually pushed at, with the client trying to go over time, it becomes a subject for discussion. Perhaps the client feels that he has never had been able to get enough, of attention, of food, of love and this is being acted out.

Alternatively the client may be frequently late. Again this has to be addressed. The obvious answer is that the client is resisting, he does not want to be there. Yet he comes: late. The two positions, not wanting to come to counselling, wanting to come, are an acting-out of Kleinian feelings of ambivalence. Both positions are valid. Counselling is painful, yet there is a hope of change. With work, these feelings can be integrated.

If the counsellor finds herself wanting to step out of the frame, offering the client more time, for example, she needs to understand what is happening. It may be that she has taken on countertransference feelings and feels overprotective to the client who is experienced as a needy child. Whatever the reasons, they should be thought about, and taken to supervision, for discussion.

Time is important in another sense. The day and time the client comes for counselling, as consistency is an issue, should be the same. Again if the counsellor finds herself juggling round the client to accommodate his changed circumstances, or new demands, she should be asking herself what it means.

Consistency extends to the counselling room. Clients are often disturbed by change. As trainee counsellors on placement in agencies will know, clients can be very disorientated by having to use a different room from the usual and will often voice it. They may say that they do not like the new room, though what they may mean, but hesitate to say, is that it does not feel safe.

Seemingly quite small things are noticed. In my counselling room are two clocks, one, which the client can see without having to move his head, one which I can see without looking as if I am clock watching. 'My' clock broke and had to be replaced. Almost every client commented on the fact that I had a new clock.

In consistency terms what the counsellor wears is significant. Do we look as if we are off to the office or the gym? And if we power dress one day and be weekend-casual the next, what message does that give to the client?

As long as the counsellor is consistent, perhaps it is immaterial if we dress up or dress down. However, clients do feel uneasy if the counsellor wears something that appears to be out of character. Normally casually dressed counsellors who appear in a suit, looking as if they are gearing up for an interview, may give the message to the client that they are preparing for something far more high powered and important than the current counselling session. The client may worry that the counsellor is to abandon him for a distant, prestigious and lucrative job.

As the counsellor we have a duty to be aware of the messages we are giving out, if only because our role is to keep safe the client within the counselling arena. I remember feeling chastened in a case discussion group, after talking about a client I had just seen, whom I thought had an erotic transference to me. A colleague remarked that my skirt was very short. I had to go away and think about whether the short skirt was an unconscious or conscious decision and my responsibility, as the counsellor, in the process.

Using the relationship

But it is not only the physical setting that determines whether the client feels safe. The ultimate test is the relationship with the counsellor and whether the client feels secure with her. As soon as the client sits down in the room, or before that if he meets the counsellor outside, he is beginning to make a judgement. Is this a person whom I can trust? Will it be safe to open myself to her?

He may ask himself, 'Can I make a relationship with her?' But this is probably the client who knows something about counselling. At this stage he is more likely to think, 'Will I like her?' Because most counsellors, particularly those starting out, want the client to like them, they may find themselves smiling and chatting to relax the client and put him at ease. The problem is that this gives the client the wrong impression and can almost turn the session into a social occasion. The client may wonder if the counsellor is being genuine, or if she is a real professional. After all, most other professionals tend to just get on with the job. It can be most confusing for the client.

The counsellor, working in a psychodynamic way, will not spend time relaxing the client or engaging in small talk. Counselling, if it is to have some meaning and purpose, is not relaxing. From being clients ourselves, we know it is hard work and often painful. Also the psychodynamic counsellor does not want to disclose too much of herself, or the client will not be unable to project his feelings on to her and use her in the transference. The counsellor needs to be there for the client, but not overwarm or reassuring. She will need to respond to him, listen and observe very carefully, maybe comment in a reflective way on what she notices, if this seems appropriate, but not press her own agenda.

As well as being available to be used in the transference, psychodynamic counsellors have to be able to make a real relationship with the client. Fairbairn's importance of a real as well as a transference relationship and Winnicott's concept of a 'true self' makes us aware that we cannot hide behind the mask of the competent expert, if we are truly to meet the client. Research maintains that the successful outcome of any counselling, irrespective of the orientation of the counsellor, depends on a meaningful relationship between client and counsellor.

This is particularly important where challenging is concerned. At the beginning of the relationship, when the counsellor challenges the client, she may be experienced, by the client, as his critical mother, and he will respond as he has always done. This may be defensively and resentfully, or compliantly with the anger concealed. If this is not worked with in the counselling, nothing will change for the client. Later as the relationship develops the client may be able to meet the counsellor as a real person, rather than a transferred authority figure.

I see the psychodynamic counselling relationship operating on several levels. Particularly at the start of the relationship, when the client may feel helpless in his plight and, as a result, dependent on the counsellor, then the transference will be more overt. He will look to the counsellor to be the mother who can protect him. As the counselling goes on, the client, with the counsellor's help, begins to get in touch with his own forgotten resources. The client, like Winnicott's toddler, will become more independent. When this happens the client will be able to use a more mutual, adult relationship with the counsellor and, for this, she has to be real.

Starting the session

In psychodynamic counselling the counsellor will let the client start. She wants to know what is uppermost in his thoughts. Even saying to a client, 'How are you?' or 'How are you this week?' sets an agenda. The client feels he has to report in. He may feel this is what is expected of him and dutifully tell you about his week, every week, before he gets down to what he really wants to say. Clients of course may decide to do this without a prompt. A client of mine always started the session by describing his week minutely. When I reflected on this, 'I'm aware that you always start by telling me about the things you've done since we last met', he replied that it made him feel safe. It was almost like a mantra, or a kind of hypnotic spell he put upon himself. It seemed to calm him. Perhaps a recount of his doings was evidence of his existence, which he often doubted.

The other problem with the 'How are you?' question is that, like the patient in the hospital bed, the client is likely to say, 'Very well thank you,' or words to that effect, however bad he actually feels. He has picked up the subtext, which is that a positive response will be most acceptable. It is hard for the client to say 'I feel so depressed, I wanted to end it all', within such a climate.

In psychodynamic counselling, counsellors look for a meaning in what the client is bringing, which may be at an unconscious level. The client who starts the session with a diatribe on his awful dentist who charged him a fortune and the filling fell out before the client got home, followed by a story about how the bank had overcharged him on an overdraft, may be making a communication to the counsellor that he is not fully aware of. The counsellor may wonder aloud if all this talk about professionals failing at their jobs, not delivering the goods and charging a fortune for it, may be a reflection of the client's disappointment about how the counselling is going. The client may not have articulated it to himself at a conscious level, he may be polite and appreciative about what the counsellor has done for him, but unconsciously he may be very angry. After all no one would choose to come to counselling, if he did not feel a need, and most of us do not like to admit to a need. Like the baby envying the good breast the client may feel he would prefer to be in the counsellor's chair and envies her position, which he feels is preferable to his.

Disclosure

A fellow counsellor told me how betrayed she felt when her therapist, while waiting to go into the counselling room, pointed to a picture in the waiting room and said that her daughter painted in a similar style. 'I didn't want to know about her daughter', said my colleague. 'I'm paying good money for this. I wanted to believe she was there for me as the good mother, and only me.' The counsellor went on to say how, normally, skilled her therapist was and how much she was getting out of the therapy. This is a useful example how at one level as clients we can be adult and objective, and at another level we can quickly become the abandoned child.

Being influenced by psychodynamic theory, whether as a would-be psychodynamic counsellor, or as a counsellor who wants to integrate some of the ideas, forces us to make certain decisions. Klein thought that therapists were there to be used, as the client wanted us to be. In phantasy we could become the rejecting mother, the authoritarian father, the successful sister. The client could use us to work through the difficulties he had, and has, with these relationships. Because the client does not want to see us as we really are, or at least not for most of the time, we have to be careful to respect this.

When we offer ourselves as clients in psychodynamic counselling, we go through a process where we hark back to childhood experiences and begin to feel those childlike feelings of dependency again. I can remember as a client standing outside the therapist's front door, repeatedly ringing the bell, hearing it echo in the empty house and feeling utterly desolate and forlorn. I was the rejected and abandoned child. In reality I had cancelled the session explaining that I was going to a conference. Except that I had got the dates wrong. The conference was the next week. I had given my therapist a date, which at an objective level I must have known was not the right date, so that I could end up on her doorstep, infantilized, angry and forsaken. You could say I was at an unconscious level spoiling the therapy, which for me, as a trainee counsellor at the time, was, I knew to be, a good thing. But perhaps part of me did not like what I was finding out about myself, did not like to feel powerless and vulnerable, so I attacked it. Remembering Klein's thoughts on the envious feelings of the baby attacking the good breast because it feels impotent, similarly I was sabotaging the 'good therapy'.

As the client puts his trust in the counsellor, so he offers part of himself, the vulnerable part. In his phantasy the therapist will be a mother who can always keep him safe. Because the phantasy includes the idea of a mother who is always there for him he does not want evidence confronting him to the contrary. The client does not want to see photographs of his counsellor cuddling her baby son, or with her arms round the baby son's father. Particularly if he is wrestling with a broken relationship the client does not want evidence of happiness and contentment on all sides. It is as if we are saying, 'Well my life is great. Sorry about yours.'

We have to be sensitive and careful. A friend who went to counselling said that the thing she hated most was the noise from the living room below the counselling room in the counsellor's quite small house. She was convinced that there was a perpetual party going on, to which of course she was not invited. In reality she knew this was highly unlikely to be true, but in her isolated, alienated state, desolate in a 'messy' divorce, said, 'I felt as if "She" (the counsellor) was rubbing my nose in it'. She did not carefully choose the words. That was how it felt. She described her life as 'shitty', going through a messy separation and then having her nose rubbed in it. Kleinian thought would suggest that her unconscious references to defecation and evacuation were symbolic of her out of control life, which made her feel like the impotent angry child, desperate to evacuate 'poisonous substances' (Klein, 1930) faeces, to make herself feel better.

Themes and patterns

Counsellors from other schools of counselling think that psychodynamic counsellors use very different skills from themselves. They have heard about interpretation and are not sure what this is. It sounds as if the counsellor, as expert, is telling the client what the client really means.

This is not something most psychodynamic counsellors would want to go along with. Like other counsellors they want a mutual relationship with the client, in which together they search for meaning. Consequently psychodynamic counsellors use most of the same skills, but they may use them in different ways. They will listen to the client, reflect on what he says, ask questions and use silence. However, any interventions and interpretations the counsellor makes to the client's responses should have an awareness of unconscious processes, in the transference. This means that the counsellor is not just working with what she sees in the here and now, but with a layered experience.

The counsellor is also looking for themes and patterns. In the example below we see the counsellor looking, with the client, at the Winnicottian idea of place and how people have to find a place in order to feel secure in their relationships.

Case Example | Donna: looking for a place

Donna has been seeing the counsellor because she feels anxious and confused. She lives with her husband Steve and her 3-year-old daughter, Amanda. Donna is expecting her second child, which she says she is thrilled about. She cannot understand why she feels as unhappy as she does. 'I should be happy.'

Case Example | (Continued)

Donna arrives looking pale and drawn. She sits down and there is a long silence.

DONNA: I feel awful. My nerves are in shreds. And it's only a month before the baby arrives. (There is another long silence.)

Steve's mad with me. I don't know what's got into him. I've been trying to organize our bedroom to take the cot, so I put his desk in a corner of the living room.

COUNSELLOR: The bedroom used to be Steve's work-room.

DONNA: Yes and he's really taken the hump.

COUNSELLOR: Are you saying Steve doesn't understand your anxiety to be prepared for the new baby?

DONNA: Too right! He's moved the desk into the garage. Says that's the only place he can get a bit of peace. He's making a statement.

COUNSELLOR: And what is the statement?

DONNA: Well.... (There is a silence while Donna thinks.) I suppose he thinks I don't understand that he has to do work at home.

COUNSELLOR: Perhaps Steve feels there isn't a place in his home for him any more.

DONNA: (Angrily) You mean he thinks I don't care?

COUNSELLOR: And you do care.

DONNA: Of course I do. It just seems I've got too many people to care about.

COUNSELLOR: It seems overwhelming. And you've got to hold it all together.

DONNA: Exactly. (Donna starts to weep. Then she briskly wipes her eyes and blows her nose.) I've made a start on organizing Amanda's room. My father looked after her while I went into town for the duvet cover for her new bed. I got what she wanted; one with dogs on. (The counsellor waits. There is a long silence.)

DONNA: Oh God. I got back to a nightmare. My father had thought he was being helpful. So he had taken down Amanda's cot. I came in and she was hysterical. She was standing in the middle of this dismantled cot, trying to put it back together. Sobbing...

COUNSELLOR: That sounds very upsetting for all of you.

DONNA: It was devastating. Poor Amanda.

COUNSELLOR: So Amanda feels that the new baby is going to take over her cot and perhaps there won't be a place for her. She wants to keep things as they are.

DONNA: I'm sure she does. I keep telling her how much I love her. But we'll all love the new baby, as well, when it comes. (There is a silence

and then Donna says, almost defiantly) After all there's more than
enough love to go round.

COUNSELLOR: It sounds as if you're not sure you believe that?

DONNA: (A long silence while she thinks) Actually, that's true. I'm
not sure.

COUNSELLOR: And I think that's the worry isn't it? That it's hard to make
room in your house for this new baby. Maybe you might not have
room in your heart.

DONNA: Yes, it does worry me. How can I love anybody as much as
Amanda. She's everything to me.

COUNSELLOR: It does seem as if everyone is worried about whether there
will be a place for them when the baby comes and everything is
changed.

DONNA: Well Steve's being very odd.

COUNSELLOR: Perhaps Steve thinks you might make him redundant and
move him out, like the desk.

DONNA: But I love him to bits. And Amanda, she's the best thing that's
happened to us.

COUNSELLOR: Maybe Amanda doesn't really understand what's
happening, but she does know she's going to have a new sister or
brother who has taken over her cot. I suppose she's frightened that
this new creature might take over you.

DONNA: But I wouldn't let that happen.

COUNSELLOR: No. Your worry is that you may not be able to love the
new baby enough. But you also feel responsible for making sure
everybody else feels loved.

DONNA: (Wearily) Yes. I suppose I do.

COUNSELLOR: No wonder you feel anxious!

Acknowledging, exploring and trying to understand her anxieties at different levels was helpful for Donna. She wanted to have
her practical fears about not being ready for the baby recognized,
but her deeper primal fears about not loving, even hating the new
baby had to be talked through. Donna's feelings for Steve were
also explored, with Donna worried about hating Steve at times. The
counselling continued until well after the birth.

In this extract the counsellor used counselling skills common
to other ways of working. Perhaps she used silence more. She was
always aware that there might be things happening below the surface and wanted to give Donna time to think about them. Sometimes
an interpretation was made which concerned levels of meaning.

Counsellors should offer any 'interpretation' in a tentative way. It can be seen as a reflection, beginning with words like 'perhaps', 'maybe', 'I wonder'. But because it is tied to what is not immediately evident on the surface, it may be rejected out of hand by the client. Particularly because an interpretation can contain an element of challenge and confrontation, it must be offered with some care.

Suppose a counsellor says to a client, 'Maybe you cancelled last week because you were angry with me. You felt I'd let you down.' In this there are suggestions of strong feelings. The client may feel angry and betrayed. The client had sent a message that he was ill. However, the counsellor feels the cancellation could be about the client's fury at the counsellor not taking his side, not championing him, when he recounted an argument with his mother. In fact the counsellor may have become the critical mother. There is much to explore here and the counsellor has to do this in a sensitive, not dogmatic way. The client may not be ready to admit to these feelings. And of course the counsellor may be wrong.

When the client tells his story there are usually several different strands, which the counsellor can pick up on. It is a bit like the children's book that says, 'If you think the children should follow the smugglers turn to page 25, if you think they should start digging for the treasure go to page 45. The different paths reach the same happy ending. The treasure is found and the smugglers get their due.'

But for the counsellor, the path she will go down could affect the ending. If she listens to the client, is aware of the transference, monitors her countertransference feelings and reflects on the encounter, she and the client should together choose a meaningful way and make a significant journey. If, however, she does not heed Winnicott's maxim on refraining from demonstrating our cleverness, she could think she knows best, and choose for the client a blind alley.

Understanding the relationship

A focus, which psychodynamic practice shares with cognitive theory, is its emphasis on thinking. This means thinking before the session, thinking in the session and thinking after the session. Before the session and after the session the counsellor will explore in her 'internal supervision' and later in external supervision the strength of the therapeutic alliance. How can the relationship between counsellor and client work better to aid the understanding of the client? Sometimes the counsellor will know she is avoiding looking at the dark side of the client. Perhaps it is too scary for both of them; much easier to stay with the positives. But if the client really wants to understand himself he will need a counsellor who can contain his bad feelings including depression and anger.

The internal supervisor

Patrick Casement (1985) argues that the therapist should be like 'a mother who is nonintrusively present with her playing child'. This means that the counsellor has to be emotionally near enough to understand what the client is feeling, yet having enough distance to function effectively as a counsellor. Casement's useful ideas on internal supervision came about when he realized that therapists need an awareness of the moment, what is happening in front of them in the client, and between the therapist and client. External supervision is invaluable but it is about the past, what happened, and the future, what could happen. Counsellors need an internal resource in the present.

Casement suggests that as part of internal supervision, trial identification, related to empathy, is important. He says that the trial identifies in different ways. He tries to think or feel the experience described by his patient. Or he may put himself in the shoes of someone his patient is referring to. He also tries to put himself in the patient's shoes in relation to himself as the therapist and tries to be the patient listening to what he, the therapist, is going to say. When he silently hears himself 'saying' something he may decide to change it, thinking that he, in the place of the patient, may find it unhelpful. Sometimes he puts himself into the client's position, and reflects on his last comment. 'Frequently this will alert me to the unintentional and unconscious communications that a patient could read into what I have just said. Then, when I listen to the patient's subsequent response, it becomes easier to see when this has been actually provoked by me, by my timing or manner of interpreting' (1985, p. 35).

Casement in talking about the capacity to be simultaneously in the patients shoes and one's own draws on the processing function of the internal supervisor, believing that it is more than self-analysis and more than supervision. This brings us into the arena of Winnicott's ideas about play. Winnicott says that therapy takes place in the overlap of two play areas, that of the therapist and that of the patient. 'If the therapist cannot play, then he is not suitable for the work' (1974, p. 63). I have already given an example of the client who could not play, where the counsellor tries to follow Winnicott's dictum that something needs to be done to help him to play; then therapy can begin (Chapter 5). The reason play is important lies in its potential for creativity.

Casement sees as part of internal supervision the capacity to use 'unfocussed listening'. This means letting the mind be free to hear the overall drift of what the client may be thinking; remembering that communication is layered and trying not to have preconceived ideas. I gave an example of this in Chapter 2 where the client appears to be angry with the vet for charging him, when the dog is not cured. The counsellor wonders if the communication is really for her, as the client feels he has been coming a long time and is no better.

Understanding the client presupposes the interplay of feeling and thinking. If we think without feeling, the process becomes an intellectual exercise with all emotion dispersed. If we feel without thinking we can lose our counsellor stance, where we seem overwhelmed and the client feels uncontained.

Rejection

In Object Relations theory, rejection is a seminal theme. Melanie Klein posited that the abandonment that a baby feels by a rejecting mother is played out through life.

Examining early childhood rejection may offer the therapist a way of better understanding what the client brings. The exploration can help clients make sense of their seemingly irrational thoughts and behaviour in the present.

Case Example | Jane: how the counsellor observes and thinks in order to understand

The first session

Jane was a reluctant client. She made no bones about it. Personal therapy was a requirement of her counsellor training. She needed to get 'the piece of paper', the counselling diploma, which would offer her a retirement plan. Therefore she had come for counselling, but she felt dragooned.

The counsellor tried not to be intimidated by her client. Jane was headmistress of a large private girls' school. She was used to giving orders and expecting that they should be obeyed. The counsellor felt uncomfortable. She realized she was on the verge of behaving like an anxious sixth former. She also recognized the transference, the response to the authoritative parent by the compliant child.

The counsellor sat opposite Jane, noting her expensive cashmere jumper, her brisk trouser suit, her glamorous shoes. They were not what her headmistress had worn. Yet there was as well an austere air about Jane, her hair firmly in a neat bun her face scrubbed of make-up. She was a handsome woman and a woman who appeared at ease with herself.

The first session was edgy. The counsellor faced the client's hostility. Jane was 'here on sufferance'. Jane was sixty and had spent her life looking after herself, protecting herself and defending herself, without recourse to therapy. She did not want to examine herself.

The counsellor wondered if Jane imagined that if she did so, she would crumble. It seemed too early to say this, so the counsellor asked why Jane thought the counselling course had required her to come to therapy. Jane replied that she supposed that it was to learn about oneself, but she had done that. 'I have spent a lifetime looking at myself. I know myself very well.'

Jane offered that her reasons for embarking on a counselling course were 'self-preservation'. After retirement Jane knew that she must find 'a satisfactory professional replacement'. She had decided that counselling would fit the bill because 'as a teacher I have spent a lot of my time counselling'. Jane had a large house and could easily accommodate a private practice.

Supervision

After the first session the counsellor went to supervision. She admitted that she had felt overwhelmed by the session and by Jane herself. She also had felt that Jane's ideas about counselling were probably suspect, as Jane had intimated that getting 'the piece of paper' was for her a paper exercise. Jane believed she had been

Case Example | (Continued)

counselling all her life and consequently knew all about it. She also felt she knew all she needed to know about herself.

The supervisor commented on the powerful transference, which had already been identified by the counsellor, when she had been swept back to a time where she was, briefly, a rebellious teenager. The summons to the head and her peers' triumphal, 'you're in for it,' suddenly seemed unpleasantly near.

The supervisor reminded the counsellor of the defensiveness of Jane and the vulnerability that could lie behind it. 'You'll make a relationship with Jane,' said the supervisor. 'Trust the process!'

Session 2

Jane was 10 minutes early. The counsellor saw her arrive in a large red sports car, which she imagined was very expensive. She wondered why she felt surprised. It did not fit with the neat bun and no make-up. It was flashy.

The counsellor watched as Jane sat in her car. As the clock struck six Jane rang the door-bell. A client who already keeps the boundaries, thought the counsellor, or perhaps Jane was bang on time for everything.

Jane started by saying, 'I have to do forty sessions for the course. What on earth am I going to talk about for nearly a year. Is it supposed that I bring a new problem each week? I solve my own problems so I shall not be doing that!'

The counsellor realized she felt deskilled already and attempted to gather her resources. She talked about the importance of personal development for trainee counsellors, and then added, 'well for all counsellors'. Jane looked sceptical, so the counsellor explained how counsellors must try to resolve their outstanding issues so they do not project them onto their clients. Counsellors must know the areas that are difficult for them. They must be aware of their own Achilles heels or they could end up trying to solve their own problems with the client.

Jane retorted that such practice was clearly unprofessional and she would never resort to like tactics. She knew very well her shortcomings and would 'keep them firmly under wraps'. The counsellor thought 'she hasn't understood', but decided to leave it for the moment. She was afraid of sounding accusatory and that Jane would feel attacked.

'Tell me about yourself,' suggested the counsellor, hoping this might make Jane feel in charge of the agenda and was taken aback when Jane said sharply, 'what do you want to know?'

The counsellor, remembering what her supervisor had said about the transference, determined not to let her feelings of inadequacy become an obstacle to her recognition of the client's vulnerability. She realized that she was anxious about the ethics of working with a client who was so fearful of engaging. Most clients are apprehensive about beginning therapy but they have usually come of their own volition. This was different. Authority, that is the counselling course regulations, had ordained it. Jane had gone along with it outwardly, but internally she was busy defending herself against what she saw as an attack. The counsellor felt protective of her client and this had the effect of making her tentative.

However, she knew that if the client was to get anything out of the sessions Jane would need to explore and challenge herself. The counsellor suggested they could begin to look at Jane's life, perhaps starting with her childhood.

At first Jane did not want to look at her childhood. It was in the past so for her there was little point. When she did start to talk about her family it was presented in a matter of fact way, without emotion.

She was the eldest of four children, the only girl, and said that she looked back on her childhood as a hard time, often spent looking after the younger children. Jane said she had always felt rejected by her mother because she was a girl. She remembers little affection from her mother, but thinks her father tried ineffectually to recognize her. But her father was, like her, lost in the omnipotence of a controlling mother and her preferred sons.

'There was a fair amount of deprivation. Obviously emotional in a family, which seemed unable to communicate with each other, but there were other sorts too. Everything was utilitarian. We were almost like a Quaker family but without the religion; plain, serviceable clothes, no treats, no fripperies. It was bleak.'

The counsellor thought of the red sports car and how it began to make sense.

Case Example | (Continued)

'Since I left home I have not seen my brothers. My parents are dead and I did not go to their funerals. I suppose that shocks you.'

The counsellor was silent for a moment; then said, 'It sounds sad.'

'It is', was Jane's response.

The counsellor's reflections

The counsellor thought about the first two sessions. Jane was so well defended and had formed a carapace around her for her self-preservation. Could she and Jane make a therapeutic alliance? Jane would resist allowing herself to be vulnerable in the therapy.

Yet there were glimpses. Jane had stated she felt rejected by her mother. She had agreed that separating from, and in effect rejecting, her family was sad.

Jane did not have a mother. Would she see the counsellor as mother? It seemed unlikely, but maybe, the counsellor thought, this is my issue. I still feel intimidated by her. I must remind myself of the transference and I must remember the vulnerability that lies behind Jane's daunting exterior.

I must also keep in mind the fact of rejection and its consequences.

Brief therapy

Although some organizations and counsellors working independently can offer long-term counselling, most organizations put a limit on the number of sessions offered. 'Brief therapy', sometimes referring to the time limit, sometimes referring to a focus, as in a lawyers' brief is now very common.

David Malan is well known for his work on brief psychotherapy. Although the psychotherapists' idea of 'brief', around 30 sessions, is very different from a counsellor working for an agency where sessions are time limited to ten or even six sessions, Malan's criteria are helpful.

(1) 'The patient's life problem can be clearly identified, and this offers a clear-cut theme or focus for the therapy,

(2) the patient has responded to interpretations concerned with this focus,

(3) the patient clearly has the motivation to work with this focus,

(4) possible dangers to brief psychotherapy have been considered, and either none can be seen, or else it seems reasonable to suppose that they can be avoided or overcome.

The four criteria for planned brief psychotherapy have been worked out from extensive clinical and research experience (see Malan, 1976a). 'The patient fulfils them all, and this is the treatment of choice' (1995).

Criterion 2 talks of interpretation. For counsellors not working in a psychodynamic way, perhaps 'reflections' would be the most apposite word.

Malan says that experience has indicated that it is best to work within a time limit, set from the beginning. From my own experience I would add that the fact of the ending has to be present from the beginning. This awareness of the ending, for both counsellor and client, should ensure that the focus is kept.

Difficulties for counsellors and particularly trainee counsellors lie when the focus, agreed by both, is destabilized by the client introducing a new and momentous issue. If the focus is return to work after a period of stress, and the client says that focusing on herself has brought her childhood abuse to the fore, and she wants to examine it, what does the counsellor do?

Clearly this issue cannot be adequately dealt with in what is likely to be the last few sessions of brief therapy. The counsellor must refer the client to another appropriate agency. This sounds self-evident, yet the reality can often be messy and distressing for both parties. The client has trusted the counsellor and feels betrayed, the counsellor feels she has somehow let the client down. The whole situation needs a deal of sensitivity and skill to handle. Both partners, in the therapeutic alliance, have to give up phantasies; the client, of a mother who can take away the pain, the counsellor, of omnipotence. It is probable that the client will be angry at the reality. The counsellor must put aside her 'but I did my best' feelings and acknowledge what it must be like for the client.

David Malan's triangles of conflict

Malan is particularly noted for a way of understanding and working with the dynamics of an individual's distress, which he calls the triangle of conflict.

The three constituents of the triangle are defence, anxiety and hidden feelings. The hidden feelings often consist of unacceptable sexual impulses.

Malan says that the therapist has to identify the mechanisms used by the patient, help him to understand them and be aware of their consequences:

- the **defence**, or devices adopted for avoiding mental pain, conflict or unacceptable feelings,

- the feared consequences, or the **anxiety**, of expressing these hidden feelings,

- the nature of the **hidden feelings** themselves (Malan, 1995, p. 16).

Malan says that a second triangle, to which Karl Menninger in 1958 drew attention, is related to the first. Menninger called it, 'the triangle of insight' but Malan says both are triangles of insight and 'triangle of person' is a better term.

The three categories of person are other, transference and parent or sibling.

The second triangle of person is interconnected with the first because hidden feelings are directed at one or more of the three person categories within time:

1. **Other** – usually current or in the past,

2. **Transference** – usually in the here and now,

3. **Parent or Sibling** – usually in the distant past.

Because there are three categories of person there are three possible links.

There is the 'Other–Parent' link where feelings directed towards other are derived from those directed towards parent or sibling.

The Other–Transference link is where similar feelings are directed towards other and the therapist (transference).

And the Transference–Parent link where feelings towards the therapist are derived from the past, connected to parents or siblings.

Malan says that the importance of the two triangles is that between them they can be used to represent almost every intervention that the therapist makes (1995, p. 91).

The following example attempts to illustrate this within time-limited counselling:

Case Example | Anne: the client who repeats her past

Rachel is a counsellor in an agency, which sees young people up to the age of 26. The agency has a policy of providing six sessions to work with a client, though the client may come back after a specified period.

Anne, aged 25, had presented with depression. When Rachel asked her how long she had been depressed it became clear that the depression was connected to what Anne saw as her failed relationships with men.

ANNE: I keep having relationships and thinking, 'this is the one', and then something happens and we split up and then I feel so depressed. I find it hard to cope.

Anne went on to say how much she wanted a stable relationship. She wanted to get married and have children and 'I am beginning to think it will never happen. I shall be a lonely, depressed woman like my mother.'

RACHEL: Tell me about your mother and you. What was it like when you were small?

ANNE: It wasn't too good. I was an only child. My father left us when I was seven. I thought it was because I'd done something wrong. Children do think that, don't they? It was only later when I was much older that I found out that my father had gone to live with a much younger woman, who had a little daughter.

RACHEL: So your father had another little girl in his life.

ANNE: The only little girl, as far as I was concerned. I never saw him after he left. My mother refused to let him see me, and he went along with it. Easier for him, I suppose.

RACHEL: That must have been upsetting for you.

ANNE: I'm sure at first it was. I got along great with my Dad. He was always doing stupid fun things. My mother used to tick him off. Told him he was irresponsible.

RACHEL: You say at first it was upsetting.

ANNE: Well, I just got used to it. Just the two of us, mum and me. She was a good mother. I didn't want for anything.

RACHEL: Except your Dad.

ANNE: Like I said, it was OK. I managed without him.

Case Example | (Continued)

RACHEL: But now you want to look at men in your life, so that you can make a good relationship, one that lasts.

ANNE: Yes. I suppose that's it.

RACHEL: Tell me about your last relationship.

ANNE: Not much to tell. We met at work, both teachers. We seemed to get along fine, similar interests, good sex. I was hoping we might think about moving in together. Then he called it off.

RACHEL: So how did that happen?

ANNE: Well he said it was far too soon to think about living together. I think he got scared.

RACHEL: So you had been the one to suggest living together?

ANNE: Yes. I suppose, when I suggested it, I really knew that he was not committed.

RACHEL: But you went ahead anyway. That makes it sound rather like a test.

ANNE: How do you mean?

RACHEL: It could sound like you were saying 'how much do you love me?'

ANNE: Perhaps I was.

RACHEL: Has that happened in other relationships, that you have had?

ANNE: That I've been too eager?

RACHEL: Well, I was thinking not just eager, but perhaps a bit reckless.

ANNE: Reckless? What do you mean?

RACHEL: Well, if you press a boy friend to live with you, guessing that really he is not ready, that he is scared. What are you doing?

ANNE: You mean it threatens the relationship?

RACHEL: Well, do you think it does?

ANNE: I suppose so. But then if he doesn't want to commit to me, aren't I better off without him?

In this extract at the beginning of the six sessions we see how Rachel, the counsellor, is trying to help the client get to the root of her depression.

Rachel has Malan's structure firmly in her head. She is thinking defence, anxiety, hidden feelings. She knows that the aim of most dynamic psychotherapy is to reach beneath the defence and the anxiety to the hidden feelings; then to try to trace the feelings back from the present to their origins in the past, usually in the relationship with the parents. What the counsellor is trying to do is to see the picture from Malan's viewpoint. She believes her task is to help the client understand her situation, learn from it and not re-enact it.

Rachel is very aware that she only has six sessions. She wonders if the client has found her too challenging, and felt too hurried in the first session. But what has come out of this session has been very useful. Rachel has learnt that Anne's depression is linked to failed relationships with men. Rachel also believes that its origin lies in the past. Anne's father left home when she was old enough to have made a strong relationship with him, yet old enough to believe that his leaving the family home was somehow her fault. Maybe, she thought he did not love her enough. Perhaps she was not lovable. Even in the first session Anne has shown that she tests her current partners to demonstrate how much they love her. Rachel has been able to help Anne to begin to understand this.

Over the remaining sessions Rachel's task will be to help Anne get in touch with her hidden feelings about her father's rejection. She has defended against these feelings by saying she was 'OK', she 'got used to it', she 'managed without him'. And of course her role model was her mother who refused to let Anne grieve and sacrificed Anne's desire to see her father, to develop their relationship, on the altar of the fury of the deserted spouse. One of Anne's hidden feelings must be resentment at her mother's selfish behaviour, as well as her father's. But her mother is 'a good mother' so those feelings are defended against; while her father is someone who can be 'managed without'.

When Anne is abandoned by a lover, as she was abandoned by her father, she tells herself she is 'better off without him'. This is tied to her desire for a total commitment that she did not have from her father. There is also the question of jealousy. Another hidden feeling may be the jealousy Anne must have felt for the new little girl in her father's life. This could now be transferred to a potential 'other woman', whom Anne may dread is keeping her partner from committing to her fully.

What has Rachel to keep in mind over the counselling and what can she and Anne hope to achieve at the end of the six sessions?

First it is important that Anne is helped to be able to identify the defensive mechanisms she uses to keep the emotional pain at bay.

Case Example | (Continued)

Her 'it didn't bother me' and 'I don't care responses' she needs to be able to see as avoidance of the anxiety. This she might feel if she looks squarely at the abandonment of the men in her life. The emotions she is fearful of acknowledging are likely too be the pain of rejection, resentment and bitterness at what she has missed out on, and maybe suppressed fury at her father, the uncommitted lovers and even her mother for letting her down.

When Anne is able to understand this and allow herself to feel the grief of abandonment, she can begin to change her behaviour. This will include not setting herself up to fail in relationships by demanding proof of commitment too soon.

Brief therapy – other ways of working

Roberts says of her experience of time-limited counselling in the Westminster Pastoral Foundation; 'How enabling, therefore, is the counsellor's pledge to back the client up in seeking, articulating and working towards their own attainable outcome of counselling.' Roberts adds, 'Therapeutically, the sense of time generated by the agreed number of sessions may serve as a considerable reassurance to the ego and the existing coping capacity of the client' (1994, p. 102).

James Mann's time-limited psychotherapy draws on the work of Winnicott, and his developmental themes of individuation and separation. Jonathon Smith says, 'Working through the loss of the therapeutic relationship in a robust and unflinching way is thus considered to be an essential prerequisite for therapeutic effectiveness' (2005, p. 271).

In contrast to the time-limited therapists who put termination at the centre of the creative process, Smith describes intermittent brief therapy. This is a way of working, where endings are mutable. Clients are told at the point of termination that they can return for further therapy if they feel they need (2005, p. 270). Smith cites both Gertrude Mander and Daniel Stern as proponents of recurrent therapy. Stern upholds the unpredictable nature of life events interacting with a changing personality (2005, p. 271).

In my practice I have found that clients sometimes come back. The reasons for this, as Stern says, are changed circumstances or changes in themselves. Often the second (or third) time round seems more 'effective', but this is probably because the focus is narrower. I think it is inappropriate to compare the results of a time-limited focused piece of work with the learning from a long-term counselling relationship.

Smith suggests that Winnicott was said to have considered his results were better with brief therapy than long analyses. Certainly he developed skills in working briefly within the context of a profound psychoanalytic framework (2009, p. 129). We know that Winnicott was flexible in his approach to therapy, meeting the client's needs rather than always adhering to a strict four-times-a-week analytic frame. He had clients in different parts of the country, and offered them therapy when they were able to see him.

Winnicott placed play at the centre of therapy. 'Here in the area of overlap between the playing of the child and the playing of the other person there is a chance to introduce enrichments' (1974, p. 58). Winnicott went on to say, 'it helps us to understand our work if we know that the basis of what we do is the patient's playing, a creative experience taking up space and time and intensely real for the patient' (1974, p. 59).

Smith offers a warning about techniques. 'One does not have to look far in the field of brief dynamic therapy to find a full range of techniques that one can apply to one's therapeutic work. Davenloo (2000) for example, elaborated a detailed method, which he termed the Central Dynamic Sequence, of relentlessly challenging the patient's defences to release hidden affects. However the very notion of the therapist being a "relentless healer" suggests hard work. The therapist who closely follows this method may be working hard and so may the patient but what may be lost is the experience of playful and creative engagement' (2009, p. 133).

It is clear that for financial, rather than ideological, reasons brief therapy will become the norm. It seems crucial that we do not privilege economy over creativity. I would strongly agree with Smith who says, 'We are increasingly working in therapeutic contexts in which techniques, however useful in themselves, are likely to become enshrined in evidence based manuals, which can become prescriptive and therefore stifle creative engagement, rather than guide the practitioner' (2009, p. 1450).

Endings

If counsellors have had difficulty in managing endings in their own lives, they will find this true of their counselling practice. Our own therapy, as a place for exploration of loss, is a necessary element in ethical management of client endings. We have to continually monitor ourselves. Is our tendency to hang on to clients too long? Or do we try to end the counselling too early because we find the issues too painful or the client too difficult?

In working with clients in brief counselling, like the lawyer, we must be conscious of the brief, and stay focused on it. And from the beginning of the counselling, we have to be aware of the ending. Clients must know where they are, in order to feel safe. In longer-term counselling, it is the responsibility of the counsellor to work with the client over feelings attached to temporary separation in the breaks. If the counselling is short term, the client must be made aware of the brevity of the counselling and the looming end, from the start.

As clients leave us at the end of the counselling, they get an additional message from us, whatever we have said formally. The unstated message may be that we are worried about their ability to manage on their own. Saying to the client, 'You know where I am if you need me', suggests that you think he will. Even saying something as anodyne as, 'Good luck!' suggests that the client is powerless in the face of fate, when the whole of the counselling has focused on the client's resources.

Probably the safest practice is to say 'Goodbye', with a handshake if it seems appropriate, and to curb ourselves from saying more. Because the extra things we say are probably more for our benefit than the client's.

It is worth spending time to think about how we manage endings. As we know with all relationships, a good relationship can be spoiled by a bad ending.

Further reading

Anderson, R. and Dartington, A. (eds.) (1998) *Facing It Out. Clinical Perspectives on Adolescent Disturbance*. Tavistock Clinic Series. London: Duckworth.

Casement, P. (1985) *On Learning from the Patient*. London: Routledge.

Casement, P. (1990) *Further Learning from the Patient. The Analytic Space and Process*. London: Routledge.

Garland, C. (ed.) (1998) *Understanding Trauma. A Psychoanalytical Approach*. Tavistock Clinic Series. London: Duckworth.

Malan, D. (1995) *Individual Psychotherapy and the Science of Psychodynamics*. Oxford: Butterworth-Heinemann.

Roberts, J. (1994) Time-limited Counselling. *Psychodynamic Counselling*, 1(1): 93–105.

Smith, J.D. (2005) Time and Again: Intermittent Brief Dynamic Therapy. *Psychodynamic Practice*, 11(3): 269–282.

Smith, J.D. (2009) Steering through Storms to Safe Havens: Playing and Reality in Brief Dynamic Therapy. *Psychodynamic Practice*, 15(2): 129–146.

Bibliography

Anderson, R. and Dartington, A. (eds) (1998) *Facing It Out. Clinical Perspectives on Adolescent Disturbance*. Tavistock Clinic Series. London: Duckworth.

Appignanesi, L. and Forrester, J. (1992) *Freud's Women*. London: Weidenfeld and Nicolson.

Balint, E. (1993) Before I was I. *Psychonalysis and the Imagination*, in Mitchell, J. and Parsons, M. (eds) London: Free Association Press.

Balint, M. (1994) *Primary Love and Psycho-Analytic Technique*. Maresfield Library. London: Karnac Books.

Barnett, M. (2007) What brings you here? An exploration of the unconscious motivation of those who choose to train and work as psychotherapists and counsellors. *Psychodynamic Practice*, 13 (3), 257–274.

Bateman, A. and Holmes, J. (1995) *Introduction to Psychoanalysis. Contemporary Thought and Practice*. London: Routledge.

Bell, D. (ed.) (1999) *Psychoanalysis and Culture. A Kleinian Perspective*. Tavistock Clinic Series. London: Duckworth.

Bell, D. (ed.) (2004) *Reason and Passion. A Celebration of the Work of Hanna Segal*. London: Karnac Books.

Bettelheim, B. (1983) *Freud and Man's Soul*. London: Chatto and Windus. The Hogarth Press.

Bion, W. R. (1967) *Second Thoughts*. Selected Papers on Psycho-Analysis. New York: Jason Aronson.

Bion, W. R. (1967) Melanie Klein Today. *Developments in Theory and Practice*, in E. Spillius (ed.) (1988). Volume 2. Mainly Practice. London: Routledge.

Bion, W. R. (1970) *Attention and Interpretation. A Scientific Approach to Insight in Psycho-Analysis and Groups*. London: Tavistock Publications.

Bion, W. R. (1982) *The Long Weekend, 1897–1919. Part of a Life*. Abingdon: Fleetwood Press.

Bion, W. R. (1989) *Experiences in Groups. And Other Papers*. London: Routledge.

Bion, W. R. (1991) *All My Sins Remembered and the Other Side of Genius*. London: Karnac Books.

Bion, W. R. (2000) *Clinical Seminars and Other Works*. London: Karnac Books.

Bleandou, G. (1994) *Wilfred Bion. His Life and Works 1897–1979*. London: Free Association Books.

Bollas, C. (1987) *The Shadow of the Object*. London: Free Association Books.

Bowlby, J. (1944) 'Forty-four juvenile thieves: their characters and home life'. *International Journal of Psycho-Analysis*, 25 (19–52), 107–127.

Bowlby, J. (1965) *Child Care and the Growth of Love*. Second Edition. London: Penguin Books.

Bowlby, J. (1971) *Attachment and Loss*. Volume 1. Attachment. London: Penguin Books.

Bowlby, J. (1975) *Attachment and Loss*. Volume 2. Separation: Anxiety and Anger. London: Penguin Books.

Bowlby, J. (1979) *The Making and Breaking of Affectional Bonds*. London: Tavistock Publications.

Bowlby, J. (1991) *Charles Darwin. A New Life*. New York: W. W. Norton and Co.

Bowlby, J. (1998) *Attachment and Loss*. Volume 3. Loss. Sadness and Depression. London: Pimlico.

Britton, R., Feldman, M., O'Shaugnessy, E. and Steiner, J. (1989) *The Oedipus Complex Today-Clinical Implications*. London: Karnac Books.

Brookner, A. (2009) *Strangers*. London: Penguin Books.

Brown, J. A. C. (1961) *Freud and the Post-Freudians*. Harmondsworth: Penguin Books Ltd.

Casement, P. (1985) *On Learning from the Patient*. London: Routledge.

Casement, P. (1990) *Further Learning from the Patient. The Analytic Space and Process*. London: Routledge.

Chodorow, N. (1978) *The Reproduction of Mothering*. Berkeley: University of California Press.

Cioffi, F. (1998) Was Freud a liar? *Unauthorized Freud. Doubters Confront a Legend*, in F. Crews (ed.) Harmondsworth: Penguin.

Clark, R. (1980) *Freud: The Man and the Cause*. London: Cape/Wiedenfeld and Nicolson.

Cohn, J., Campbell, S., Matias, R. and Hopkins, J. (1990) Face-to-face interactions of postpartum depressed and nondepressed mother-infant pairs at 2 months. *Developmental Psychology*, 26 (1): 15–23.

Coles, P. (2003) *The Importance of Sibling Relationships in Psychoanalysis*. London: Karnac Books.

Crews, F. (ed.) (1999) *Unauthorized Freud. Doubters Confront a Legend*. Harmondsworth: Penguin.

Davies, R. (2000) in Sandler, A.-M. & J. (eds.) *Clinical and Observational Psychoanalytic Research: Roots of a Controversy* a collection of conference papers exploring the work of discussants Green, A. & Stern, D. in the Psychoanalytic Monograph Series, London: Karnac Books.

Davis, M. and Wallbridge, D. (1983) *Boundary and Space. An Introduction to the Work of D. W. Winnicott*. London: Penguin Books.

Demos, V. (1986) *Crying in early infancy. Affective Development in Infancy*, in Brazelton, T. B. and Yogman, M. W. (eds), Norwood, NJ.

Deurzen-Smith, E. van (1988) *Existential Counselling in Practice*. London: Sage Publications.

Dryden, W. (ed.) (1996) *Handbook of Individual Therapy*. London: Sage Publications.

Dunn, J. (1984) *Sisters and Brothers*. London: Fontana.

Eichenbaum, L. and Orbach, S. (1982) *Outside in . . . Inside Out. Women's Psychology: A Feminist Psychoanalytic Approach*. Harmondsworth: Penguin.

Erikson, E. (1965) *Childhood and Society*. Harmondsworth: Penguin.

Fairbairn, R. (1952) *Psycho-Analytic Studies of the Personality*. London: Routledge and Kegan Paul.

Fara, P. and Patterson, K. (eds) (1998) *Memory*. Cambridge: Cambridge University Press.

Ferenczi, S. (1988) *The Clinical Diary of Sandor Ferenczi*, in Judith Dupont (ed.). Michael Balint and Nicola Zarday Jackson (trans.). Cambridge, MA: Harvard University Press.

Fernyhough, C. (2008) *The Baby in the Mirror. A Child's World from Birth to Three*. London: Granta.

Fonagy, P., Target, M., Gergely, G. and Jurist, E. (2004) *Affect Regulation, Mentalization and the Development of the Self*. London: H. Karnak (Books) Ltd.

Freud, S. (1900) *The Interpretation of Dreams*. Penguin Freud Library. Volume 4.

Freud, S. (1901) *The Psychopathology of Everyday Life*. London: Ernest Benn Limited (1966 edition).

Freud, S. (1905) *Three Essays on the Theory of Sexuality*. Penguin Freud Library, Volume 7.

Freud, S. (1906–1908) *Jensen's Gravida and Other Works*. Standard Edition, Volume IX. London: Hogarth Press.

Freud, S. (1910) Five lectures on psychoanalysis, in *Two Short Accounts of Psychoanalysis* (1962). Harmondsworth: Penguin.

Freud, S. (1914) *On Narcissism: An Introduction*, in P. Gay (ed.) (1995) London: Vintage.

Freud, S. (1915a) *The Unconscious*. Penguin Freud Library, Volume 11.

Freud, S. (1915b) *Observations of Transference Love*. Standard Edition, Volume XII. London: Hogarth Press.

Freud, S. (1916) *Introductory Lectures on Psychoanalysis*. Penguin Freud Library, Volume 1.

Freud, S. (1917) *Mourning and Melancholia*. Penguin Freud Library, Volume 11.

Freud, S. (1920) *Beyond the Pleasure Principle*. Penguin Freud Library, Volume 11.

Freud, S. (1923) *The Ego and the Id*. Penguin Freud Library, Volume 11.

Freud, S. (1924) *Three Essays on the Theory of Sexuality* (enlargement of 1905 Three Essays), in P. Gay (ed.) (1995) London: Vintage.

Freud, S. (1925) *An Autobiographical Study*. Standard Edition, Volume XX. London: Hogarth Press.

Freud, S. (1930) *Civilisation and Its Discontents*. Penguin Freud Library, Volume 12.

Freud, S. (1933) *New Introductory Lectures on Psychoanalysis*. Penguin Freud Library, Volume 2.

Frosh, S. (1999) *The Politics of Psychoanalysis*. London: Macmillan.

Garland, C. (1998) Thinking about Trauma. *Understanding Trauma. A Psychoanalytical Approach*, in C. Garland (ed.). London: Duckworth.

Garland, C. (ed.) (1998) *Understanding Trauma. A Psychoanalytical Approach*. Tavistock Clinic Series. London: Duckworth.

Gay, P. (1988) *Freud: A Life for Our Time*. London: J. M. Dent and Sons Ltd.

Gay, P. (ed.) (1995) *The Freud Reader*. London: Vintage.

Gerhardt, S. (2004) *Why Love Matters: How Affection Shapes a Baby's Brain*. Hove: Routledge.

Gill, G. (1990) *Agatha Christie. The Woman and her Mysteries*. London: Robson Books.

Gomez, L. (1997) *An Introduction to Object Relations*. London: Free Association Books.

Greenberg, J. R. and Mitchell, S. A. (1983) *Object Relations in Psychoanalytic Theory*. Cambridge, MA: Harvard University Press.

Grosskurth, P. (1986) *Melanie Klein: Her World and Her Work*. London: Hodder and Stoughton.

Guntrip, H. (1995) *Personality Structure and Human Interaction. The Developing Synthesis of Psychodynamic Theory*. Maresfield Library. London: Karnac Books.

Holmes, J. (1993) *John Bowlby and Attachment Theory*. London and New York: Routledge.

Holmes, J. and Lindley, R. (1998) *The Values of Psychotherapy*. Revised Edition. London: Karnac Books.

Holt, R. (1989) *Freud Reappraised. A Fresh Look at Psychoanalytic Theory*. New York: The Guilford Press.

Hopkins, J. (1996) The dangers and deprivations of too-good mothering. *Journal of Child Psychotherapy*, 22 (3), 407–422.

Howard, A. (2000) *Philosophy for Counselling and Psychotherapy*. London: Macmillan.

Jacobs, M. (1988) *Psychodynamic Counselling in Action*. London: Sage Publications.

Jacobs, M. (1992) *Sigmund Freud*. London: Sage Publications.

Jacobs, M. (1995) *D. W. Winnicott*. London: Sage Publications.

Jacobs, M. (1998) *The Presenting Past*. Second Edition. Buckingham: Open University Press.

Jones, E. (1954) *Sigmund Freud. Life and Work*. Volume 1. The Young Freud, 1856–1900. London: Hogarth Press.

Jones, E. (1958) *Sigmund Freud. Life and Work*. Volume 11. Years of Maturity, 1901–1919. London: Hogarth Press.

Jones, E. (1974) *Sigmund Freud. Life and Work*. Volume 111. The Last Phase, 1919–1939. London: Hogarth Press.

Jung, C. G. (1968) *Analytical Psychology: Its Theory and Practice*. Hove: Routledge

Kahr, B. (1996) *D. W. Winnicott. A Biographical Portrait*. London: Karnac Books.

Kennedy, R. (1993) *Freedom to Relate. Psychoanalytic Explorations*. London: Free Association Books.

Klass, D., Phyllis, R., Silverman, S. and Nickman, L. (1996) *Continuing Bonds-New Understandings of Grief*. Washington: Taylor and Francis.

Klein, J. (1987) *Our Need for Others and its Roots in Infancy*. Reprinted 1993. London: Routledge.

Klein, M. (1930) The importance of symbol-formation in the development of the ego. *Love, Guilt and Reparation, and Other Works 1921–1945*, in M. Klein (ed.) (1988). London: Virago.

Klein, M. (1937) Love, guilt and reparation. *Love, Guilt and Reparation, and Other Works 1921–1945*, in M. Klein (ed.) (1998). London: Virago.

Klein, M. (1940) Mourning and its relation to manic-depressive states. *Love, Guilt and Reparation, and Other Works 1921–1945*, in M. Klein (ed.) (1988). London: Virago.

Klein, M. (1946) Notes on some Schizoid mechanisms. *Envy and Gratitude, and Other Works 1946–1963*, in M. Klein (ed.) (1988). London: Virago.

Klein, M. (1952) Some theoretical conclusions regarding the emotional life of the infant. *Envy and Gratitude, and Other Works 1946–1963*, in M. Klein (ed.) (1988). London: Virago.

Klein, M. (1957) Envy and gratitude. *Envy and Gratitude, and Other Works 1946–1963*, in M. Klein (ed.) (1988). London: Virago.

Klein, M. (1959) Our adult world and its roots in infancy. *Envy and Gratitude, and Other Works 1946–1963*, in M. Klein (ed.) (1988). London: Virago.

Klein, M. (1963) On the sense of loneliness. Posthumous paper. *Envy and Gratitude, and Other Works 1946–1963*, in M. Klein (ed.) (1988). London: Virago.

Klein, M. (1997) *The Psychoanalysis of Children*. London: Vintage.

Klein, M., Heimann, P. and Money-Kyrle, R. E. (eds) (1985) *New Directions in Psychoanalysis*. London: Karnac Books.

Kovel, J. (1991) *A Complete Guide to Therapy. From Psychoanalysis to Behaviour Modification*. London: Penguin Books.

Krause, I.-B. (1998) *Therapy across Culture*. London: Sage Publications.

Leader, D. (2000) *Freud's Footnotes*. London: Faber and Faber.

Leader, D. and Groves, J. (1995) *Lacan for Beginners*. Cambridge: Icon Books.

Loewenthal, D. (2001) Should all psychotherapists have personal therapy? *European Journal of Psychotherapy, Counselling and Health*, 4, 1–6.

Lorenz, K. (1967) *On Aggression*. London: Methuen and Co. Ltd, University Paperback Edition.

Maciejewski, P. K., Zhang, B., Block, S. D. and Prigerson, H. G. (2007) An empirical examination of the stage theory of grief. *Journal of the American Medical Association*, 297 (7), 716–723.

Malan, D. H. (1976a) *The Frontier of Brief Psychotherapy*. New York: Plenum.

Malan, D. H. (1995) *Individual Psychotherapy and the Science of Psychodynamics*. Oxford: Butterworth-Heinemann.

Mander, G. (2004) The selection of candidates for training in psychotherapy and counselling. *Psychodynamic Practice*, 10 (2) May, 161–171.

Mann, D. (1997) *Psychotherapy, an Erotic Relationship: Transference and Countertransference*. London: Routledge.

Marcuse, H. (1972) *Eros and Civilisation*. London: Abacus.

Marris, P. (1978) *Loss and Change*. London: Routledge and Kegan Paul.

Masson, J. (1993) *Against Therapy*. London: Harper Collins.

Mbiti, J. (1969) *African Religions and Philosophy*. London: Heinemann.

McLoughlin, B. (1995) *Developing Psychodynamic Counselling*. London: Sage Publications.

Mearns, D. and Thorne, B. (1988) *Person-Centred Counselling in Action*. London: Sage.

Melanie Klein Trust. *Memories of Melanie Klein: Part 1. An interview with Hanna Segal* by Daniel Pick and Jane Milton, both psychoanalysts belonging to the British Psychoanalytical Society http:/www. melanie-klein-trust.org.uk/segalinterview2001.htmPublications.

Mitchell, J. (1974) *Psychoanalysis and Feminism*. Harmondsworth: Penguin.

Mitchell. J. (ed.) (1991) *The Selected Melanie Klein*. Harmondsworth: Penguin.

Mitchell, J. (1998) Memory and psychoanalysis. *Memory*, in P. Fara and K. Patterson (eds). Cambridge: Cambridge University Press.

Mitchell, J. (2000) *Psychoanalysis and Feminism: A Radical Reassessment of Freudian Psychoanalysis*. New York: Basic Books.

Mitchell, J. (2003) *Siblings*. Cambridge: Polity Press.

Moore, H. L. (2007) *The Subject of Anthropology*. Cambridge: Polity Press.

Mullan, B. (ed.) (1996) *Therapists on Therapy*. London: Free Association Books.

Parkes, C. M. and Prigerson, H. G. (2010) *Bereavement. Studies of Grief in Adult Life*. London: Penguin Books.

Pfeiffer, E. (ed.) (1972) *Sigmund Freud and Lou Andres-Salome Letters.* London: The Hogarth Press.

Phillips, A. (1988) *Winnnicott.* London: Fontana Paperbacks.

Phillips, A. (1994) *On Kissing, Tickling and Being Bored. Psychoanalytic Essays on the Unexamined Life* (pbk). London: Faber and Faber.

Pines, M. (ed.) (1985) *Bion and Group Psychotherapy.* London: Routledge and Kegan Paul.

Reid, S. (ed.) (1997) *Developments in Infant Observation. The Tavistock Model.* Hove: Routledge.

Robertson, J. and Bowlby, J. (1952) Responses of young children to separation from their mothers. *Courr. Cent. Int. Enf.* 2, 131–142.

Robertson, J. and Robertson, J. (1967–1973) *Film Series, Young Children in Brief Separation: No. 2 Jane, 17 Months in Fostercare for 10 Days, No.3 John, 17 Months, 9 Days in a Residential Nursery.* London: Tavistock Institute of Human Relations.

Robertson, J. and J. (1989) *Separation and the Very Young.* London: Free Association Books.

Rogers, C. (1967) *On Becoming a Person. A Therapist's View of Psychotherapy.* London: Constable.

Rogers, C. (1990) *The Carl Rogers Reader.* London: Constable and Company Limited.

Roith, E. (1987) *The Riddle of Freud.* London: Tavistock Publications.

Roth, A. and Fonagy, P. (2005) *What Works For Whom*, 2nd edition. New York: Guilford Press.

Rutter, M. (1991) *Maternal Deprivation Reassessed.* London: Penguin Books.

Ryle, A. (1990) *Cognitive-Analytic Therapy: Active Participation in Change.* Chichester: Wiley.

Samuels, A. (1993) *The Political Psyche.* London: Routledge.

Sandler, J., Davies, R., Green, A. and Sandler, A. M. (2000) *Clinical and Observational Psychoanalytic Research. Roots of a Controversy.* In Andre Green and Daniel Stern. London: H. Karnac (Books) Ltd.

Sayers, J. (1992) *Mothering Psychoanalysis.* London: Penguin.

Sayers, J. (2000) *Kleinians: Psychoanalysis Inside Out.* Cambridge: Polity Press.

Schore, A. N. (2002) *Affect Regulation and the Origin of Self. The Neurobiology of Emotional Development.* USA: Psychology Press.

Allan Schore in an interview in 2001 with Roz Carroll, before a lecture to the United Kingdom Council for Psychotherapy, (UKCP) on July 21st, entitled, *Neuroscience – why should therapists be interested?* http:/www.thinkbody.co.uk/papers/interview-with-allan-s.htm.

Schore, A. (2003) *Affect Dysregulation and Disorders of the Self.* New York: W.W Norton and Co.

Segal, H. (1988) *Introduction to the World of Melanie Klein*. London: Karnac Books.

Segal, H. (2003) From Hiroshima to 11th September and after. *Psychodynamic Practice*, 9 (3), 257–265.

Segal, J. (1992) *Melanie Klein*. London: Sage Publications.

Sinason, V. (1992) *Mental Handicap and the Human Condition. New Approaches from the Tavistock*. London: Free Association Books.

Skultans, V. and Cox, J. (eds) (2000) *Anthropological Approaches to Psychological Medicine*. Crossing Bridges. London: Jessica Kingsley Publishers.

Spillius, E. (1996) *Melanie Klein Today. Developments in Theory and Practice*. Volume 1. Mainly Theory. London: Routledge.

Spillius, E. (1996) *Melanie Klein Today. Developments in Theory and Practice*. Volume 2. Mainly Practice. London: Routledge.

Stern, D. N. (2002) *The First Relationship*. Cambridge, MA: Harvard University Press

Storr, A. (1968) *Human Aggression*. London: Penguin Books.

Storr, A. (1989) *Freud*. Oxford: Oxford University Press.

Stroebe, M. and Schut, H. (1999) The dual process model of coping with bereavement.in *Death Studies*, 23 (3), Abingdon: Routledge.

Suttie, I. D. (1960) *The Origins of Love and Hate*. London: Penguin Books.

Swales, P. (1999) Freud's Master Hysteric. *Unauthorized Freud. Doubters Confront a Legend*, in F. Crews (ed.). Harmondsworth: Penguin.

Symington, N. (1986) *The Analytic Experience. Lectures from the Tavistock*. London: Free Association Books.

Turner, J. (2000) *On the Origin of Human Emotions*. Palo Alto: Stanford University Press.

Waddell, M. (1998) *Inside Lives. Psychoanalysis and the Growth of the Personality*. Tavistock Clinic Series. London: Duckworth.

Wertheimer, A. (1991) *A Special Scar. The Experiences of People Bereaved by Suicide*. London and New York: Routledge.

Wheeler, S. and Schroder, T. (2005) Does accreditation make you rich? This and other tales of counsellors and psychotherapists. *BACP Research Conference*, Nottingham, May.

Wheeler, S. (2007) What shall we do with the wounded healer: the supervisor's dilemma. *Psychodynamic Practice*, 13 (3), 245–256.

Whyte, L. (1962) *The Unconscious Before Freud*. London: Tavistock.

Winnicott, D. W. (1945) Primitive emotional development in (1975) *Through Paediatrics to Psychoanalysis*. Collected Papers. London: Karnac Books.

Winnicott, D. W. (1947) Hate in the countertransference in (1975) *Through Paediatrics to Psychoanalysis*. Collected Papers. London: Karnac Books.

Winnicott, D. W. (1952) Anxiety associated with insecurity in (1975) *Through Paediatrics to Psychoanalysis*. Collected Papers. London: Karnac Books.

Winnicott, D. W. (1956) Primary maternal preoccupation in (1975) *Through Paediatrics to Psychoanalysis*. Collected Papers. London: Karnac Books.

Winnicott, D. W. (1963) The development of the capacity for concern in (1965) *The Maturational Process and the Facilitating Environment*. London: Hogarth Press.

Winnicott, D. W. (1964) *The Child the Family and the Outside World*. London: Penguin Books.

Winnicott, D. W. (1965) *The Maturational Process and the Facilitating Environment*. London: Hogarth Press.

Winnicott, D. W. (1974) *Playing and Reality*. London: Penguin Books.

Winnicott, D. W. (1975) *Through Paediatrics to Psychoanalysis*. Collected Papers. London: Karnac Books.

Winnicott, D. W. (1980) *The Piggle*: *An Account of the Psychoanalytic Treatment of a Little Girl*. London: Penguin Books.

Winnicott, D. W. (1986) *Holding and Interpretation*. London: Karnac Books.

Wollheim, R. (1971) *Freud*. Glasgow: Fontana/Collins.

Index